CITIZENSHIP AND EXCLUSION

Für den Kollegen
Udo Sautter
mit besten Wünschen
für weitere gute
Zusammenarbeit
April 99 Dirk Hoerder

Citizenship and Exclusion

Edited by

Veit Bader
Universiteit van Amsterdam
The Netherlands

First published in Great Britain 1997 by
MACMILLAN PRESS LTD
Houndmills, Basingstoke, Hampshire RG21 6XS and London
Companies and representatives throughout the world

A catalogue record for this book is available from the British Library.

ISBN 0–333–71243–9

 First published in the United States of America 1997 by
ST. MARTIN'S PRESS, INC.,
Scholarly and Reference Division,
175 Fifth Avenue, New York, N.Y. 10010

ISBN 0–312–17587–6

Library of Congress Cataloging-in-Publication Data
Citizenship and exclusion / edited by Veit Bader.
p. cm.
Includes bibliographical references and index.
ISBN 0–312–17587–6 (alk. paper)
1. Citizenship. 2. Emigration and immigration. 3. Social policy.
4. Aliens—Civil rights. 5. Immigrants—Civil rights. I. Bader,
Veit-Michael.
JF801.C568 1997
323.6—dc21   97–11684
                                                          CIP

This book is printed on paper suitable for recycling and made from fully managed and
sustained forest sources.

10   9   8   7   6   5   4   3   2   1
06 05 04 03 02 01 00 99 98 97

Printed and bound in Great Britain by
Antony Rowe Ltd, Chippenham, Wiltshire

Contents

Acknowledgements

Citizenship and Exclusion publishes revised versions of new papers or lectures presented at an expert colloquium in Amsterdam, April 9-12, 1996. Distinguished scholars from different countries, disciplines and theoretical perspectives focused on moral, political, historical, social and legal aspects of citizenship as exclusion, particularly on immigration-, refugee-, asylum- and naturalization policies in a comparative perspective. Three characteristics made the colloquium a distinctive event: (i) It was truly international and interdisciplinary, particularly in combining normative disciplines (moral and political philosophy, law) with descriptive and explanatory ones (history, anthropology, sociology, political science). (ii) As the subtitle of the colloquium: *Towards practical knowledge* indicated, all scholars have been confronted with urgent practical questions. (iii) Its organization allowed extended conversations and mutual learning. Not only were all articles distributed long in advance, written auto-comments by the authors as well as comments, responses and replies were also distributed and read in advance. Time was available for extensive debate during the sessions.

In session I on 'European and Multicultural Citizenship: Recent paradoxes of sovereignty and citizenship in an historical and comparative perspective', the following texts were discussed: Will Kymlicka (Chapter 2. 'The Politics of Multiculturalism' from his *Multicultural Citizenship* (1995) and his 'Update' (1996), commented on by Marlies Galenkamp ('Sitting on the fence'); Verena Stolcke ('The "Nature" of Nationality', in this volume), commented on by Jessurun d'Oliveira and Rainer Bauböck. Roel de Lange ('Paradoxes of European Citizenship', 1995), commented on by Cees Groenendijk; Danielle Juteau ('Beyond Multiculturalist Citizenship', in this volume), commented on by Will Kymlicka. Session II on 'Citizenship and Exclusion: Why not open borders?': Robert Goodin ('If People Were Money' (1992); 'Auto-Comment: Free Movement: Further Thoughts' (1996), commented on by Thomas Pogge; Thomas Pogge ('Globalizing the Rawlsian Conception of Justice' (Part Three of his 'Realizing Rawls' (1989)), commented on by Rainer Bauböck. Rainer Bauböck ('Changing the Boundaries of Citizenship' (1995), commented on by Robert Goodin. Veit Bader ('Citizenship and Exclusion' (1995); 'Auto-Comment' (1996), commented on by Thomas Pogge and Rainer Bauböck; response to Pogge's comment by Bader: 'A Multilayered Concept of Citizenship' (1996a). Session III on 'Immigration, Asylum, Naturalization and their Consequences in Past and Present'; Aristide Zolberg ('Wanted but not Welcome' (Ch. 2 of 1987) and 'Who is a Refugee?' (Ch. 1 of 1989)), commented on by Leslie Page Moch. Leslie Page Moch ('Moving Europeans' (1995)), commented on by Jan Lucassen. Jan Lucassen ('The Netherlands, the Dutch and Long Distance Migration in the Late Sixteenth to Early Nineteenth Centuries' (1994)), commented on by Dirk Hoerder. Veit Bader ('The Arts of Forecasting and Policy Making' (in this volume)), commented on by Ton Korver. Session IV on 'Concepts and Modes of Incorporation': Aristide Zolberg ('Modes of Incorporation', in this volume), commented on by Robert Goodin. Stephen Castles (Ch. 8 'New Ethnic Minorities and Society', from *The Age of Migration* (1993); 'Auto-Comment'), commented on by Danielle Juteau. Yasemin Soysal (Ch. 3: 'Explaining Incorporation Regimes', from her *Limits of Citizenship* (1994)), commented on by Stephen Castles. Dirk Hoerder ('Segmented Macrosystems, Networking Individuals, Cultural Change'; in this volume), commented on by Leslie Page Moch. Session V on 'Immigration-, Refugee- and Naturalization Policies: Programmatic Alternatives and Strategies': Hans Ulrich Jessurun d'Oliveira ('Expanding External and Shrinking Internal Borders' (1994)), commented on by Aristide Zolberg. Cees Groenendijk ('Three Questions on Free Movement of Persons and Democracy in Europe' (1993)), commented on by Roel de Lange. Dilek Çynar ('From Aliens to Citizens' (1995)), presented by Rainer Bauböck and commented on by Dirk Hoerder.

This volume contains all the new articles and the public lecture by Thomas Pogge: 'Poverty and Migration: Normative Issues'.[1] For reasons of space it has been impossible to include all lectures, summaries of all articles and all the comments, auto-comments and responses. I asked all authors to take comments and discussions into account in rewriting their contributions and I myself tried to do justice to the debates in session II in my chapter on 'Fairly Open Borders' written for this volume. Still, only a very small part of the stimulating and productive exchange of ideas during the colloquium can be made accessible here.

I take the opportunity to thank all participants who made the colloquium a success and, I hope, enjoyed it as much as I did. I would like to

[1] The lectures by Robert Goodin, Rainer Bauböck and Leslie Page Moch are published, for different reasons, elsewhere: Goodin, R (1997) 'Inclusion and Exclusion. The very Ideas', in: *Archives Européennes de Sociologie*, Dec. 1996 . Bauböck, R.: 'Group Rights for Cultural Minorities: Justifications and Constraints', in: Lukes, S. and Garcia, S. (eds.) *The Quality of Citizenship: Social Inclusion versus Multiculturalism?* Page Moch, L. (1997) 'Foreign Workers in Western Europe: 'The "Cheaper Hands" in Historical Perspective', in: Klausen, J. and Tilly, L. (eds.) *European Integration as a Social Process: Historical Perspectives, 1850-1995.* Boulder: Roman and Littlefield.

thank the following institutions for financial support: Directie Coördinatie Minderhedenbeleid, Ministerie van Binnenlandse Zaken; Ministerie van Volksgezondheid, Welzijn en Sport; College van Bestuur van de Universiteit van Amsterdam; Koninklijk Nederlandse Academie der Wetenschappen; Dutch Research School for Practical Philosophy; Faculteit der Wijsbegeerte en Faculteit der Politieke en Sociaal Culturele Wetenschappen, Universiteit van Amsterdam. Special thanks to Tom Nieuwenhuis and to Klaske de Jong for their help in organizing the Colloquium.

Contributors

Veit Michael Bader is currently Professor of Sociology at the Faculty of Political and Social Cultural Sciences at the University of Amsterdam (Department of Sociology and Institute for Migration and Ethnic Studies) and Professor of Social and Political Philosophy at the Faculty of Philosophy of the same University. His recent areas of research cover sociology of work and industrial relations, political sociology (particularly of inequalities and collective action and of ethnic relations) and normative problems of multi-ethnic and -national societies. His books include: *Ungleichheiten (Inequalities,* 1989, Opladen, Leske&Budrich; together with Albert Benschop), *Kollektives Handeln (Collective Action,* 1991, Opladen, Leske&Budrich), and *Rassismus, Ethnizität, Bürgerschaft (Racism, Ethnicity, and Citizenship,* 1995, Münster, Westfälisches Dampfboot).

Stephen Castles is Professor of Sociology and Director of the Centre for Multicultural Studies at the University of Wollongong. He was and is a member of many Australian Advisory Boards. He has been studying migration, ethnicity and racism for many years and has worked in Germany, Britain and Southern Africa. He has been responsible for a wide range of studies on immigration and multiculturalism in Australia. His current research interests include changing models of citizenship in countries of immigration, and the social and political consequences of new migrations in the Asia-Pacific Region. His books include: *Here for Good: Western Europe's New Ethnic Minorities* (London, Pluto Press, 1984); *The Age of Migration: International Population Movements in the Modern World* (with Mark J. Miller, London, Macmillan, 1993); *The Teeth are Smiling: The Persistence of Racism in Multicultural Australia* (co-edited with Ellie Vasta, Sydney, Allen and Unwin, 1996).

Dirk Hoerder is Professor of History at the University of Bremen. His areas of interest are European labour migration in the Atlantic economies, worldwide migration systems, and migrant acculturation. He has been director of the Labor Migration Project and is currently working on a survey of worldwide migration systems and on a study of immigrant experiences as reflected in Canadian immigrant life-writings. His publications include *Labor Migration in the Atlantic Economies: The European and North American Working Classes during the Period of Industrialization* (Westport, Ct.: Greenwood, 1985) and *European Migrants: Global and Local Perspectives* (Boston: Northeastern UP, 1995).

Danielle Juteau is Professor of Sociology at the Université de Montréal ; she holds a Chair in Ethnic Relations at the Center for Ethnic Studies. Her work focuses on the construction and transformation of ethnic social relations. She has published extensively on the building of nations in Canada and on the production of ethnicity. Her recent interests comprise the interconnections between sex/ gender and ethnic/ national relations as well as the relations between citizenship and pluralism. Her publications include: J. Burnet, D. Juteau et. al. (ed.), *Migration and the Transformation of Cultures*, Toronto, Multicultural History Society of Ontario, 1992. 'Reconstructing the Categories of Race and Sex', preface to C. Guillaumin, *Racism, Sexism, Power and Ideology*, London, Routledge, 1995. 'Theorising ethnicity and ethnic communalisations at the margins: from Quebec to the world system', *Nations and Nationalism* 2(1) 1996: 45-66.

Thomas Pogge is associate Professor of philosophy at Columbia University in New York and has published extensively in moral and political philosophy as well as on Kant. He is currently at work on a comprehensive book on global justice which will extend and unify his essays of the last few years. His publications include: *Realizing Rawls* (1989, Ithaca, Cornell University Press); *Cosmopolitanism and Sovereignty* (1992b, in: Ethics 103(1): 48-75); *An Egalitarian Law of Peoples* (1994, in: Philosophy and Public Affairs 23(3): 195-224).

Verena Stolcke is Professor of Social Anthropology, Universidad Autonoma de Barcelona. Her research topics are anthropological history of structures of exclusion and the articulation of nationality, class and gender in a comparative perspective (Cuba, Brazil, Europe). Her publications include *Marriage, Class and Colour in Nineteenth Century Cuba*, Cambridge University Press, 1974 (2nd edition by Michigan Univ. Press, 1989; *Coffee Planters, Workers and Wives: Class Conflict and Gender Relations on Sao Paulo Coffee Plantations, 1850-1980*, St. Antony's College/Macmillan, 1988; *Europe: New boundaries, new rhetorics of exclusion*, in: *Current Anthropology* 36 (1): 1-24, 1995.

Aristide Zolberg is currently Professor of Politics, Department of Political Science, New School for Social Research and director of the International Center for Migration, Ethnicity and Citizenship in New York. His publications include: 'Wanted But Not Welcome: Alien Labor in Western Development' (1987, in: Alonzo, W. (ed.) *Population in an Interacting World*. Cambridge, Harvard University Press, pp. 36-73); *Escape from Violence: The Refugee Crisis in the Developing World* (1989, New York, Oxford University Press, with A. Surhke and S. Aguayo); *Crowding at the Gates: The Past and Present Immigration Crisis* (1996, Free Press).

Introduction

Veit Bader

People have always been on the move. States claim sovereignty over people, territories and borders. Modern, democratic (nation) states in particular implemented stricter rules of state-membership and naturalization and enacted stronger policies of border-control whenever it seemed to be in their interest. However, two fairly recent developments seem to challenge the effectiveness and legitimacy of "national" sovereignty and of citizenship.

Contrary to the legal and political myth of absolute, unitary, and indivisible *sovereignty*, states have never been as sovereign as that. Recently, their legal sovereignty and their factual powers are undermined by two processes: first, by the *reconstruction of sovereignty* on supra-national levels (e.g. the EU) and the increasing moral and legal limitation by international law, asking for a redefinition of "nationhood" and for more multi-layered conceptions of sovereignty and citizenship. Secondly, by the speed of unbound *capitalist globalization* in combination with triumphant neo-liberal economic policies, which have considerably weakened national economic policies (monetary, fiscal, tax, trade, investment, employment, social security policies) as well as international economic governance. Under such conditions, states have trouble in controlling money, credit, investment, goods, services, ideas and information, but they still have considerable powers to control the transborder movements of people (see Hirst/Thompson 1996, p. 181 ff., 141: Goodin 1996).

Migration may be enforced (slave-transfer, indentured labour, refugees) or more or less free (migrant workers, highly qualified specialists, entrepreneurs, family reunification). Till the early 1970s, people moving into the rich Northern States roughly belonged either to the class of "wanted and welcome" ones (cold war political refugees and official immigrants) or to the class of "wanted but unwelcome" ones (manual workers under *Gastarbeiter* regimes). This in-migration has considerably increased the ethnic diversity of (nation) states and contributes to the need for redefining the predominant conceptions of nationhood and citizenship, particularly the ethnic ones, in less ethnocentrist or nationalist ways. At least in Europe, the migration-pattern has changed dramatically since this time: apart from a tiny group of wanted and welcome professionals and businessmen (and a tolerated group of "wanted" illegal workers), the

1

bulk of those that manage to get in are either "unwanted and not welcome legal" ones (legally binding family reunification, recognized refugees) or "unwanted and unwelcome" illegal refugees (see Zolberg et al. 1989; Castles/Miller 1993). The rich Northern States and the European Union have developed into fortresses with electronically controlled borders, struggling to keep all unwanted people out, to reduce legal obligations with regard to refugees and asylum seekers by harmonizing their deflection regimes, and to get rid of all unwanted illegal workers. At the same time, as a consequence of gross violations of civil and political rights, of (civil) wars and ethnic cleansings, of ecological catastrophes and severe poverty, the numbers of those forced to move are growing fast all over the globe (see Gurr 1993). And the national and transnational institutions and mechanisms of governance are obviously inadequate to deal with these interconnected root causes of forced migration.

Citizenship always meant the exclusion of non-members. However, under such conditions, democratic citizenship in the rich and safe Northern States which, internally, has become ever more inclusive (T.H. Marshall), increasingly is a privilege. The exclusion of billions of desperately poor and uprooted people "out there" becomes morally more scandalous the harder one thinks about it.

The contributions in this volume address the associated issues of first admission policies (immigration, asylum and refugee policies) and of incorporation of ethnically and culturally diverse residents (denizens and citizens). Problems of migration, refugees, asylum seekers, of first admission policies, of incorporation and naturalization are among the *hottest contested political issues*, and this won't change in the foreseeable future. Governments and mainstream parties in rich Northern States as well as the EU and intergovernmental committees increasingly try to stem migration flows and develop deflection regimes regarding refugees and asylum seekers. To legitimize these policies a whole barrage of well-known arguments is used: the "flood" of overwhelming numbers of migrants and refugees; the "boat is full"; the sovereign legal right of states to decide how many and whom to admit; public order problems; unemployment and ethnic segmentation of labor markets; stress or breakdown of the social security system; serious overload of public social services like education, housing, health; serious political backlashes (welfare backlash, growing xenophobia and racism, immigrant fundamentalism); dangers for social and political stability and, particularly, political culture; erosion of the national culture up to threats for racial purity. The *defenders of closed borders* stress state-sovereignty and use a mix of prudential, particularist ethical arguments (*eigen volk eerst*) and realist arguments. They accept the legitimacy of the national and international institutional status quo and ask for tougher policies.

An unstable coalition of (representatives of) UN organizations, international and national NGOs, small opposition parties, some dissenters in mainstream parties and administration, organizations and movements of migrants, asylum seekers, committed citizens and critical professionals tries to challenge these policies. To legitimize their endeavours they try to show that states do not live up to their international legal, let alone moral obligations, that their rhetoric of human rights is hollow and that they violate the most simple demands of humanity and generosity. The *defenders of fairly open borders* underscore universalist moral arguments (like a right to free movement, basic needs, international distributive justice), criticize the international economic and political order and institutions, particularly the "moral standing of states", and look for alternative institutions.

It is an important task of *moral and political philosophy* to critically assess and balance the variety of normative arguments implicit in political discourse (Part I: Citizenship and Exclusion, Philosophical Perspectives). However, for a long time, most moral and political philosophers have simply neglected questions of international justice and citizenship (philosophy in the rearguard). As from the 1970s the issue has got some attention and recently a steady stream of publications can be seen. Still, the subject is fairly underdeveloped. Many, often too many questions are being asked while controllable theoretical strategies to answer them are scarce. Furthermore, these strategies and answers are at least as hotly contested as those in practical politics. There is no consensus, not even within different approaches, either with regard to the question of how to tackle normative issues of first admission or with regard to the answers. Starting from such a description of the "state of the art", Thomas Pogge and Veit Bader nevertheless try to achieve some minimal overlapping consensus among divergent traditions in recent moral philosophy in order to show that recent institutions and policies are morally wrong.

Thomas Pogge has developed such a minimalist strategy of overlapping consensus among divergent traditions in recent moral philosophy to show that gross international inequality, in particular extreme poverty, constitutes a global core injustice. However, he criticizes the link between poverty and severe inequality and fairly open borders. In 'Migration and Poverty', he starts from the indubitable truth that our resources and political energy are scarce. Given this fact, he tries to convince us that those who accept a weighty moral responsibility toward foreigners in desperate need should not devote their time, energy, and resources to the struggle of getting more of them admitted into the rich countries, but rather to the establishment of an effective programme of global poverty eradication. He does not deny that the richer states ought to admit more needy persons and ought to give equal citizenship to foreigners already here but explains that this is not a very effective strategy because, even under the best of circumstances, their numbers are ridiculously small, they are generally not really among the worst-off, and because it is a very costly strategy in terms of the political effort necessary to get them in and in terms of the hostility and anger they generate among our compatriots. The first priority should therefore be given to the effectuation of programmes directed at the straightforward eradication of poverty. The first task of such programmes should be the creation (by treaty) of suitable global institutional mechanisms for raising a stable flow of international financing up to one per cent of the combined GNP of 25 OECD countries. To achieve this, Pogge presents a Global Resource Dividend: states, while retaining full control over the natural resources in their territories (e.g. oil; other non-renewable resources; air, water, soil for the discharching of pollutants), would be required to pay a dividend proportional to the value of any of the resources they decide to use or sell. The second task consists in the design of alternatives to governmental development aid in order to spend these funds effectively. In Pogge's view, the full spectrum of possible channels should be exploited in a competitive way: to give funds directly to the poor themselves or to their local organizations, to spend funds through specialized organizations such as UNICEF and Oxfam, and to transfer funds to poor-country governments.

In 'Fairly Open Borders' *Veit Bader* also starts from an overlapping consensus with regard to poverty and severe global inequalities. He accepts that policies aimed at the eradication of poverty and gross inequality should have moral and strategic priority. Nevertheless he links these issues to the problem of first admission. The nature of this link is indirect and strategic: as long as states oppose direct policies or to the degree that such policies are not effective, their moral standing is undermined and this fact seriously qualifies all the well-known moral, ethico-political and realist arguments in favour of closed borders, because moral priority should be given to compatriots; because states have to play a fundamental role in the allocation of imperfectly allocated global obligations; because this is the only way to guarantee fundamental civil rights, democratic rights and cultures, and social rights and domestic equality. Commonly, these arguments are related to strong particularist arguments claiming that states should close their borders in order to protect thick ethnic or national cultures. He concludes that these arguments are strong enough to rule out the bogey of completely open borders. However, in our world of severe international injustice, restrictive first admission policies or closed borders are morally wrong. Rich Northern States have a double moral obligation seriously to fight global poverty *and* to let in "more, much more".

The articles in Part I focus exclusively on moral problems of first admission in our recent global (dis)order, bracketing more advanced and well-known philosophical discussions of incorporation and multiculturalism which will be taken up in Part III. The chapters in Part II, Citizenship, Migration and Incorporation: Historical Perspectives broaden the scope of problems. Critical historians have shown that different forms of migration are of all times and places. Many that are "hosts" now have been "strangers" in the past, not only in all officially so-called "immigration states" of the New World but, contrary to the cultivated image, also in the supposed ethnically and culturally homogeneous "nation-states" like France and Germany. Processes of democratization of state-sovereignty lead, paradoxically, to internal homogenization of citizens, to legal regulations of state-membership and admission and to increasing legal and actual powers of states to exclude "aliens" whenever that seems prudent.

Verena Stolcke addresses this paradox. In her 'The "Nature" of Nationality' she examines how nationality or state-membership became naturalized in the process of nineteenth-century nation-building in Germany, France and Britain. Membership in a nation-state comprises three analytically distinct dimensions: first, nationality in a strictly juridical sense as a legal relationship of state-membership *(Staatsangehörigkeit)*; second, citizenship which warrants the unqualified enjoyment of civil, political and social rights *(Staatsbürgerschaft)*; and, third, the inner, subjective sense of shared national identity. Stolcke focuses on the first dimension which she thinks has received little attention because, with the modern idea of the nation-state, nationality generally became naturalized, almost taken for granted. Stolcke shows a contradiction intrinsic in the very origin of modern rules of membership: on the one hand liberals and democrats advocate a universalist, voluntarist idea of citizenship while on the other hand, in a world of competing nation-states, states ascribe membership, using a mix of *jus sanguinis* and *jus soli*. Modern nationality laws were designed to overcome this contradiction between the original cosmopolitan, democratic and voluntarist ideal of citizenship and the imperative boundedness of the polity. Contrary to the frequent contrast established between the French, universalist, republican *Staatsnation* based on political consent and predominant *jus soli* and the German, particularist *Kulturnation* based on ethnic descent and predominant *jus sanguinis,* Stolcke shows that the rules of nationality and naturalization in both countries unite, in changing ways, both rules. By the 1880s the similarities between French and German nationality law outweighed the differences. In both states *patrilineal jus sanguinis* was the foremost rule conferring state membership. Subsidiary criteria contrasted, however, more markedly. In

France birth-place qualified descent while the German Empire allowed for naturalization by an act of state. In Britain, to the contrary, unconditional *jus soli* - in combination with the vertical bond of indelible allegiance to the Crown and its Parliament - prevailed until after WW II. Only the British Nationality Act of 1981 severely curtailed unconditional *jus soli* in response to the "colonial vengeance" transforming Commonwealth immigrants into aliens. Finally, Stolcke shows that parallel to the development of modern nation-states, nationality, citizenship and national identity became properly the domain of men though this gendered "nature" of nationality has passed largely unnoticed. France and Germany no less than Britain in the 19th century became "fatherlands" in the most literal sense. A woman's nationality was submerged into that of her father or husband by a double *patrilineal "matrix"*. European women conquered independent nationality only in the 1960s whereas women's nationality rights in the Americas developed quite differently from the 1930s onwards.

In his 'Segmented Macrosystems, Networking Individuals, Cultural Change' the historian *Dirk Hoerder* presents a differentiated frame to analyse migration as a balancing process. Specific for his approach, enriched by many examples, is the attempt to connect macrosystems, commonly emphasized by economic world system approaches, with the meso-level of regionally and sectorally segmented labour markets and networks of families, larger kin groups and neighborhoods (communities) on the one hand, and the micro-level of choices of individuals and families in a biographical and generational perspective on the other hand. *Migration* is conceived as an interactive balancing process within unequal power relationships. An extended economist approach to explain migration decisions is also applied in Hoerder's analysis of *incorporation and acculturation* as interactive change within unequal power relations. Migration always implies rapid cultural change. Focusing on culture and acculturation, Hoerder shows that one has clearly to distinguish between "experienced" and "reported" cultural reality. After migration, migrants do usually not experience pre-migration culture, which becomes "frozen in time", but develop their own *"ethnic culture"*. Interaction in the new society and pressures for adaptation lead to a change in behavioural patterns. What ethnic immigrants seek to maintain is clearly not the culture of origin but an intermediate culture, a lived multifaceted ethnic culture which is heterogeneous and varies according to class, social status and gender. In an ideal-typical sketch of stages of acculturation Hoerder discusses several options for the *formation of ethnic group identities* using examples from Canada: strict retention of pre-migration cultural characteristics and self-segregation by ethno-religious groups or political refugees; cooperation or merging with other ethnic groups to the detriment of ethnic specifics, partly as a result of categorizations by the receiving society ("the Galicians", "the Orientals", etc.), partly as an attempt to pool resources (Scandinavianism in the US); differentiation or diversification of resources when they are ready to rely on their own; the kind of homogenization by which different German tribes turned into Germans, Toscani and Lombardi into North Italians etc.; development of a hyphenated, ethno-Canadian culture when ethnics begin to move out of the ethnic language into the hegemonic one, out of the ethnic enclave into the suburbs; finally the merging of ethnic cultures in mainstream society if ethnics did not belong to a "visible minority" or are locked into underclass positions: symbolic or flag-waving ethnicity.

In Part III, Modes of Incorporation and Politics of Multiculturalism: Sociological Perspectives the scope is narrowed again. Now the focus is not on first admission but on mechanisms, processes and politics of incorporation of newcomers (and of indigenous people). Danielle Juteau, Stephen Castles and Aristide Zolberg all share a pro-theoretical frameworks similar to that of Hoerder stressing interactive changes in situations of specific power relationships. All three authors also share some crucial common principles of morally defensible politics of incorporation, most directly addressed by Castles, which seem to emerge from normative discussions of politics of multiculturalism in different countries and philosophical traditions.

In 'Beyond Multicultural Citizenship: The Challenge of Pluralism in Canada', *Danielle Juteau* presents a sociological approach to the understanding of the complex interaction between normative, structural, and cultural pluralism, highlighting unequal power relations among different national groups (in contexts of conquest and colonization) and ethnic groups (in contexts of migration). *Normative* pluralism accepts the legitimacy of multiple ethnic collectivities and solidarities and opposes institutionalized domination, assimilationism and syncretic integration. *Structural* pluralism presupposes a social structure characterized by institutional duplication. Ethnic *cultural* pluralism is related to cultural differences tied to the presence of different ethnic groups. Juteau's objective is to show that distinct goals of different groups cannot be explained in terms of cultural differences. Differentiated levels of power are "the basis for a dynamic understanding of ethnic and national diversity in Canada". This approach enables her to explain the process of nation-building, the challenge of ethnic and national pluralism and the origin, development and limits of multicultural policies in Canada. While the two colonizing groups called themselves "founding" peoples, they excluded or tried to assimilate the First Nations. French-Canadians developed an organic, ethnic model of the national community. British Canada developed a national model of a *Staatsnation*, trying to keep the French fact relegated to Quebec. Three simultaneous processes challenged this dominant vision of Anglo-Conformity after WW II: the increasing rate of immigration, the rise of *Québécois* nationalism, and the political emergence of First Nations. The eventual outcome has been the policy of *multiculturalism* in the 1970s, which did not emerge "naturally" or result from the application of a principle defining the just society. It should rather be viewed as a terrain of struggle opposing interrelated, yet differentiated and hierarchized ethnic and national groups. In its first stage, the policy set out to recognize symbolic rather than material interests, emphasizing prestige and ethnic honour. Since the 1980s it also embraced social issues. Juteau defends multicultural politics against increasing criticisms in the 1990s which hold it responsible for disuniting Canada, for creating too much heterogeneity, for encouraging discrimination through racial labelling, for essentializing societal dynamics, etc. She shows that what is "wrong" with multiculturalism is not to be found in what it does: it marks a passage from assimilationist liberalism to cultural pluralism and another step towards social inclusion. Rather, the problems must be found in what it cannot do and should not be expected to do: responding to the demands of collectivities defining themselves in national terms, such as First Nations and the *Québécois* which claim control over their boundaries, over economic, political and socio-cultural institutions. In her view these problems can only be solved by building a multicultural and multi-national country beyond the nation-state model which would include multiple forms of structural pluralism.

Stephen Castles, in his 'Multicultural Citizenship: the Australian Experience', analyses challenges to the predominant model of the nation-state and different models for managing increasing ethno-cultural diversity: the *differential exclusion*-model, the *assimilationist* model, and the *pluralist* model. Only the latter accepts ethno-cultural diversity and demands equal rights in all spheres of society. In its first variant, the *laissez-faire* approach of the USA, difference is tolerated but the state does not assist with settlement and does not support the maintenance of ethnic cultures. In the second, explicitly multiculturalist variant, typical for Canada and Australia from the 1970s and Sweden, the recognition of cultural pluralism is combined with policies designed to secure minimum economic and social standards for all. All different versions of *multiculturalism* run into four *dilemmas*: (i) the dilemma of formal inclusion: failure to make immigrants into citizens contradicts liberal-democratic principles, but making them into citizens questions the supposed ethnic and cultural homogeneity of the nation; (ii) the dilemma of substantial citizenship: where immigrants are socio-economically marginalized and are targets for racist violence, granting formal citizenship does not guarantee full civil, political, and social rights; (iii) the dilemma of recognition of collective cultural rights; (iv) the dilemma of the appropriateness of liberal-democratic institutions. Castles draws four *principles* of multicultural citizenship from the international debate on multiculturalism: take equality of citizenship rights as a starting point; recognize that formal equality of rights does not necessarily lead to equality of respect, resources, opportunities or welfare; establish mechanisms for group representation and participation; differential treatment for people with different characteristics and needs. Against this backdrop he analyses to what extent *multiculturalist policies in Australia* correspond with this notion. In 1973 the ALP (Labor) Government first introduced explicit multicultural policies rejecting assimilationism. This "ethnic group approach" emphasized cultural pluralism and the role of ethnic organizations in providing welfare services. During the 1980s the Government developed 'a citizenship model of multiculturalism' adding cultural rights to civil, political and social rights. Principles and rhetoric of government policy documents indeed correspond to Castles' four principles. A critical inquiry into implementation and practices of multicultural policies, however, reveals some *major problems*. First, multiculturalism has not addressed the needs of indigenous Australians. Secondly, multicultural policies directed at the combat of social disadvantage and the removal of labour market barriers run against the unresolved tension between principles of social justice and economic efficiency, poorly masked by the new notion of "productive diversity". Judged by different criteria the improvements have been painfully slow. Thirdly, multiculturalism became part of the mainstream of government service delivery and showed the deficiencies of bureaucratic practices. Finally, it led to a decline of ethnic mobilization and to the cooptation of leaders of ethnic organizations into government consultative bodies.

Aristide Zolberg presents the outlines of a comparative framework in his 'Modes of Incorporation'. Large-scale immigration and incorporation tend to provoke contentious *confrontations* and to produce politically confusing alignments cutting across the usual line-up of interests and established political parties. This is not surprising because immigration involves two very different dimensions of concern and interest. On an *economic axis*, the putative effects on material conditions are at stake: immigrant workers are welcomed by employers and resented by resident workers; immigrant entrepreneurs are viewed as undesirable business competitors or welcomed as providers of unusual goods and services at lower prices. Immigrants as customers of goods and services may be welcomed as buyers and taxpayers as well as resented as extra clients crowding public services. On a *cultural axis*, the putative impact of immigrants on the receiving country's national identity, its cultural character and social cohesion, is at stake. The dominant national formula defining the identity of the nation always incorporates negative criteria of identity, the "others" being commonly close neighbours, or outsiders within one's society, or remote and culturally "distant" aliens. Zolberg focuses on one specific manifestation of the *dialectics of the two axes*, the "wanted but not welcome" syndrome (economically wanted migrant labour which is, culturally and politically, not welcome) which is a key source of the tensions related to immigration in most of the post-industrial democracies today. Selected according to economic criteria (willingness to work for very low wages under harsh and dangerous conditions) immigrant labor is usually drawn from some less developed country or region, which belongs to the world of "others". Compared to historically earlier methods to keep immigrants out of the receiving society (extreme segregation, slavery or hierarchically stratified "plural societies" in the "plantation belt"), milder forms of control have been developed to prevent settlement (like preventing family unification, rotating recruitment, job-restrictions, exclusion from naturalization or very long waiting periods and expensive procedures). Most of these practices, however, conflict with liberal, social, and democratic norms that apply to residents as well as citizens. Even if ongoing immigration were to be sharply reduced in the near future, receiving societies have to face the challenge of successfully *incorporating* the large wave of recent decades. Zolberg looks for the most appropriate *balance* between the *obligation of newcomers* to respect the identity and cohesion of the host society, and the *obligation of the hosts* to respect the dignity and distinctive identity of immigrants. Zolberg concedes that, apart from alarmist fears, concern with the preservation of the host society's cultural character and social cohesion is not in itself illegitimate and that the settlement of a substantial group of people who diverge markedly from a country's established cultural norms does raise legitimate concerns which should not be dismissed as mere xenophobia. Some may deplore changes in the mainstream culture and fear that the "give" by the hosts leads to unmanageable cultural diversity but such an outcome is very unlikely because the hosts retain overwhelming advantages: incorporation is taking place on their turf, within an institutional framework which they control. The burden of change and adaptation remains squarely on the immigrants' shoulders. Zolberg concludes with a plea for a *differentiated politics of incorporation*. However, there has to be some bottom line: equalization of rights and politics to prevent the formation of ethnic underclasses. The task of incorporation cannot be left to the free play of market forces but requires a major commitment of public action. The neo-liberal and conservative dismantling of the public sector is highly counterproductive. Democracies cannot survive as "separate and unequal" societies.

In Part IV some 'Dilemmas of Migration- and Incorporation Policies' are addressed. Moral philosophers, critics of predominant institutions and policies as well as mainstream policy makers and administrators all ask for more comprehensive, long-term, internationally coordinated migration- and incorporation policies. In 'The Arts of Forecasting and Policy Making' *Veit Bader* tries to address two huge gaps: the gap between an increasing demand for knowledge and information and the actual knowledge about the future available, on the one hand, and the gap between the increasing demand for steering and control and the very limited capacities of international and governmental organizations in this regard, on the other hand. Criticizing constructivist rationalism and the arrogant truth-power of forecasting he opts for a critical interaction among scientific expertise and democratic politics, difficult to achieve. Criticizing neo-liberal "dethronement of politics" as well as hot republican "enthronement of politics" and "expertocratic politics", he opts for the development of new institutions and mechanisms of governance in the tradition of "associative democracy" to address the mismatch between increasingly global problems and the increasingly weakened capability of governance of the existing international, intergovernmental and state institutions.

Problems of migration, of first admission and of incorporation, in this volume, are analysed from different perspectives and disciplines by scholars from different countries: "Crossing the boundaries". As if looking into a hologram, I hope that these different beams of light may show some aspects of the many ways in which these issues are interconnected. Furthermore I hope that this view from many angles heightens the awareness and sensitivity - both on the part of scientists as well as on the part of policy makers and the general public - for the many serious moral and political dilemmas and the inevitable trade-offs in this hotly contested political area. Practical judgement and politics is a difficult art of balancing and the contributions in this volume can stimulate critical public debate and democratic decision making and action by clearly showing that predominant institutions, cultures and politics urgently need to be changed and alternative institutions and policies need to be developed to be able to address these burning problems of the 21st century.

1 Migration and Poverty*

Thomas Pogge

Many privileged and influential persons and governments hold that they have no weighty moral responsibility toward foreigners in desperate need. I have attacked this view elsewhere, arguing that we do have such a responsibility.[1] Of those who accept a weighty responsibility toward needy foreigners, most advocate that more such persons be admitted into the richer states and that more be done to ensure that those already here gain equal citizenship with ourselves in the fullest sense. I will argue here that such advocacy is not a good way of discharging our responsibility.

This argument may be a little hard to understand, because I agree with what I say we should not advocate. I agree that the richer states ought to admit more needy persons and ought to give equal citizenship to foreigners already here. But I question whether we should expend our scarce political energy and resources on these issues. Rather than try to get our compatriots to support admitting more needy foreigners and to support equal citizenship for foreigners already here, we should instead try to enlist them for other moral projects with regard to which our mobilizing efforts can be much more effective. What these other moral projects are will become clear in due course.

For purposes of the present argument, I can take for granted a moral concern for needy foreigners, many of whom would like to be admitted into the rich countries. To get a sense of the real-life dimensions of this issue, we must ask: Who are the persons seeking admission? Why do they want to come? And what moral claims do they have on us?

The answers to the first two questions are familiar. Very large numbers of persons live under truly terrible conditions: desperately poor and without effective rights of any sort. Every now and then, one can learn about some such lives through the media.[2] One can learn, for example, about the other side of the sex tourism advertisements — about the young girls and boys who, after being kidnapped, or sold by their parents, spend their teenage years enslaved in brothels in Bangkok or in Bombay or in any one of hundreds of cities in the so-called Third World. One can learn about the other side of those beautiful oriental rugs by reading about that little boy who was relinquished by his parents to settle a debt of $15 and who was then chained to a loom and forced to make carpets during every waking hour of his life. He escaped and tried to mobilize world public opinion in order to rescue other children forced into a similar fate. But his campaign did not last long: He was shot and killed in his native Pakistan still only twelve years old. One can read, finally, the latest Amnesty International annual report, detailing how some 150 national governments imprison and torture their political opponents.

We know at least vaguely that such things are going on, and this knowledge lends moral urgency to our conviction that the rich states have a moral obligation to take such people in, to rescue them from their dreadful situation. But before we act on this conviction, before we publicize it and try to win the support of our compatriots and governments, we should reflect upon two further facts.

The first further fact is the sheer extent of desperate need, which can be grasped by looking merely at the problem of global poverty. Some 20 million deaths per year — mostly female and mostly children[3] — are attributed to poverty: "Nearly 800 million people do not get enough food, and about 500 million people are chronically malnourished" and about 1300 million people (24 per cent of humankind) live below the international poverty line[4] — which is defined as "that income or expenditure level below which a minimum, nutritionally adequate diet plus essential non-food requirements are not affordable"[5] and currently corresponds to an annual *per capita* income of ca. $75. With hundreds of millions falling significantly below this line, we can assume that the income of the poorest fifth (1100 million) of humankind is about 1/4 per cent of world income, or $50 *per capita* annually — while the richest fifth has over 90 per cent of world income, or $19000 *per capita* annually, nearly 400 times more than the poorest fifth.[6] With regard to wealth, the disparity is even greater, because the poor tend to have much less wealth than annual income, while the rich tend to have much more wealth than annual income. The wealth of the richest five persons suffices to match the combined annual income of the poorest fifth, and the wealth of the richest 358 (the dollar billionaires) suffices to match the combined annual income of the poorest 45 per cent.[7]

Two important lessons may be drawn from these amazing statistics — one piece of bad news and one piece of good news. The bad news is that the number of desperate foreigners whom the rich countries now admit every year, and also the larger number of desperate foreigners they might conceivably come to admit under the best of circumstances — these numbers are ridiculously small in comparison to the number of those who are in desperate need and would like to come. The good news is that, despite the huge number of the global poor, it would be quite possible to improve their conditions decisively, if the rich countries were willing to make a concerted effort. Remember: just one per cent of the income of the richest fifth is nearly *four times* the income of the poorest fifth of humankind.

I will now discuss each of these two points, before drawing the obvious conclusion from them, which is: other things being equal, those who accept a weighty moral responsibility toward needy foreigners should devote their time, energy, and resources *not* to the struggle to get more of them admitted into the rich countries, but *rather* to the struggle to institute an effective programme of global poverty eradication. The rider "other things being equal" is meant to exclude those whose jobs or expertise give them special opportunities to support needy foreigners who are seeking or have gained admission into one of the rich countries. My argument may not apply to them.

The first point — the bad news — was that the admission of needy foreigners into the rich countries cannot possibly protect all who now live under dreadful conditions and would want to come. One reason for this is that the number of needy persons in the world — including at least those 1300 million who cannot afford "a minimum, nutritionally adequate diet plus essential non-food requirements" — is simply out of all proportion to the number of needy foreigners which the rich countries admit or could admit. To see this, compare the 1300-million figure to two other numbers

a The number of refugees legally admitted in 1995 by all the countries of the European Union combined: ca. 25000.

b The number of legal aliens from all outside countries estimated to be now living in the European Union: ca. 10 million.[8]

For every person we can persuade some rich country to admit, there will be hundreds, if not thousands, left in desperate need.

There is another reason why the admission of needy foreigners will not solve the problem. This is the second further fact I had wanted to mention, namely: not many of those whom the rich countries admit are really among the worst-off. It is quite obvious, on reflection, why this should be so: it helps a very great deal, in the scramble to gain admission, to have money for bribing officials, for paying smugglers, and for hiring a lawyer; to have some education, professional skills, and language training; to have some relative who has already succeeded in gaining admission; and also to be well endowed: bright, tall, healthy, and good looking. But persons with these advantages will rarely be among the neediest. In whatever way the rules for admitting needy foreigners may be designed — in this or that rich country, now or in the future — the truly worst-off always compete at a great disadvantage against more privileged persons from the poor countries who will often be able to elbow them aside.

This important second fact also helps to put into perspective an argument often made in favour of admitting needy foreigners. When admitted and allowed to work in one of the rich countries, so it is said, they are likely to send money back home to their families. This is true. But the families to whom this money is being sent are often among the more privileged in the poor country in question. Of course, some of these funds may "trickle down" to the poorest. But some will also be used to cement and entrench the oppression of the poorest by Third-World "elites". In any case, these funds are far more likely to increase than to reduce domestic inequality in the poor countries and therefore are a mixed blessing at best.

I must respond at least briefly to one prominent objection against my claim that the task of persuading our compatriots and governments to admit more needy foreigners has less moral urgency than we tend to suppose. The objection is this: there is a small class of needy foreigners whose admission is of much greater moral importance than that of the desperately poor. These are *political refugees*, fleeing persecution for their expressed beliefs or peaceful political activity. In response: I cannot see why the moral importance of admitting political refugees should be any greater than that of admitting so-called economic migrants. For one thing, the politically persecuted are not, in general, worse off than the desperately poor. Being imprisoned for one's beliefs is not, in general, worse than working 16-hour days while being permanently hungry. Being beaten to death for participating in a demonstration is not, in general, worse than dying of diarrhoea or simple starvation. Second, the politically persecuted are generally better educated and more resourceful, hence better able to protect themselves. Third, the desperately poor are *also* the victims of political oppression, for they are excluded from all better economic opportunities through the coercive power of governments. Their plight is produced by the present national and international economic order which is coercively upheld by their governments and ours.[9] And fourth, even if this third reason did not hold and desperate poverty were not then imposed upon the global poor by others, there would still be no moral reason to discriminate. For protecting one person from being killed by an attacker is not, in general, morally more important than protecting another from drowning. There may be special circumstances, of course, as when our own government has played a role in the attack — for example, by delivering arms to a government that now uses them to oppress its opponents. But such special circumstances often obtain also in regard to desperate poverty, as when our market demand for coffee and flowers causes land use in some poor country to be converted toward these export crops, thereby driving the prices of rice and beans beyond the means of the local poor.

So much in support of the first point. There are hundreds of millions of needy people in this world. Helping to protect them is of great moral importance. Getting such persons admitted into one of the rich countries does indeed protect them. But by this method only a ridiculously small fraction of those in desperate need can be protected, even under the most optimistic assumptions about what we can get our governments and compatriots to accept.

Let us now attend to the second point, the *good* news, which is that it is quite possible to protect most of those in desperate need by other means. You may remember my estimate that the annual *per capita* income of the poorest fifth of humankind is around $50. You may have thought this estimate misleading because, as is well known, one dollar buys much more in a poor country than it would buy in a developed country. Economists take account of this fact by converting annual income figures in terms of "purchasing power parities" (PPP). Instead of saying of some poor textile worker in India that she is earning one dollar a week, they say that she is earning, say, five dollars PPP per week. Behind this lies the following thought. While the 36 rupees this woman earns weekly are equivalent to one dollar at the market exchange rate, these 36 rupees can buy much more in India than one dollar can buy in the developed countries. So the translation of 36 rupees into five dollars PPP means that this woman can buy with her 36 rupees about as much as we can buy with five dollars.[10]

I mention purchasing power parities for two reasons. First, to respond to the suspicion that I have shamelessly overstated the severity of global poverty. I plead guilty. So instead of saying that the annual income of the global poor is around $50, let us instead say that it is around $250 PPP.[11] But this surely does not invalidate what I have said about the severity of global poverty. Having on average as much purchasing power as $250 annually would supply in the developed countries, the poorest fifth are still desperately poor. They can perhaps, in normal times, afford just enough basic foodstuffs to survive — but virtually nothing else by way of vacations, education or medicines, presents for the children, or savings. Any small mishap — such as an illness or a rice shortage with increase in price — can spell disaster.

My second reason for getting into purchasing power parities is to reinforce my plea for the alternative strategy toward protecting the global poor. The fact that 36 rupees buys much more in India than one dollar buys in the developed world presents a golden opportunity. This is so, because in the currency market one can actually receive 36 rupees for a dollar and thus multiply the purchasing power of one's funds. It is therefore much cheaper than one might think to reduce global poverty despite the huge number of persons affected by it. Ironically, those who like to claim that eradicating world poverty would impoverish the developed countries do not know how incredibly poor the global poor really are. Thus Rorty, for example, doubts that we are able to "help" the global poor by appealing to the claim that "a politically feasible project of egalitarian redistribution of wealth, requires there to be enough money around to insure that, after the redistribution, the rich will still be able to recognize themselves — will still think their lives worth living."[12] Rorty can rest assured: the total amount of money that the poorest 1300 million persons are lacking toward being able to satisfy their basic needs is exceedingly small. For them $75 billion a year would make a phenomenal difference — it could *double* their current income — while for us it is just 0.4 per cent of the GDP of the developed countries (or 1/7 of the value of annual crude oil production or 1/3 of US military expenditure).

Of course, in the real world things are not so simple. Even if $75 billion could be raised in or from the rich countries, there would be no possible way of spending this money, in a concentrated way, toward the emancipation of the global poor. This is so for at least three reasons. First, there will be transaction costs, as the disbursement of the funds in dozens of countries must be planned and organized. Hundreds of people would need to be hired, including economists and accountants, and the money would have to be exchanged and transported to where it is needed, generally by hand. Second, there will be targeting costs, as some of the funds will inevitably benefit persons not in desperate need. And, third, there will be corruption costs as well: Members of the local "elites" will try very hard to divert some of the funds into their own pockets, for instance by demanding payment for all sorts of bureaucratic licences and authorizations; and some of the persons involved in the distribution will inevitably be tempted to engage in extortion, passive bribery, or theft.

Because of these costs, considerably more than $75 billion per year would be needed to double the income of the global poor. Nevertheless, getting the rich countries and their citizens to support such a project is still vastly more effective than getting them to support the admission of more needy foreigners — effective, that is, toward the purpose of protecting those in desperate need. And the same holds on a smaller scale as well: with the political effort it would take to pressure some Western government to admit an extra hundred needy foreigners, we could alternatively pressure this same government to allocate a few extra million dollars to global poverty eradication. And these few extra million dollars, if effectively spent, could protect not a hundred, but thousands or even tens of thousands of desperately poor persons.

Let me be clear about the conclusion I want to draw from the two points I have developed thus far. My conclusion is *not* that we should oppose the admission of needy foreigners into our richer countries. *Not at all.* Nor am I denying that persuading our governments and compatriots to accept more needy foreigners is a worthy cause. But if this *is* a worthy cause, it is so in virtue of the protection it affords to persons who are very badly off. Protecting such persons from the oppressive conditions imposed upon them by current institutional arrangements is indeed a principal moral priority. I have argued, however, that we can do much more in respect to this priority by attempting to promote better living conditions in the poorer countries than by attempting to promote the admission of needy foreigners. Through efforts of the first kind we can protect many more, and more needy, people than through efforts of the second kind.

What then should we try to persuade our compatriots and governments to do? First, we should probably not spend our time and resources on advocating more governmental development aid. It is now abundantly clear to those who care to know that such aid is generally ineffective in protecting the global poor and is rarely even intended to do so.[13] This should not be surprising. Our government officials have some public-relations reasons to care about our country's overall foreign aid allocation as a percentage of national income. Charts with these percentages are compiled and circulated widely in the media. But why should they be concerned whether foreign aid projects they are funding now will help alleviate severe poverty in the long run? Who will evaluate those projects, keep track of who authorized them, and hold these officials accountable for their decisions in two or five or ten years' time? The only incentives our officials have toward spending foreign-aid funds well are *moral* incentives, and among politicians these are, alas!, somewhat of a rarity. Moreover, these moral incentives are opposed by powerful prudential incentives. When a rich country's government has at its disposal funds targeted for foreign aid, it has opportunities to spend them so as to promote its own interests and perhaps those of its country. Such a government can, for example, use its foreign aid funds to buy political support from domestic creditor banks and exporters, or from "elites" in strategically important Third-World countries. Moreover, such a government is likely to gain more recognition and prestige from large, high-visibility projects, which tend to benefit the poorest segments of the recipient country's population only very indirectly, if at all. A large new power plant affords nice photo opportunities, and it may also provide lots of cheap electricity. But the poorest of the poor have no electric outlets or appliances and need safe drinking water much more urgently in any case. Pressing for additional governmental development aid is not, then, the most promising idea. The rich countries are already spending some $60 billion under this rubric,[14] but the effect of this spending on the global poor is rather slight.

It is a much better idea, secondly, to persuade our compatriots to support the more efficient anti-poverty organizations such as UNICEF and Oxfam. At very low cost, these organizations provide what the poorest really need — for example, oral rehydration therapy to combat diarrhoea, wells for safe drinking water, elementary education so people can read and write and understand their rights, micro-loans to break the dependence on local landlords and loan sharks, quality seeds to increase crop yields and to reduce the need for fertilizers, stoves for fuel-efficient cooking, medical and family-planning services. The proven effectiveness of these organizations entails, on a small scale, that we as individuals have strong moral reasons to support them: we can help protect many more persons by collecting a few thousand dollars for UNICEF or Oxfam than by getting a few additional needy foreigners admitted into our country; and we are also far more likely to succeed with the first project than with the second. The proven effectiveness of these organizations entails, on a larger scale, that severe global poverty could be largely eradicated in a matter of years, if such organizations had anything like the money now available for official development aid.

This suggests a third idea about what we might persuade our compatriots and governments to do with respect to global poverty. This idea would seek to combine the best of what we already have. Official development aid is mostly inefficient, but it does provide an amount of money — about $60 billion per year — that is at least in the right ballpark. The better anti-poverty organizations are quite effective, but they do not have anything like the funds they would need to succeed on a large scale.[15] The third idea is then to create by treaty suitable global institutional mechanisms for raising a stable flow of international financing for global poverty eradication. The funds to be raised should initially be between $65 and $200 billion a year (or between 1/3 and one per cent of the combined GNP of 25 OECD countries).

Let me indicate, just very briefly, how these funds might be raised and spent. The simplest way of raising the funds would be to oblige the governments of the rich countries to pay them out of general tax revenues. But other ways of raising the funds are better by being morally more compelling and/or by having positive collateral effects. One such idea has been floated for many years by the Nobel laureate James Tobin. He proposes a half-per-cent tax on currency transactions in order to discourage currency speculation. The specific intent of this tax is to reduce speculation-induced exchange rate fluctuations and thereby to enable national governments and central banks better to adapt their monetary policy to domestic economic conditions. But the tax would also raise revenues, which Tobin proposes to use for global poverty eradication.[16] Presently the volume of currency transactions is an incredible $1.5 *trillion per day* . Even if the tax achieved its purpose by reducing this volume dramatically, by a factor of 25, say, down to $60 billion a day, this tax would still raise $300 million per day or $110 billion annually — enough to eradicate malnutrition, trivial diseases, and severe poverty in a matter of years.

Another, quite plausible idea almost became reality. It was the basic principle of Part XI of the 1982 *United Nations Convention on the Law of the Sea* that natural resources on the ocean floors beneath international waters "are the common heritage of mankind" (Article 136), to be used "for the benefit of mankind as a whole ... taking into particular consideration the interests and needs of developing States [through an] equitable sharing of financial and economic benefits" (Article 140), which was to have been effected by sharing of seabed mining technologies and profits (Annex III, Articles 5 and 13) under the auspices of the International Seabed Authority, or ISA (Annexes III and IV). How could anyone have wanted to oppose this idea, to exclude the global poor, who are literally starving, from the value of seabed resource? Three successive US administrations have tried quite hard to secure the great benefits of the treaty in "protecting and promoting the wide range of U.S. ocean interests"[17] without the sharing regime. Shortly before the Convention was to come into force (November 28, 1996), the Clinton Administration succeeded in having the sharing provisions replaced by a superseding *Agreement*.[18] This *Agreement* endorses the US view that the common-heritage principle really means that the oceans and their resources "are open to use by all in accordance with commonly accepted rules."[19] Accordingly, it frees mining companies from having to share seabed mining technologies[20] and greatly reduces the sharing of profits.[21] The *Agreement* further accommodates US demands by "1) guaranteeing a U.S. seat in the Council [the executive organ of the ISA]; 2) allowing ourselves and a few other industrialized nations acting in concert to block decisions in the Council;...."[22] In managing to renegotiate the *Law of the Sea Convention* — by pressing the Reagan era threat of founding a competing seabed resources regime with a few like-minded countries[23] — the Clinton Administration won a great victory for the US and any other countries that will have the capital and technologies for profitable seabed mining. The reaction in these wealthy countries was quiet relief: their governments raised no objections and their media largely ignored the event. The governments of the poorer countries went along as well in the interest of making the treaty universal. It is the poor persons, in any case, who can least afford being shut out from this common heritage of humankind. And so, for rather trivial gains,[24] one viable and morally plausible opportunity of raising funds for poverty eradication through the sale of seabed mining rights has been lost.[25] A mobilization in defense of the common-heritage idea could have achieved much more for foreigners in desperate need than any comparable mobilization for the sake of having more of them admitted into the rich countries.

A Global Resources Dividend or GRD offers yet another alternative for raising the requisite funds.[26] Here states, while retaining full control over the natural resources in their territories, would be required to pay a dividend proportional to the value of any of these resources they decide to use or sell. The word 'dividend' is meant to suggest that all human beings, including those now excluded, are viewed as owning an inalienable stake in all limited natural resources. As with preferred stock, this stake confers no control over whether or how natural resources are to be used, but merely a claim to share in their economic benefits. Take crude oil for example. Every state extracting crude oil might be required to pay a $2 dividend per barrel ($0.0125 per litre) extracted, which would be, for the most part, passed along to the end users of petroleum products. The current global crude oil production is about 4 trillion litres (or four cubic kilometres) per year. From just the consumption of this single resource, the GRD scheme could therefore raise $50 billion annually — or somewhat less if, as is desirable, crude oil demand would decline as a consequence of its slightly increased price. The GRD could be extended to other nonrenewable resources and also, importantly, to the use of air, water and soil for the discharging of pollutants. It would then not only raise the needed revenues, but would also tend to slow down the depletion of natural resources and the pollution of our environment.

I can speak only briefly about how the funds raised for global poverty eradication should be spent. Here the most obvious idea — transferring the funds to the governments of the poorest countries — is clearly problematic: many Third-World governments and officials are even less interested in effective poverty eradication than most rich-country politicians in charge of foreign aid funds. Making them the recipients of funds raised from seabed mining, or through a Tobin tax or GRD, would greatly dilute, if not erase, their intended benefits.

To make development funds effective, the full spectrum of possible channels must be explored and exploited in a competitive way. The most important possibilities are to give funds directly to the poor themselves or to their local organizations, to spend funds through specialized organizations such as UNICEF and Oxfam, and to transfer funds to poor-country governments. The idea of competitive allocation provides that fund flows be directed and redirected to where they have the greatest effect in enabling the global poor to fulfill their needs and to defend their basic interests on their own. The effects of fund flows in terms of poverty eradication are to be closely monitored and the allocation of funds is to be adjusted accordingly, pursuant to clear rules announced in advance, so that funds flow through *those* channels and to *those* countries which lead them to their most effective use. By formulating the allocation rules in this way, incentive effects are created and mobilized. Thus, the political and economic elite of any poor country has an interest in attracting funds to its country because it, too, will benefit from these funds in various ways. The rules governing fund disbursement should be designed to take full advantage of this interest — making it clear to such elites that, if they want to benefit from their society's receipt of funds, they must cooperate in making these funds effective toward improving the conditions and opportunities of the domestic poor. In general terms, the rules for the disbursement of funds must be designed so as to stimulate a worldwide peaceful competition in poverty eradication.[27]

It is time to take stock. We have organized our social world — and, in particular, our world economy — so that it produces and reproduces truly monstrous poverty and inequality. Over 20 million persons die each year from poverty-related causes, hundreds of millions are in desperate need. It is quite understandable, and noble actually, that our first reaction to this suffering should be to insist that we must take these people in.

> *Give me your tired, your poor,*
> *your huddled masses yearning to breathe free*
> *the wretched refuse of your teeming shore ......*

I have argued that this first reaction is nevertheless mistaken. If there were no political resistance to open or fairly open borders, if our compatriots and governments were quite ready to receive the moral argument for them and to act on it, then things might be different. But as things stand, the needy foreigners we manage to get admitted are very costly indeed in terms of the political effort necessary to get them in and in terms also of the hostility and anger they generate among our compatriots, which makes it ever harder to enlist their support for *any* initiatives on behalf of the global poor. We can be vastly more effective in protecting those we are concerned to protect by adopting a different strategy.

Having presented the argument that this is so, it strikes me that this argument is not particularly difficult or unobvious. This raises the question why people do not generally see things my way. Why do most of those who care about needy foreigners at all think in terms of taking people in, rather than in terms of alleviating the terrible conditions that make them want to come here in the first place? To make my argument complete, I should be able to explain why this is so and also to show that any reasons others might have for thinking as they do are not good reasons.

One possible explanation is patriotism. Here I have in mind not the silly view that our country is so wonderful that no one can be happy outside of it — though I must say that this view does have its adherents e.g. in France and the US. Nor do I have in mind the chauvinist view that only Europeans with their rich history and political traditions can govern a country well, though this view, too, seems to have some adherents, albeit a dying breed. What I mean by patriotism, rather, is the idea that we have more moral reason to promote the justice and moral perfection of our own country than those of the rest of the world. The idea is that the hostility many of our compatriots harbour against the admission of foreigners is a flaw in them that we ought to correct quite independently of the effects this correction would have on the fate of needy foreigners. We have a special responsibility, as it were, for the sentiments and prejudices of our compatriots which can seem to trump the more general responsibility we feel for global poverty.

I can surely feel the emotional force of this idea. I certainly share the moral preference for living in a country where needy foreigners are welcomed. But reversing the moral priority I have been arguing for on this ground is nevertheless, I believe, a gross mistake — for two reasons: First, it is true that our countries are often actively involved in turning away needy foreigners. But it is just as true, if much less obvious, that our countries are also actively involved in upholding the prevailing world order and, in particular, the present structure of the world economy which, quite regularly and predictably, produces and reproduces severe global poverty and inequality. In the latter case, the active involvement of the officials who purport to act in our name is so much less obvious, because the present global economic order is already in place and appears to reproduce itself without any human agency, and also because we and our officials are no more involved in its reproduction than millions of persons from the other rich countries. You feel awful, if one desperate asylum seeker is turned away by a consular official purporting to act in your name. But you feel much less awful if your government, like all the others, shows no interest in supporting or defending global economic reforms and thereby collaborates in continuing Third-World starvation and disease at current levels. The economic exclusion of 1300 million persons is brought about by the citizens and governments of the rich countries, together with corrupt Third-World elites, and, though we clearly are collectively responsible for it, we have a tendency not to feel particularly responsible, because no one is really in a position to alter this exclusion, to change the world economy. The fact that so many are maintaining this exclusion together creates the illusion that no one is really doing it, that it just happens, naturally, as it were.

A second explanation of the widespread mistaken priority is somewhat related to the first. We tend to think of refugees and asylum seekers as particular individuals, as persons with a face. We think of them as having stepped forward and knocked on our door and told us their story. How can we slam the door in their face? Of course, no one will deny that the 1300 million global poor are also persons with faces. But we think of them as an anonymous, amorphous mass. Since they have not stepped forward, they can become persons with faces only if *we* reach out to *them*, selecting them from the crowd. This requires an initiative that few of us ever take. Fundraisers, by the way, know about this quirk in our psychology and, instead of requesting a donation for poverty-stricken children in the Third World, often ask us to sponsor some *particular* child, picture enclosed. With such an appeal, the project of protecting needy children can gain some of the psychological urgency that we tend to attach to not turning back needy foreigners asking for admission.

Two other sample contrasts display the same psychological propensity of ours. Think back to the Second World War, of those forced to live under the terror of German occupation. Imagine what it was like to know Jews threatened by deportation while also knowing about some reasonably safe places to hide or routes of escape. It is *much* easier, psychologically, merely to fail to approach any of the Jews one knows with the offer to help than to turn away a Jewish family standing on one's doorstep. — Or think of a person trapped in a cave or in a well. In such a case, we are willing to move heaven and earth, to spend millions of dollars and thousands of hours to save a human life. Do we feel the same moral urgency about installing a guard rail on a busy highway which we know would save two or three lives a year? Or about reducing emissions from a plant which we know would prevent several cancer deaths? No, we do not. We have a tendency to accept much greater costs for the sake of protecting someone we think of as a determinate individual — though on reflection this seems quite irrational, especially in a case like global poverty, where the only distinction of the determinate individuals is that they have asked for admission or have somehow managed to come here — which, if anything, tends to show that they are *less* in need than many others.

A third explanation why people might think it morally more important to work for the admission of more needy foreigners than for global poverty eradication projects is that they take the former itself to be the most effective means for promoting the latter. Once persons from the poor countries are living among us, so one might reason, they can influence those around them to be more sympathetic to the plight of Third-World populations and they can also work through our political process to initiate the kind of global poverty eradication mechanisms I have proposed. While some may accept this line of thought, I do not think there is much evidence for it. In Europe's recent experience, the influx of poor foreigners has made the population in general *less* sympathetic to suffering in foreign lands. And in the US, which has a much longer history of significant Third-World immigration, there is little indication of such immigrants even *attempting* to influence government policy in favour of their former compatriots (in contrast to Polish-, Irish-, and Jewish-Americans, for example, who make considerable political efforts on behalf of, respectively, Polish, Irish, and Israeli causes).

I have taken a position that goes against the moral beliefs, sentiments, and conduct of many persons I respect. I have tried to show, in a rudimentary way, that their contrasting view can be explained in a way that does not provide reasons against mine. For the moment, then, I believe that my view is correct. Let me say clearly, one last time, what my view is and what it is not. I have *not* argued against the admission of needy foreigners into the rich countries, nor against equal citizenship for those already here. I have *not* denied that it is wrong to refuse admission to truly needy foreigners. What I have argued is, *first*, that awful living conditions abroad are due, for the most part, to the economic exclusion of the global poor as practised by the citizens and governments of the rich countries; and, *second*, that there are much more effective ways of protecting these poor persons from the deprivations they now suffer than by trying to get them admitted into the rich countries. Given that we — those who recognize a weighty moral responsibility toward foreigners in desperate need — have only limited resources at our disposal and cannot possibly devote ourselves to every worthy political goal, we should focus our efforts to where we can achieve the most toward overcoming the greatest injustice of our time: the impoverishment and starvation of hundreds of millions of people. We should stop attempting to get more needy foreigners admitted into the rich countries and instead concentrate on improving the local living conditions of the global poor through international institutional reforms, like the Tobin Tax or the GRD, and through effective international aid organizations, like UNICEF and Oxfam.

Notes

*   Many thanks to Dagfinn Føllesdal for the kind invitation to join him at the Centre for Advanced Study in Oslo, where this essay was written, and to Veit Bader and Bente Puntervold Bø for highly instructive criticisms and suggestions. In this essay, the $-sign refers to US dollars throughout, and "billion" and "trillion" stands for 1000 million and 1000 billion, respectively.

1   Pogge 1989, Chapter 6; Pogge 1992a; Pogge 1994b; Pogge 1995c; Pogge 1997a; Pogge 1997b.

2   For example: 'Asia's Plantations of the '90s', *International Herald Tribune* , April 15, 1996, p.2; 'The Flourishing Business of Slavery', *The Economist* , September 21, 1996, pp.43-4.

3   Some 3 million children annually die of simple diarrhoea because their parents cannot obtain a 15-cent oral rehydration pack. Lack of vitamins and antibiotics leads to another 3.5 million deaths from pneumonia, one million deaths from measles, and so on. See Grant 1993.

4   UNDP 1996, p.20.

5   *Ibid.* , p.222.

6   What I say here may seem to conflict with a prominent statement in the Report: "The poorest 20% of the world's people saw their share of global income decline

from 2.3% to 1.4% in the past 30 years. Meanwhile, the share of the richest 20% rose from 70% to 85%. That doubled the ratio of the shares of the richest and the poorest — from 30:1 to 61:1" (*ibid.*, p.2). These ratios were, however, calculated from country aggregates. The two relevant fifths were formed by simply taking the populations of the richest and poorest *countries*, with each set of countries selected so that it represents one fifth of world population (according to the written explanation I received from Mr. Selim Jahan, Deputy Director of the UNDP Human Development Report Office, New York City). But this yields the ratio between the average income in the richest countries and the average income in the poorest countries, not the income ratio between the richest and poorest fifths of "the world's people." The former ratio is obviously a very bad estimate of the latter: the income of the richest fifth is underestimated, as many poor in the richest countries are much poorer than many rich in non-rich countries (so the latter, not the former, should be included in the top fifth). And the income of the poorest fifth is hugely inflated as the poorest in middle-income countries such as Brazil are excluded in favor of more affluent persons in the poorest countries (among them, for instance, President Mobutu Sese Seko, whose income is a rather considerable part of the Zairian national income).

7   *Ibid.*, p.13.

8   These two figures are from the *International Herald Tribune*, March 5, 1996, p.5.

9   See Pogge 1997b.

10   The 5:1 ratio is realistic, in that India's 1993 GDP *per capita* is $250 (calculated from GDP and population; UNDP 1996, pp.179, 185) and its real GDP (PPP) *per capita* is given as $1240 (*ibid.*, p.136). The weighted average ratio for all poor countries is close to 5:1, though the ratios given for individual poor countries differ significantly — ranging from 2:1 (Mali) to 8 :1 (Tanzania).

11   Similarly, the international poverty line should then be expressed not as annual *per capita* income of $75 (20¢ a day), but as annual *per capita* purchasing power of $375. Being poor means having less purchasing power than $1 a day affords in the developed countries. 1300 million persons, 24 per cent of humankind, are poor in this sense (UNDP 1996, 27). (Mr Selim Jahan, Deputy Director of the UNDP Human Development Report Office, has confirmed orally that the $1-per-day figure printed in the Report represents purchasing power, not income. This squares with figures given in Dasgupta 1993, pp.79-80.)

12   Rorty 1996, pp.14-15. Rorty's essays are, of course, to be taken as "narratives".

13   There are important exceptions, notably the Scandinavian countries and the Netherlands. The present paragraph does not apply to them.

14   Official development assistance by the rich countries was $59 billion, or 0.3 per cent of their combined GNP, in 1994. Of this, less than one quarter went to the least developed countries. Norway was the most generous country, allocating 1.05 per cent of its GNP (0.44 per cent for the least developed countries). The US was the least generous, allocating 0.15 per cent of its GNP (0.04 per cent for the least developed countries). Though Norway, Sweden, Denmark and the Netherlands together have only 13 per cent of the US population and 12 per cent of US GNP, they spend more than the US on aid for the least developed countries. For all these 1994 data, see UNDP 1996, pp. 199, 203, 208. In 1995, the US reduced its official development aid by more than one quarter, from $9.927 billion to $7.367 billion (written communication from Sigismund Niebel, OECD, Paris).

15   The entire United Nations Organization with its dozens of agencies has an annual budget of $1.3 billion and is undergoing drastic cut-backs this year as a result of unpaid membership dues. The UN is owed some $3 billion in back dues, about half of this by the US.

16   For a brief statement of the idea, see Tobin 1994, where he acknowledges that "raising revenues for international purposes was not a primary motivation of my proposal."

17   Ambassador David A. Colson, Deputy Assistant Secretary of State for Oceans, in testimony before the Subcommittee on Oceanography of the Merchant Marine and Fisheries Committee of the US House of Representatives (April 26, 1994).

18   *Agreement Relating to the Implementation of Part XI of the United Nations Convention on the Law of the Sea of 10 December 1982*. Its Article 2(1) says: "In the event of an inconsistency between this agreement and Part XI, the provisions of this agreement shall prevail."

19   US Department of State: *Commentary on the Law of the Sea Convention including the 1994 Amendments*, p.3. "The Agreement fully meets the objections of the United States and other industrialized states to Part XI" (*ibid.*, p.2), which were that: "it established a structure for administering the seabed mining regime that does not accord the industrialized States influence in the regime commensurate with their interests; it incorporated economic principles inconsistent with free market philosophy; and its specific provisions created numerous problems from an economic and commercial policy perspective that would have impeded access by the United States and other industrialized countries to the resources of the deep seabed beyond national jurisdiction" (*ibid.*, pp.2-3).

20   The provisions of Annex III, article 5, of the Convention shall not apply." Section 5(2) of the Annex to the *Agreement* (cited in note 18).

21   Section 7(1) of the Annex to the *Agreement* (cited in note 18) limits the sharing of profits to "economic assistance" to "developing countries which suffer serious adverse effects on their export earnings or economies resulting from a reduction in the price of an affected mineral or in the volume of exports of that mineral, to the extent that such reduction is caused by [seabed mining]." Section 8(3) halves the application fee for exploration and exploitation of sites to $250,000 and Section 8(2) eliminates the $1,000,000 annual production fee as well as the profit-related financial contributions (all of which were mandated in the *Convention*'s Annex III, Article 13).

22   Colson, *op.cit.* (note 17).

23   Germany and Great Britain were especially willing to go along with such a move.

24   At current metals prices, seabed mining is not expected to become commercially worthwhile for quite some time.

25   One may object that any funds Part XI of the *Convention* might have raised for the least developed countries would — like so much official development aid — have ended up in the pockets of corrupt Third-World politicians and bureaucrats. But, surely, the choice of throwing money at corrupt Third-World elites versus ignoring global poverty does not exhaust the available options. Clinton might well have pressed for terms that ensure that the funds raised are spent on effective poverty eradication.

26   For an elaborate statement of this proposal, see Pogge 1995c.

27   Pogge 1995c, section 3, develops these points in more detail.

2 Fairly Open Borders*

Veit Bader

Practical philosophy had much trouble in dealing with problems of first admission.[1] In this chapter I do not give a comprehensive overview of the state of the art. Instead, I will present a committed, non-technical plea in favour of fairly open borders. Broadly speaking, two different moral arguments in favour of fairly open borders can be developed: the first one tries to show that free mobility is an inherent moral principle and should, therefore, be recognized as a universal and basic human right (Dummet 1992, Carens 1992). The second is a more indirect one which tries to show that states have a moral obligation to let people in as long as and to the degree that they do not live up to their moral obligations to guarantee universal and basic human rights to safety and subsistence. In this argument, free movement and open borders are not seen as intrinsic moral principles but rather as instrumental devices.

Arguments based on free mobility as a human right may seem preferable because they see open borders as a moral end in itself, they are direct and straightforward, they imply strong individual rights to migrate and moreover, they even hold in an ideally just world. Arguments based on distributive justice, on the contrary, are indirect, instrumental, overtly conditional, more collective and they are silent in an ideally just world.[2] I will nevertheless try to show that, in the present world, arguments from safety and subsistence are eventually stronger and more convincing. In many areas, these two approaches seem compatible: free movement can be seen as a 'reduction of political, social and economic inequalities' (Carens 1992: 26) and open borders are morally required to the degree that severe international inequalities persist (see Goodin 1992). However, they are bound to conflict as soon as one asks 'whether affluent countries should give [...] priority in accepting immigrants to those who are poorest and most in need, if all who wish to enter cannot be admitted'.[3] In that case one has to make a choice which argumentative strategy to follow.[4]

Critics of closed borders quite often link restrictive first admission policies to questions of basic security and subsistence.[5] The link between standard threats to security and first admission is direct, obvious and not

28

only morally, but legally acknowledged in the Geneva Convention Relating to the Status of Refugees, the 1967 protocol and the various rights of asylum seekers: states do have a moral and legal obligation, however badly allocated, co-ordinated and sanctioned, to let at least some in. The link between poverty and open borders however, though the argument is strictly analogous,[6] is far from obvious and rarely explained. The nature of this link may be *remedial, causal, or moral.*

Open borders, an unlimited right to external free movement or immigration is no *effective remedy* against poverty. It might even be outrightly counterproductive and there are obvious reasons to be skeptical with regard to the effectiveness of extensive immigration as an anti-poverty strategy:[7] (i) the proportion of the world's poor who might be helped in this way will be very small; (ii) it will be imperfectly targeted: those who have an opportunity to move are far from being among the worst off; (iii) free migration may lead to a brain-drain, leaving the worst-off even worse off; (iv) it may weaken pressures on corrupt governments to address problems of poverty. As a device to reduce poverty 'immigration is at best one strategy among several' (Woodward 1992: 67), it may be not even a 'second best' (Goodin 1992) or 'third best stop gap' nor a realistic option at all.

Is the link between poverty and international migration, then, a *causal* one? I think that one has to concede that extreme poverty is only one of the many *direct motivational causes* explaining migration. It cannot in itself explain 'why people move', let alone when and where they move (see Bader, 1997:158). Extreme poverty, together with violence, are however the two most important indirect, structural or *root causes* of forced migration. "If" extreme poverty could be overcome, many fewer people would be forced to move and would be able to stay 'where they were born and raised, a place whose language, customs, and ways of life are familiar' (Carens 1992: 34). Furthermore, standard threats to security and to subsistence are highly interconnected and reinforce each other in a vicious circle. As a consequence, the traditional distinction between involuntary, political refugees and voluntary, economic migrants, seems to collapse.[8]

The perceived threat of huge "waves" of hundreds of millions of economic and political refugees serves as the main argument in the dominant political talk to close borders. The argument, linking poverty and borders, is intended to undermine the moral legitimacy of policies to close borders. The link is a specific *moral, negative, and indirect* one. Its logic is nicely phrased by Goodin, using a simplified picture of international inequalities (economic) and of foreign aid (money):

'If we cannot move enough money to where the needy people are, then we will have to count on moving as many of the needy people as possible to where the money is... Of course, there is likely to be even more political resistance to that policy than the other... But that, in a way, is precisely the *political point underlying exercises in moral philosophy on this topic.* The goal of such exercises is precisely to put rich countries on the spot. The aim is to argue that, if arguments for international distributive justice are valid and if rich countries do not want to give generously of their money to meet the demands that those arguments impose, then they are morally obliged to pay instead in a currency that they hold even dearer. Morally, rich countries faced with strong moral arguments for global redistribution have only two options. Ideally, they should provide the poor with substantial sums of foreign aid; failing that, as a moral minimum they must alternatively be willing to admit substantial numbers of immigrants from the poorest countries.' (1992: 8f.).

The argument puts the finger on the festering sore of poverty and severe injustice and urgently asks for effective policies in this regard. It is intended to *weaken and undermine standard arguments in political rhetoric and practical philosophy in favour of closed borders*: they can only be morally legitimate, whatever their internal value, if, and to the degree to which, states live up to the minimal moral obligations following from humanitarian obligations and from distributive justice. Under conditions of rough, complex international equality, normative arguments in favour of closure (be they moral, ethico-political, prudential or realist) would in turn gain in practical legitimacy because closure would lose its sting. *"If"* citizenship in rich and safe states ceased to be a privilege, exclusion would be less a prima facie moral wrong.[9] This "if" has two aspects. First a *temporal* one: "as long as" measures to fight poverty are not taken or as long as they are not really effective, "we" (individuals, organizations, states) in the rich countries of the Northern hemisphere have no moral right to close borders. And secondly, a *gradational* one: to the degree that "we" do not live up to our international moral obligations, we have no moral right to close borders. This double "if" makes all other arguments *conditional* upon the fulfillment of our moral obligations with regard to security and subsistence.

In the first section I will try to show, in an initial, minimalist step, that severe global *poverty* calls for immediate help and, in a second, still minimalist step, that existing gross international inequalities are seen - from divergent moral traditions - as a kind of global core *injustice* which demands international redistribution. I conclude that the rich countries of the Northern hemisphere in no way fulfill their moral obligation to address these urgent problems. In the second section I will try to show that this state of affairs seriously undermines the moral and ethico-political arguments to close borders which may be quite legitimate in a context of rough international equality: (i) moral priority should be given to compatriots; (ii) states have to play a fundamental role in the allocation of imperfectly allocated global obligations; only by closing borders can states guarantee (iii) security and fundamental civil rights; (iv) democratic rights and democratic culture; (v) social rights and domestic equality. Commonly, these arguments are linked with strong particularist arguments (vi) that states should close borders to protect thick ethnic or national cultures. I conclude that these six arguments, the most prominent ones in political philosophy and political discourse, are strong enough to rule out the bogus arguments of completely open, instead of fairly open borders. However, in our world of severe poverty and gross global inequality, restrictive first admission or closed borders are morally wrong. Rich Northern states have a double moral obligation to seriously fight global poverty and to let more people in.

I POVERTY, JUSTICE, INTERNATIONAL REDISTRIBUTION AND OPEN BORDERS

Severe global *poverty* creates humanitarian moral obligations to help even if it were not the result of unjust and gross inequalities. The most modest and minimalist argument could thus focus exclusively on poverty and neglect matters of global justice and the much stronger moral obligations resulting from severe *injustice*. A further advantage would be that in this way many tricky questions could be avoided: there are too *many competing theories of justice* around. Some of them have been applied to international relations.[10] The fact that the existing global economic and political order systematically leads to an unfair distribution of resources and political power, has been demonstrated from a utilitarian approach (Singer), from a theory of legitimate appropriation like Locke or Nozick, from Rawlsian contractarianism (Beitz, Barry, Pogge), from a theory of basic rights to security and subsistence (Shue), from a needs and rational obligation approach (O'Neill). These approaches differ in their theoretical strategies and, moreover, they are highly critical with regard to the internal consistency and plausibility of the competing approaches. In spite of these disagreements, I don't think it is necessary to avoid matters of global justice completely because it is possible to find some *minimal 'overlapping consensus* among divergent and competing moral approaches' (Pogge 1995c: 200).[11]

An approach like this can draw freely from more elaborate treatments within different traditions as long as they are not incompatible. It is less *minimalist* than an approach focusing just on poverty and humanitarian obligations[12] but it is still quite modest and minimalist in its moral assumptions, in its empirical and explanatory assumptions, in its argumentative steps, and in its institutional and practical alternatives. The *minimal moral assumptions* (I.1) are those implicit or explicit in the common core of the social, democratic and constitutional state, formulated in international treatises on civil, political and economic, social, and cultural rights. They have to be the core of all moral theories compatible with "our" deepest moral intuitions.[13] The empirical and explanatory assumptions of radical inequality are a kind of "*minima sociologica*"(I.2), shared by all reasonable approaches in the social sciences and backed by a flood of official and semi-official reports and studies. The argumentative steps to show that these "facts" constitute severe injustice can be seen as some kind of *minima moralia* (I.3) of recent theories of justice. Wherever one is able to plausibly demonstrate more, the urgency to develop alternative institutions or, minimally, other *policies* (I.4) is more pressing.

I.1   Minimal moral assumptions

(1) Egalitarian plateau

Recent moral theories compatible with our constitutions share a common core of universalist egalitarianism (see Kymlicka 1990: 5; Goodin 1992: 7). The *egalitarian* principle of equal liberties criticizes all ascriptive privileges. It is incompatible with the strong exclusionary effects of citizenship in a world of separate nation(states): citizenship laws combine criteria of descent (*jus sanguinis*) and territory (*jus soli*) and these criteria are *prima facie* morally no more defensible than sex, age, residence, language, religion, social class, and so on. The *universalism* of the moral point of view, even in its considered and weak versions, does not allow *prima facie* moral privilege to the members of particular communities or states (see II.1). I take it for granted that refutations of universal moral equality cannot be defended rationally.

(2) Citizenship, exclusion and radical international inequalities

State-membership, combined with - only marginally restricted - powers of legally sovereign states to decide who to let in is, in the present situation of radical inequalities among states, one of the crucial mechanisms to defend, guarantee and sanction these inequalities (see Beitz 1991: 243). The awareness is growing among political philosophers that this is hard to justify: 'Citizenship in Western liberal democracies is the modern equivalent of feudal privilege - an inherited status that greatly enhances one's life chances. Like feudal birthright privileges, restrictive citizenship is hard to justify when one thinks about it closely'.[14] To refute this, one would have to show that predominant concepts of state-membership and state-sovereignty would be neutral with regard to severe international injustice.

(3) Morally arbitrary natural and social contingencies
One of the basic assumptions of recent moral theories is that people should not benefit or suffer from morally arbitrary natural and social contingencies like natural talents or handicaps or the good or bad luck to be born of rich or poor parents. For quite a while, the discussion has focused on contingencies *inside states* and has neglected the natural and social contingencies *among states*:

a Nobody deserves to be born into a rich or a poor country. This too is a matter of good or bad luck which has very important effects on one's life-chances.[15]

b The distribution of natural resources - in the broadest sense possible - among states is morally just as arbitrary.[16]

c The moral legitimacy of the inheritance of all other advantages of "national economies" - like advanced means of production, good systems of communication, administration, education etc. - must be very limited.[17]

To refute these claims, one would either have to challenge the strong intuition that we are morally responsible only for our own actions and choices and their consequences, or one would have to dispute "facts" about poverty and unequal distribution.

I.2 *Minima sociologica*: poverty

Thomas Pogge has recently spelled out ten steps to show that citizens and governments of rich Northern countries have more than just a positive humanitarian responsibility to fight extreme poverty. Poverty and affluence are continuously reproduced by an unjust global order which is enforced and maintained by the rich states that profit from it. These therefore have a negative moral responsibility which is more narrowly confined and implies much stronger obligations.[18] "Facts" and explanations of radical international inequalities are in a specific way linked to moral argument. Let me first summarize some well-known and well-documented facts:

Absolute poverty (step 1). In the 1980s about 1.3 billion people in the world lived under conditions of severe poverty, hundreds of millions in nearly unimaginable poverty whichever standards one uses: infant mortality, life-expectancy; access to food, clothing, shelter, education and minimal health care; personal security, rights, liberties, opportunities; political influence; hygiene; income, wealth, spare time (see Pogge 1997).

Relative poverty (step 2). The desperately poor are very unevenly spread among countries: although the moral scandal of extreme poverty persists or is even growing in the richest Northern states, particularly the United States, it is concentrated in the former "Third World countries".

There is a huge gap between affluence and poverty, which is also grow-ing relatively, by whichever standard of measurement.

Extreme poverty is permanent (step 3), not simply momentous: those who deserve the most remain worst off and the prospects of changing their predicament on their own are utterly bleak.

Extreme poverty is all-encompassing (step 4): the deprivation concerns all aspects of life in mutually reinforcing vicious circles (see Shue, 1980: 29 ff.).

Extreme poverty is not an unalterable given of nature, an inevitable ne-cessity of the human condition, it *can be prevented* (step 5).

These five statements constitute "rock bottom facts" of any defensible and plausible description of the international situation. They are couched in terms of "poverty"/"affluence", "poor/rich", "worse off/better off" without referring to any explanatory relationship between these oppo-sites. Even those who refute the claim that the worse off are worse off be-cause the better off are better off, have to face the humanitarian moral obligations following from these five statements.

I.3   *Minima moralia*: gross international inequalities

This *extreme poverty* constitutes a moral challenge and a *moral scandal* as soon as one accepts that those able to help - without excessive sacri-fices - have a moral duty to so. However, poverty and inequality would not constitute a *severe injustice* and therefore no more demanding duties to avoid these deprivations or to protect from deprivation. There are at least *three plausible approaches* that can show why, and under which conditions, this radical inequality is an injustice for which the better off are negatively responsible. All have in common that some morally rele-vant relation between poverty and affluence can be established which at the very least presupposes that they are interconnected. The deserving poor out there are inhabitants of the planet Earth and not some imagin-able deserving poor out there on Venus. The rich and the poor live presently in a *global order with common institutions* (I.3.I), they make use of the *natural resources* of a common planet (I.3.2), and they have a common *history* (I.3.3).

I.3.1   Radical inequality, global order and common institutions

Co-existence in one global economic and political order and in one sys-tem of common institutions, for which we are morally responsible (step 6). The deserving poor in the Southern hemisphere live in a global eco-nomic order and their prospects are seriously affected not only by poli-cies of their own governments but also by world-market prices, interna-tional division of labour, investment and policies by multi-national corpo-rations, by policies of international organizations like the IMF, the World bank, WTO, and UN Organizations, by foreign economic, "aid" and the military policy of powerful Northern states, and recently by global (sex) tourism. This economic (dis)order is maintained by a global political order and guaranteed by international law and treatises. The claim that all, but particularly the better off in such a system of interdependencies, are morally responsible for this order and these institutions, is at least widely shared among different moral theories.[19]

The structure of this system produces and reproduces avoidable poverty and there are better and practically feasible alternatives (step 7). The poor of this world are not only poor and often hungry, 'they are made poor and hungry, so to speak, by our common institutions' (Pogge 1995c: 189; see Beitz 1985: 296f). This *empirical claim* that the better-off are better off due to the current system is, of course, susceptible to the objections that the poor are poor because they have miserable governments and are exploited by corrupt ruling elites. In my view, extreme poverty is not only the historical product of colonialism, imperialism and capitalist strategies of modernization, or only due to factors internal to Third World countries, but it is also - at least partly - the inherent result of the working of the recent global order. Such a claim has to be founded by explanatory approaches like theories of unequal exchange, of world systems theories etc. All who want to free themselves of negative responsibility have to refute these empirical and explanatory claims.[20]

Radical inequality cannot be explained by extra-social factors (step 8). Most attempts to legitimize radical inequality by stressing natural causes, like "racial" or genetic inabilities, climate or natural catastrophes, have lost all credibility. The social causes of poverty are too obvious and visible to be ignored by any credible social and moral theory.

The statements 6, 7 and 8 are shared basic assumptions of *different traditions* in moral theory which try to show not only that radical inequalities are severe but that minimal compensatory measures and institutional readjustments are a matter of justice.[21]

I.3.2 Radical inequality and international distribution of natural resources

Even if one starts from the assumption that statement 6 (and consequently statements 7 and 8) is not fulfilled, this does not mean 'that our *only* moral ties are those with whom we share membership in a co-operative scheme' (Beitz 1985: 292). Even if (nation) states were completely self-contained entities, there is a strong case for international moral obligations in situations where the distribution of natural resources among states is radically unequal.

The better-off have considerable advantages and the worse-off are *excluded from the use and the benefits of natural resources without adequate compensation* (step 9). The internal steps of this argument are simple: (i) The distribution of natural resources is morally completely arbitrary (see above); (ii) Natural resources should be, in principle 'the joint possession of the human race as a whole' (Barry 1989: 450).[22] (iii) The present distributional system 'makes the economic prospect of a country dependent, to a significant degree, on something for which its inhabitants (present or past) can take absolutely no credit and to whose benefits they can lay no just claim, namely its natural resources - including in this soil, water, minerals, sunlight, and so on.' (Barry 1989: 451); (iv) State sovereignty over natural resources is morally legitimate only if (a) the appropriation was just; (b) resulting inequalities are adequately compensated for.[23]

I.3.3 Radical inequality and historical injustice
The first two approaches are present and future-oriented approaches to justice, this third one is particularly relevant for all retrospective approaches.

The starting positions of the better off and worse off are a result of a historical process of massive crime, of force and fraud (step 10). Any reference to the history of conquest, colonialism, imperialism should be sufficient as a demonstration of the plausibility of this claim. The moral consequences of this fact can be far-reaching, especially for libertarian theories of fair appropriation and transfer (strong claims for retribution), but all other theories should also be sensitive to the idea 'that we should not allow radical inequalities of social starting positions if the distribution of these positions is a result of historical processes in which the most elementary legal and moral rules and principles have regularly been violated' (Pogge 1995c: 191).

I.4   Institutional and practical alternatives: from moderate to radical
Each of these three approaches (fair co-operation, fair distribution of the use and benefit of natural resources, compensation for historical injustice), is in itself sufficient to show that radical international inequalities constitute severe injustice and each invites us to allocate our moral duties. Furthermore, these approaches need not be mutually exclusive and often (but not in all cases) may reinforce each other. All three approaches accept the moral duty to design alternative institutions or policies to prevent these inequalities or to compensate for them. I will present some examples here of measures that can be taken. They range from fairly moderate to extremely radical:

(1) Proposals which accept recent global capitalism and a system of fairly sovereign states, but ask for urgent policies to address standard threats to security and subsistence, particularly extreme poverty: (i) a global dividend to be paid by governments, proportional to the value of any natural resource it chooses to extract (see Pogge 1994: 200 ff.;

1995c: 192 ff.; 1997). Such a GRD follows directly from the second approach but it is consistent with the two other approaches. (ii) A 'tax on the governments of rich countries, assessed as a proportion of gross national product that increases with per capita income, the proceeds to be distributed to poor countries on a parallel basis of negative income tax' (Barry 1989: 454). Such a GNP tax follows directly from the first approach.[24] (iii) Any other taxes to be paid by governments on foreign trade, on trade in fossil fuels, or on all currency transactions (Tobin-tax).[25] (iv) A tougher version of so-called developmental aid, up to two or three percent of GNP which should be obligatory to express that it is not aid but moral obligation to redress severe injustice; another option would be the measures proposed in the Social Development Agenda (see Goodin 1996).

These and similar proposals, moderate as they are, still seem much too radical for governments of the affluent countries who do not accept that ought implies costs.

(2) Proposals and strategies to intervene in cases of gross violations of essential civil (and political) rights and in cases of gross violations of subsistence rights. These policies do not confine themselves to redistribution and overrule sovereignty of governments.[26]

(3) Proposals for more or less far-reaching changes in international organizations and institutions, like a much stronger and more effective UN and an organization of WTO, IMF, World bank which gives poorer countries much more say.

(4) Proposals to change the structure of the global economic order, e.g. the design of institutions of some global, Keynesian welfare-capitalism or of models of global economic governance in theories of associative democracy.[27]

(5) Proposals to change the structure of the international political system, e.g. some world-state or the design of overlapping political units with limited, delegated, multi-layered sovereignties.[28]

Proposals (3), (4) and (5) can, of course, be combined. They address the systemic and institutional causes of radical international inequalities and imply far more radical and long-term political strategies. If they are not combined with more moderate and short-term proposals (see 1) this radicalism is their essential political weakness.

It is obvious that the countries of the rich Northern hemisphere in no way live up to the minimal moral obligations resulting from extreme poverty, let alone to the more demanding ones from severe global injustice. I completely agree with Thomas Pogge that our first moral priority ought to focus on projects that address poverty and global injustice directly, instead of fully opening our borders. However, I do not consider policies to eradicate poverty directly and policies of fairly open borders to be exclusive alternatives. On the contrary, I start from the observation that - now and in the foreseeable future - we do not succeed in 'alleviating the terrible conditions that make them want to come here in the first place' (Pogge 1997: 22). As long as this is the case, and to the degree that this is the case, our moral and political projects, given the scarcity of our energy and resources, still have to include moral criticism of policies of closed borders. We cannot, counterfactually, presume our policies to address poverty and global injustice to be successful in the long run and in the meantime close our eyes.[29]

II   WHY NOT CLOSED BORDERS?

Arguments based on justice are not the only relevant moral, let alone practical arguments. In this section, I briefly and critically assess the six most prominent and often heard arguments in favour of closure of borders. As mentioned earlier, it is often said that borders should be closed (II.1) because moral priority should be given to compatriots, (II.2) because states have to play a fundamental role in the allocation of imperfectly allocated global obligations; because only in such a way, fundamental civil rights (II.3) could be guaranteed, together with democratic rights and cultures (II.4), and social rights and domestic equality (II.5); (II.6) to protect thick ethnic or national cultures. All these - moral, ethico-political and realist - arguments have strong implications for practical judgements. They need not be only thinly veiled welfare-chauvinism.[30] I do not intend to dismiss these arguments for closed borders completely, but to put them into perspective.[31] Taken together, they should demonstrate why fairly open, instead of fully open borders, is my preferred option.

II.1   Morality of concentric circles: priority for compatriots?

Most arguments qualifying or denying universal obligations criticize the bloodless world of cosmopolitanism which would not recognize any special moral ties or obligations.[32] My intention here is not to discard these arguments as anything more than a form of special pleading; I am only trying to qualify them.[33]

Henry Shue has shown marvellously how these arguments, when they are made more explicit, invoke the metaphor of a morality of concentric circles: If a person were a pebble thrown in a pond, his or her duties would be 'exactly like the concentric ripples around the pebble: strongest at the centre and rapidly diminishing towards the periphery' (1988: 691). What is wrong and highly misleading in this image 'is the *progressive* character of the decline in the priority as one reaches circles farther from the centre' (p. 694).[34] The morality of concentric circles, according to Shue, cannot be used to legitimate a '*priority for compatriots*': 'Once the centre has been left behind, however, I see insufficient reason to believe that one's positive duties to people in the next county, who are in fact strangers, are any greater than one's positive duties to people on the next continent, who, though they are distant strangers, are not any more strangers than the strangers in the next county: a stranger is a stranger.' (p. 692f)

Now not only unreconstructed communitarians may think that something crucial is lacking in Shue's analysis of special obligations: common practices and common history (even of bitter conflicts that create special ties) so important for national communities,[35] and this lack obviously weakens his critique of the priority to compatriots. In this case, it cannot be love or care and it commonly is not shared principles that may create special moral obligations but, depending upon how one defines compatriots, shared cultural practices and a common political history. There is more space between intimates and complete strangers and this in between may give rise to a more multilayered model of moral obligations than only towards intimates or humanity.[36] However, such a possible priority for compatriots has to be carefully delineated:

(1) The argument in favour of compatriots cannot easily be extended to modern states without forthrightly underwriting the belief in the mythology of strong democratic nation-states: only if states were "communities" of shared language, culture, ethnicity and civic and democratic culture, would such an argument make sense at all.[37] In many prominent aspects, the relationship of state-members is one among strangers and the adequate public morality is a morality of strangers.[38]

(2) Even in the case of ideally democratic (nation) states, the relevant sentiments would not be love and care (versus all misguided blood and family-analogies) but those based on a common political culture and a common history.[39]

(3) Excessive stress on historical relations would be incompatible with the time-orientation of liberal democratic constitutions which is more future-oriented.[40] Moral obligations following from legitimate expectations are deeply conservative and tend to block urgent moral changes.[41]

(4) The relevant historical ties are not limited to compatriots but transcend the borders of states: the histories of colonialism and imperialism create special obligations towards specific "foreigners" and the same holds for new relations as a consequence of rapid and encompassing globalization.[42]

(5) Many of the special obligations we owe to compatriots are a mixed blessing and imply some kind of negative priority: we have to treat foreigners better than we need to treat our compatriots. [43]

What would follow from such a qualified priority for compatriots? It seems clear to me that any defensible theory of multilayered special obligations has to rule out an unconditional priority for compatriots (like my country right or wrong). However "thin" or "reiterative" one conceives of the universalism of the moral point of view, one has to agree that special obligations towards compatriots may not prevent the fulfillment of duties correlative to basic rights of security and subsistence of foreigners.[44] In all such cases they have to be overruled, because statements that universal and special obligations can and normally do 'peacefully coexist' (Perry 1995: 109) are wishful thinking: ought implies costs and resources are limited.[45]

Abstract cosmopolitanism on the other hand, neglecting the moral significance of particular, special relations, suffers not only from serious problems of allocation of duties and from problems of moral compliance, it is unnecessarily abstract.[46] If the moral minimum is fulfilled, there is much scope for morally legitimate special obligations based upon special historical, cultural, linguistic, political ties.[47]

Our moral obligations may not only give qualified *priority for* compatriots but for all *residents*, particularly for asylum seekers and immigrants. Morally defensible and realistic *policies of incorporation* are often put forward as an important argument to close borders and they may really ask for controlled immigration. Now I think one has to concede that there is a moral and political trade-off between how many would-be immigrants and refugees a state takes in and how much it is willing to do for each. Contrary to common use, however, this argument should extend to all residents, including long-term illegal residents. Even then, the legitimate claims of asylum seekers, recognized refugees and immigrants should not be allowed unconditional priority over those "out there". There may have to be a ceiling to first admissions but this cannot be an alibi for closed borders.

My approach, like any other who accepts such multilayered moral obligations, including some qualified priority for compatriots and residents, is confronted with serious problems only unreconstructed utilitarians can avoid: if the moral minimum is fulfilled, how to balance conflicting moral claims concretely, given the fact that these qualified priorities are very abstract and leave wide discretionary margins? How to measure and weigh them? What would morally acceptable double standards mean?[48]

II.2   Moral standing of states and their role in allocating duties

Declaring and proclaiming universal basic *rights* to security and subsistence without adequately allocating the corresponding *duties* is 'hypocrisy and fraud' (Shue 1988: 695).[49] No comprehensive theory is available of what such an allocation ideally would look like and what would follow for the existing allocation. Particularly, the role *states* should play within such an allocation of corresponding duties, is hotly debated. From an abstract universalist and cosmopolitan point of view, states, sovereignty, borders, and state-membership can only be justified in a strictly instrumental way as means to fulfill universal human rights, or to maximize utility or basic needs. From the opposite point of view, the common mix of particularist communitarianism and political realism states are seen as moral entities in their own right and universal obligations are either neglected or downplayed. A more convincing approach ought to find some reasonable middle ground which should minimally include the following points:

(1) A reasonable scheme of multilayered moral obligations has to give priority to the rock-bottom moral minimum of global obligations without neglecting or sacrificing domestic obligations.

(2) It should critically discuss states internally: do they fulfill the obligations corresponding to civil, political, and social rights of their citizens; and, in particular, it should assess the existing international system of states: does this system, and if so, to what degree, live up to the global demands of basic security and subsistence? Such a critical distance implies that states are not to be taken as self-justifying or superior moral entities. They have to be justified on the basis of a very general notion of individual autonomy. For all moral approaches compatible with social, liberal democracy, only individuals, historically and socially situated as they are, are subjects of ultimate moral concern.[50]

(3) Such a critique should not be blocked by realist accusations of utopian idealism: if one can show that the existing international system is deficient by any reasonable standard and, particularly, that the existing international organizations and institutions are underdeveloped and inefficient, one has a duty to design alternative institutions.[51]

(4) If, and to the degree to which states live up to their domestic and minimal international moral and legal obligations, states can play an important and not only strictly instrumental role with regard to a problem which plagues solutions to poverty, refugees and migration: they may help to address the problem of *unallocated duties*. In the cases of unallocated, or better *imperfectly allocated obligations* 'we can clearly identify the right and its bearers, but not who has to comply with the corresponding obligation' (Bauböck 1994: 308). The universal individual human right not to be exposed to starvation normally correlates with special obligations.[52] States, which normatively can be seen as 'institutional ensembles for resolving the problem of imperfectly allocated obligations within a territorially limited population' (Bauböck 1994: 309),[53] may also help to alleviate this problem beyond their borders. States would have 'to accept obligations that reach beyond those toward their own citizens' and would have to 'recognize special obligations [...] towards specific populations that may result from active involvement in the affairs of another

country, from geographical proximity, or from historic ties' (p. 315). Being a "compatriot" is not only a mixed blessing internally, it also includes costly external obligations as well and contributes to transform otherwise unallocated duties to help needy foreigners into special moral obligations. The *domestic obligations* of states extend beyond their citizens and include all residents, denizens as well as long-term "illegal" residents. Their *transnational obligations* include not only family members of citizens but of immigrants and refugees as well, e.g. in the case of family reunification. Their colonial history has created moral obligations towards immigrants from their former colonies and their involvement in the affairs of other states creates special responsibilities with regard to refugees fleeing from those countries (e.g. US and refugees from Cuba, Haiti, Vietnam).[54] Their *international obligations* towards other states, resulting from treaties, from historical ties and past injustice, may create specific obligations, e.g. of some moderate version of redress[55] or of some prospective, targeted development or special "aid" programme towards ex-colonies. States also have *supranational obligations*, resulting from common institutions like the EU which create specific obligations (e.g. for internal redistribution from rich to poor states or poor regions). Finally *global obligations,* resulting from membership in UN organizations or from signing global covenants, may imply allocated special obligations, e.g. minimum quotas for asylum seekers and rules for burden-sharing. All these special transdomestic obligations of states would, of course, not solve the problem of the vast amount of remaining unallocated obligations towards those who cannot claim special relations or those who are not covered by global schemes. However, they would alleviate the problem considerably by reducing its amount, particularly if one were convincingly able to translate a lot of unspecified and unrelational "deprivation" or "poverty" into more specific contexts of exploitation and oppression. The deserving poor out there would then be seen as people and countries whose universal basic rights have been violated and there would be known bearers of the corresponding duties to be addressed.

If one is more pessimistic regarding the possibility of domesticating existing states - these 'wild organizations' (Shue 1988: 698) - into performances of currently unfulfilled duties, and if one is convinced that the existing international institutions are 'primitive and clumsy' (p.702) one should at least complement transnational obligations of states and transnational citizenship by the design of better suited international organizations and institutions.[56] Such mediating institutions would have to fill the remaining gap of imperfectly allocated duties and they would have to play a major role in *co-ordinating* the required activities by states and other organizations in an efficient and effective way.[57]

II.3 Closed borders to guarantee public security and civil rights

'The primary reason which can legitimate restrictions on immigra- tion is the maintenance of a comprehensive system of civil, demo- cratic and social rights of citizenship' (Bauböck 1994: 320)

The most legitimate arguments in favor of closure refer to the three pil- lars of liberal, democratic, social constitutions: closure would be required to protect and guarantee the rule of law and essential civil rights (II.3), to protect and develop political democracy (II.4), and to maintain adequate welfare arrangements (II.5).[58]

A favorite legitimation to close borders is the threat the overwhelming numbers of asylum seekers and immigrants would pose to public order and social stability. This is a contested realist argument with serious moral implications because the maintenance of public order belongs to well-allocated duties of states to guarantee the basic (civil) right to secu- rity.[59] What is supposed to be commonly threatening is a mix of (i) sheer numbers and their consequences for employment, social security and public services; (ii) supposed or real opposition to principles, institutions and culture of social, liberal democracy (see II.4); (iii) supposed or real ethno-cultural distance (see II.6).

It is impossible to address these effects in general without taking into account specific demographic, economic characteristics and politics of the different states, on the one hand, and supposed or real characteristics of refugees and immigrants on the other hand. I would like to stress only some points:

(1) As already noted, I accept as a given that the tension between first admission and incorporation policies is growing the more people one lets in. There may be much alarmist reasoning in this regard but there is a context specific ceiling which cannot be surmounted without serious negative effects.

(2) I also accept that it is completely irresponsible to let people in with- out minimally adequate incorporation policies which may include affir- mative action policies for specific groups of (second and third generation) immigrants with regard to employment, education, housing (see Bader 1995c) in order to prevent the formation of permanent ethnic under- classes and related forms of criminality. Again there is much alarmist reasoning around, particularly when it comes to the ethnicization and culturalization of presumed "propensities to crime", but it would be ut- terly naive to neglect obvious facts in this regard.

(3) To the degree that threats to civil rights, public order and social sta- bility can be plausibly demonstrated for specific states in specific con- junctures, the whole argument for closed borders would only strengthen the imperfectly allocated duty to guarantee minimal safety and subsis-

tence for all those uprooted foreigners out there. At present, the typical combination is exactly the opposite one: the "overwhelming numbers" of those actually in are far below any reasonable ceiling or threshold and at the same time the ever more exclusionary states do not live up to their minimal moral obligations with regard to basic security and subsistence abroad.

II.4 Democracy and closure

Political democracy, in itself of utmost moral concern,[60] may legitimate closure in two different ways: democratic decision making and *membership*, and democratic political *culture*.

(1) I think one has to agree with the following statements, carefully elaborated by Bauböck (1994: 178 ff.): (i) stable *democratic decision making in general*, not only in political democracy, presupposes some well-defined and relatively stable rules of membership;[61] (ii) democratic *polities* cannot 'decide democratically on who is to be a member of this very same polity' (Bauböck 1994: 180), and non-members cannot democratically decide to become members; (iii) all *states* use (some mix of) descent (*jus sanguinis*) and/or birth on their territory or residency (*jus soli*) as criteria for state-membership and all liberal-democratic states should include at least some permeability and flexibility regarding borders and membership and they should introduce as much voluntary consent as possible.[62] (iv) Only in a democratic *world-state* with exclusively global citizenship would it be possible to overcome the fact that membership-rules in political units have to rely on territorial borders which are historically contingent and morally arbitrary.[63] (v) In a *world of multiple states* membership rules would be 'premised upon the notion of a territorially bounded society' as long as one insists on minimal residency requirements, even if one would have highly permeable borders, easy first admission, reduced periods of residency, easy naturalization, and dual citizenship.[64]

However, the conclusions to be drawn from these more or less indubitable statements do not legitimate what the defenders of closed borders expect from them.

(i) The fact that some form of closure has to be allowed somewhere for democratic decision making to be stable, neither determines the form nor delineates the place. Bauböck, on the contrary, criticizes fixed and restrictive state-membership and closed borders and argues at length for a multi-layered concept of transnational citizenship and for blurred boundaries.

(ii) Even in a world of *multiple states with fairly open borders under conditions of rough equality* state membership implies insiders and outsiders and rules to decide who is a non-member; it is therefore, inevitably, exclusionary. Many committed universalists try to avoid all exclusionary aspects by opting for global citizenship, for a world state and a world constitution as a legal utopia: 'a system that finally denies citizenship: by suppressing it as a privileged status associated with rights not recognized to non-citizens, or instead by instituting universal citizenship, and thus in either case overcoming the dichotomy between "the rights of man and the rights of citizens"' (Ferrajoli 1995: 31). Apart from questions of desirability or feasibility, this option is not the only one to overcome the illegitimate exclusionary aspects of existing citizenship practice. An institutional design of overlapping political units with delegated, limited and differentiated sovereignties and with multiple citizenship-statuses in local, provincial, state, federal political units and an international 'polity of polities' (Bauböck 1994: 248) may achieve the same end. Such a design would shift the emphasis from citizenship rights to universal human rights without replacing citizenship rights by human rights. It would de-emphasize statecentred citizenship and shift the focus or the center of gravity of political citizenship both upwards and downwards: let us be both more localists and more rooted cosmopolitans at the same time.

(iii) However, under such conditions of fairly open borders and rough equality among states, this remaining exclusionary aspect would lose its sting and democratic closure would not only be morally permitted but would be perfectly legitimate. If, and to the degree to which states do not live up to these requirements, arguments based on democracy cannot be used to legitimate their exclusionary practices.

(2) Arguments from democracy as decision making, disentangled from *democracy as political culture*, and from all stronger particularist communitarian arguments, in my view cannot counter arguments based on justice in favour of fairly open borders. Stronger exclusionists, consequently, will argue along the culturalist line, stressing two points: (i) letting so many foreigners in who are not accommodated or even hostile to civic and democratic culture will inevitably threaten the maintenance and flourishing of democracy; or (ii) any liberal-democratic political culture has to be based upon a common history and common practices which are deeply embedded in particular ethnic, national, religious cultures. Even civilized democratically minded foreigners would threaten our specific ways of doing democracy.

Being unable to discuss both strategies at length,[65] I must confine myself to short qualifying remarks: (i) it seems very unfair, to say the least, to confront a normative textbook *model* of shared and vivid democratic culture among compatriots, to the construction of a dramatized *muddle* of foreign enemies of democracy swamping our democratic paradises. (ii) Different groups of immigrants and refugees may have more or less practised democracy in their home countries; outright opposition to principles, culture, virtues and practices of liberal democracy in the form of ethnic and religious fundamentalism is a common reaction to very illiberal and anti-democratic practices of discrimination, oppression, exploitation, marginalization in the receiving states and, in particular, to miserable state policies of incorporation.[66] (iii) Liberal democratic political culture should stimulate a wide variety of ways of doing democracy, embedded in different and diverging ethnic, religious or other conceptions of the good life. However, there may be limits to the amount of variation that is bearable and these limits may legitimate some thresholds or ceilings to first admission if one takes into account that it takes time to learn and accommodate to the specific ways of doing democracy in France, the USA, England or the Netherlands. (iv) The background argument, that political stability would require fairly high degrees of (ethnic or national) cultural homogeneity leads us right into the heart of strong exclusionary republican nationalism or communitarianism which are both at odds with modern, liberal democratic principles and which are, obviously, completely out of phase in our world of migration (see II.6).

To sum up, the maintenance and flourishing of a civic and democratic culture may require some ceiling to the admission of culturally unaccustomed newcomers. However, one should be wary of slippery slope reasoning: states who cultivate the myth of (ethnic or national) cultural homogeneity and who lack thoroughly rooted civic and democratic political cultures (e.g. Germany or Japan) can easily use these arguments to legitimize their illiberal, exclusionist policies.

II.5 Social rights, welfare and closure

The maintenance of adequate welfare and social rights is one of the strongest reasons in favour of restrictive migration policies.[67] Commonly, two lines of argument can be found to legitimate higher standards of social security and welfare inside states and, consequently, closure of these systems 'against an environment in which no similar systems exist' (Bauböck 1995: 21 f.). On the one hand, higher standards may be directly derived from the priority for compatriots discussed above.[68] On the other hand, a specific normative relation is invoked between political democracy and domestic socio-economic equality, and between democratic self-governance and external inequality.

(1) The relationship between *political democracy and domestic socio-economic equality* is a tricky one: for *normative* reasons it is evident that maintenance and flourishing of political democracy needs some minimal socio-economic equality though it is still hotly debated how much inequality is tolerable.[69] The *empirical* claim is contested that representative democracy in capitalist, sexist, ethnocentrist societies has an inherent

equalizing tendency and leads to more and more domestic equality and it is at least much weaker.[70] Anyhow, both political philosophers and social scientists should, in my view, avoid what I call *crypto-normativist* conclusions derived from what "democratic polities" should do, e.g. reduce domestic inequalities, to what recent states actually do. It is obvious that restrictive immigration policies in states in which domestic inequalities are growing cannot be legitimated morally or ethico-politically with reference to their "normative task". At present, both domestic and international inequality are growing at the same time.

(2) As long as *democratic sovereignty*, as it is traditionally understood, is linked to (nation) states, it is obvious that 'sovereignty regarding domestic matters can come into clear conflict with *transborder claims to equality*' (Føllesdal 1995: 21). Then 'our concern for equality comes into conflict with another important interest: democratic self-governance, leading to a diversity of equally just social arrangements' (p. 5) 'Differences, enacted democratically' would be a matter of 'equally just ways of maintaining a public order' (p. 22) and different standards should be accepted as an expression of democracy, not only of *différance*. The defensibility of this argument depends upon two assumptions: first, that the present system of guaranteeing social rights as exclusive rights of state-members (citizens) or residents by means of welfare bureaucracies of 'sovereign states' is the only thinkable or feasible one. Secondly, that states would have to live up to their minimal international obligations, however high their domestic standards may be.

Again, one is left with a couple of intriguing questions regarding definitions, measurement and comparison of these standards:[71] how high is this minimal global standard? How do we balance arguments based on global justice and on the maintenance of legitimate differences in democratically decided upon domestic standards? How big a difference between the global and the domestic standards is legitimate and tolerable?[72]

I doubt that we ever will be able to provide contextfree, general and exact answers to such questions, but I think we can reach some basic agreement. For instance: at present, no state lives up to the global moral minimum (and some, like the US and the UK, much less than others). As long as this is so obviously the case, and as long as these states do not live up to the demands of "domestic" equality either, such arguments from social rights and welfare arrangements are morally pointless and only mask continuing injustice.[73] "If", and to the degree to which states actually would live up to these global and domestic requirements, the exclusionary arguments would become more plausible and the same states would gain democratic and social legitimacy. But states who do not want to pay 'in a currency that they hold even dearer' would have to face their global moral obligations directly.

II.6 Thick ethnic or national culture and closure

In everyday discourse as well as in much political theory arguments based on security, democracy and welfare in favour of closure are inextricably interwoven with protection and maintenance of thick ethnic or national cultures. In my discussion I have tried to separate them as far as possible. Civil, political and social rights belong to the core moral principles of modern constitutions and mainstream liberal theory teaches us that they are "ethnically blind". Even if this turns out to be untenable because civil and political culture cannot be completely disentangled from thicker ethnic or national ones,[74] the modern state as a liberal state should be as neutral as possible in ethnic terms with regard to kinship, descent, sex and gender, "race", age, regions, specific languages, religion, political affiliation etc.

This is not the place to reiterate well-known critical arguments against communitarian or "strong perfectionist" defences of closed borders for which the central purpose of the state is simply to serve and protect the "shared culture".[75] However, even thoroughly liberal arguments, based on individual autonomy and universalist justice, can legitimate some degree of closure for the maintenance and development of ethnic or national culture:

(1) *Minority-protection.* Justice requires some closure and differential treatment in favour of negatively privileged ethnic or national groups in situations in which the economic, social, legal, political and cultural chances are grossly unequal. Not only for reasons of severe historical injustice (as in the case of indigenous peoples) but also to tackle recent and prospective severe inequalities which are a consequence of the working of specific institutional translations of "strictly neutral" and "difference-blind" principles and mechanisms.[76]

(2) *Realists* assume that *stability* requires 'a certain degree of cultural stability and cohesiveness... to preserve either general social and political stability or the liberal/democratic character of existing political institutions' (Perry 1995: 113f), and that first admission should be restricted accordingly. If qualified in four ways, this argument has to be taken seriously. *Firstly*, stability and cohesiveness should not be misunderstood as mythical cultural homogeneity. *Secondly*, cultural continuity is not only 'perfectly compatible with cultural pluralism', cultural stability also includes cultural change. The core issue is 'the rate of cultural change, not the preservation of an existing culture or cultural mix. What is at stake is cultural continuity rather than the substance of the dominant culture or cultures' (Perry: 114). The realist proviso can only mean that cultural change has to be 'sufficiently gradual' to 'avoid excessive cultural disruption'. This, of course, is a terribly open-ended formula in urgent need of context-specific delineation. *Thirdly,* contexts make all the difference

and realistically necessary ceilings to first admission may 'vary from state to state' (Perry: 114f). However, this context-dependency should, in my view, itself be further specified in two ways: on the one hand, there should be, as already mentioned, much space for legitimate variety of the institutions, the cultures, habits and virtues, and traditions of good practices of the social and democratic, constitutional state. The different ways to live democracy and the rule of law may need some protection (which I personally doubt very much). However, such an argument can never legitimately be used in a way that lower degrees or even absence of civic and democratic political culture can serve as an excuse for more closure. On the other hand, there is legitimate space for varying degrees of ethnic or national heterogeneity of states: not all the world has to be America.[77] However, this argument is often used as the main avenue to legitimate exclusionary policies of the most exclusionary states: 'A less open, culturally homogenous society might not be able to absorb the same levels of immigration without the occurrence of social unrest' (Perry: 115). This kind of realism would exempt Japan or Germany or France or Israel (or what have you!) from all the burdens of immigration.

"If" closure to maintain culture would take place under conditions of rough international equality, it would cease to be a pressing moral problem. In the real world today, restrictions on first admission that are intended to preserve cultural stability and continuity can be morally legitimate, only if states really fulfill their minimal global moral obligations. To put it simply: the more closed, the more they would have to pay in normal currency to keep their imagined sanctuaries as culturally clean and sterile as possible and prevent all those hybrid, cosmopolitan and devilish cultural blendings.

III FAIRLY OPEN BORDERS

The six arguments discussed in the last section, combined with other realist and prudential reasons, explain why completely open borders are neither feasible nor desirable: let us remove the bogus of an open border scenario from the political agenda! Some degree of closure is morally permitted and ethico-politically required. However, do not these same arguments, taken together, add up to an impressive overall plea for complete closure or at least for fairly closed borders instead of "bounded openness" and fairly open borders? Or, to put it differently: 'does not "fairly open" actually mean exactly the same as "fairly closed"?' (Bader 1995: 216) In my view, one has to concede that no exact answer to these questions is possible: it is simply impossible to measure, weigh and compare exactly the diverging moral arguments and to calculate the sum total of these moral arguments against countervailing ethico-political, prudential and realist arguments. We have to admit that not only no comprehensive practical philosophy dealing with problems of first admission and incorporation is available, but that it is impossible to calculate the different practical arguments that point in opposite directions, in any strict or quantitative manner. "Qualified priority", "limited veto", "degrees of preference", like any other formula, suffer from the same indeterminacy and vagueness.[78] Moral philosophers are simply unable to tell exactly how high the "ceilings" or how low the "thresholds" are, what exactly the "point" is "below which" states do not fulfill their minimal global obligations, what exactly the different domestic and global standards would mean and how great the distance between them may be to be morally acceptable.

One may deplore this or, as I do, one may welcome a situation in which moral philosophers, economists and social scientists are unable to prescribe or calculate exactly what we have to do practically. Only democratic public talk and decision making can legitimately close this inevitable indeterminacy of moral reasoning taking all these different arguments into account, using all available and relevant context-specific information, all educated guesses and comparisons - however insufficient and contested they may be - and developing the difficult art of balancing moral, ethico-political, prudential and realist arguments as components of our practical political judgement.[79]

I am convinced that - in our present world - the rich states of the Northern hemisphere do everything but live up to their minimal global moral obligations and I hope that this educated guess is shared by most reasonable people. "If" - as soon as and to the degree to which - they did fulfill these obligations, the well-known arguments for closure would become more plausible and their policies would gain in legitimacy. As long as they do not, and - realistically speaking - I am afraid this will be the case for a very long time, their moral standing is miserable. All talk about special responsibilities, security, democracy, domestic welfare in this global context only serves to avoid that "ought implies costs". Moral philosophers can and should play a modest role in convincing citizens, politicians, and bureaucrats that a radical change in *both policy areas, poverty and first admission*, is urgently required. Fighting global poverty asks for more drastic policies of international redistribution. At the same time and as long as that takes, wealthy Northern states have to admit more people: the increasing turning away of refugees and asylum seekers has to be reversed, which at the very least would mean living up to the letter and the spirit of the Geneva Convention, and all rich Northern states have to acknowledge that they are immigration countries and should, therefore, accept binding obligations to let much higher numbers of migrants in, e.g. in the form of constitutionally protected large immigration quotas of, for example, 1.5 % of the total population annually. Fairly open borders or "bounded openness" in practical terms means taking in "more, much more" (Carens) whereas "fairly closed borders" means keeping more, much more out.

Both policy changes would be costly but, in my view, would not - minimalist as they are - ask unacceptable sacrifices. Both policy changes may be easier and more plausible if a shift would take place in public discourse from citizenship rights towards human rights, from domestic towards transdomestic obligations, from democratic state sovereignty towards more powers to international, democratic organizations.

Notes

*   In the notes to this chapter I have tried to incorporate many comments, replies and debates from session II of the Amsterdam-colloquium which explains their number and length. I would like to thank Rainer Bauböck, Ewald Engelen, Gijs v. Oenen, Pieter Pekelharing, Thomas Pogge, and the members of the department of Practical Philosophy of my Faculty for their productive and critical comments. Special thanks to Klaske de Jong who streamlined the text and corrected my English. Thanks also to NWO *Ethiek en Beleid* for a generous grant.

1   See Singer 1972, 1993; Barry 1973, 1989; Beitz 1979, (ed.) 1985, 1991; Dowty 1987; Carens 1987, 1989, 1991, 1992, 1992a, 1995, 1996; Shue 1980, 1988; Goodin 1988; Pogge 1989, 1992, 1994, 1995c, 1997; Shklar 1991; Barry/Goodin (eds.) 1992; Nardin/Mapel 1992; Rawls 1993; Schwartz (ed.) 1995

2   See Carens 1992, III; Woodward 1992; Bauböck 1994; Pogge 1996a. A serious problem with this argument is that the right to free movement is not recognized as a legal right in any of the International Covenants. There is no symmetry between "right of exit" and "right of entry", and internal freedom of movement is not analogous to external movement (see Barry 1992: 283f. vs. Carens, Goodin 1992: 12; Dummet 1992: 173.). This may be morally arbitrary, at least in part (see Carens 1992: 26 ff.) but it nevertheless weakens the force of the rights-argument. I think Woodward is right that 'much of the force of Carens' advocacy of relatively unrestricted freedom of movement really derives from the second rationale' (1992: 62), i.e. from justice.

3   Woodward 1992: 61. See Pogge 1996: 'we should ask, however, why borders need be only *fairly* rather than *fully* open. How does the fact that we have admitted a large number of desperately poor persons from Third World countries into our midst make it easier for us to justify continued exclusion of others who would also like to come? After all, those still excluded even by fairly open borders would benefit greatly from fully open borders. It is not even clear why the equalization at the top, which fairly open borders would effect, is any moral gain at all, if those at the bottom continue to be just as badly off as they are now.'

4   Both approaches share two very broad and general assumptions:
     (1) All productive moral reasoning has to tackle the *tension* between the *universalizing* trend of *moral principles* on the one hand, the *particularizing* trend of normative *institutions, cultures and practices* on the other hand. There has to be some "critical, *reflexive equilibrium*", some back and forth connecting "our" moral intuitions which are always intuitions of a historically and socially situated moral community to more universally shared moral principles. Otherwise two dangers are imminent: (i) the danger of abstract, merely stipulated universalism; an imaginary

moral view from nowhere would not have any plausibility, let alone binding force; (ii) the dangers of unreflected particularism or of an uncritical acceptance of "our" particular institutions and practices as morally right or at least as defensible 'first approximations' (Coleman/Harding 1995: 38). Particularly in our case the existing international order and the institutional *status quo* may turn out to be not first or second best but 'fifteenth best or worse' (Tushnet 1995:149. Vs. Coleman/Harding 1995: 11, 18, 34. 38). In our times it is crucial to widen the gap between principles and practices. I share this conviction with Pogge, Goodin (1988: 686), Barry (1989: 447), Beitz, and many others.

(2) It is crucial to approach practical arguments from *moral, instead of a realist* premises and to start moral arguments with questions about what ideally would be requested to gain critical distance towards existing institutions, to widen the gap between ideal and real world before trying to "bridge" it (here I disagree with Carens overly "permissive" attitude (1996: 169 'no single correct starting point')). Most moral philosophers agree that it is important to distinguish between 'what ideally would be just' and what practically is required in the real world (see Beitz 1985:306; Pogge 1989:259 ff., Carens 1987:262; 1992:VIII; Bauböck 1994:327 ff.). I see four main advantages to such an approach: (i) if institutional settings are severely wrong from a moral point of view, one needs to gain critical distance. Stretching the tensions, inherent in all societies, between rhetorically invoked principles and existing institutions and practices allows for such distance without losing contact with "our" world. Take the institutional setting of liberal-democratic constitutions in welfare states as an example. The indeterminacy of moral principles of egalitarian liberalism allows for two polar strategies and, of course, many in-betweens. On the one hand, it is common practice to accommodate these principles to the predominant institutional translations (capitalist world market, existing system of states and international institutions) and to attack the construction of ideal moral worlds, whenever the resulting moral requirements do not fit given practices (see Woodward 1992, § 4 or Barry 1992: 179f.). On the other hand, one can radicalize the universalism and inclusiveness inherent in these principles, and criticize the predominant order and institutions. (ii) This approach allowsstretching of the limits of what is possible and feasible. Surely, ought implies can, but what can be done is very often prematurely closed by taking for granted "false necessities" in history and society. (iii) "Ought implies can" still holds but it has changed its meaning. Our discussions of what can be done should no longer be restricted to what is possible given the existing institutional setting. The "reality-check" realism rightly asks for, and should take into account real historical and actual possibilities, and we should make sure that "starting" from the world as it is does not mean "ending up" with the world as it is. (iv) Moral idealism is an important practical device with far reaching strategic consequences: if futures are not closed and predictable but open, it makes sense to reinterpret realism like Fourier: 'let's be realistic, ask for the impossible'. The fact that we cannot know whether better institutions and policies are really impossible or whether our alternatives would worsen things does not justify closing the world more than necessary.

5   See Carens 1987: 270; 1992 III; 1995a: 8f; Goodin 1992; Perry 1995; Tushnet 1995: 148, 151f; Treblicock 1995: 243.

6   Both start from (i) threats to a basic right (security, subsistence) which (ii) challenge the moral standing of the system of states; (iii) the preferred policies in both cases are direct policies (to prevent gross violations of civil and political rights; to eradicate poverty); (iv) as long as, and to the degree to which these policies are not effective, we have an indirect moral obligation to help the victims (moral and legal obligation to let refugees in; moral obligation not to close borders against forced migration).

7 See Carens 1992: p. 35 ff.; Woodward 1992: 64 ff.; Barry 1992: 282. See Pogge
   (1996a: 4). See Pogge 1997. Perry, on the contrary, thinks that there would be
   'strong arguments that tend to favor immigration over foreign aid' (1995: 103).
8 See Zolberg et al. (1989: 30 ff.) for a broader definition of refugees than the statu-
   tory one: refugees are 'persons whose presence abroad is attributable to a well
   founded fear of violence, as might be established by impartial experts with adequate
   information' (33), including not only fear of persecution: 'But flight inducing violence may also be an incidental consequence of external or internal conflict, or some
   combination of both, and affects groups that are not even parties to that conflict.
   Violence may also be inflicted indirectly, through imposed conditions that make
   normal life impossible.' See also Carens 1995, Hathaway 1995 and Goodwin-Gill
   1994.
9 Closure under conditions of rough equality can be legitimate and must be permitted
   'somewhere' (see Bader 1995, note 25; Bader/Benschop 1989: 136-41; see Barry
   1995: 16 ff. for private clubs).
10 For overlapping attempts to distinguish traditions regarding international justice and
   free movement see Nardin/Mapel 1998: 297f (consequence oriented traditions
   (utilism, realism, marxism) vs. rule-oriented traditions (natural law, rights, contractarianism)); Barry 1989 (generosity versus justice as reciprocity (fidelity, requital,
   fair play) or justice as equal rights); 1995 (justice as mutual advantage, as reciprocity, as impartiality); Barry/Goodin 1992 (liberal egalitarianism, libertarianism,
   marxism, natural law perspective, political realism; see critically: Goodin 1996);
   O'Neill 1991 (consequentialism (utilism) vs. rights (libertarianism, compensatory
   justice, welfare and international justice) vs. Kantian obligation/needs); Perry 1995
   (justice as mutually advantageous co-operation, as reciprocity vs. subject-centred
   theories of basic rights or needs).
11 This overlapping consensus is different from Rawls' concept, on a higher level and
   still more concrete (Pogge 1995c: 200). My argument in this section is very much
   influenced by recent texts of Pogge (1994, 1995c) in which he takes more distance
   towards his earlier critical reconstructions of a Rawlsian approach. In two respects
   my argument is different: (i) I restrict my hope for an overlapping consensus on
   core moral and sociological arguments, to show why radical international inequalities impose strong moral duties on rich countries and leave alternative institutions
   and policy-proposals more open. Pogge hopes that overlapping consensus can also
   be reached for his GRD proposal. (ii) I try to link this strategy to arguments in favor
   of fairly open borders. Pogge has put forward critical objections against this link.
12 Which, in my presentation, is integrated into the arguments based on justice but can
   easily be singled out: steps 1, 2, 4 and 5 in section 1.2 below.
13 See Bader 1997c:33 and note 2. See Shue 1980: 23, 25, 30 for a minimal and limited list of 'basic rights' near the 'moral rock-bottom' (p. 123) and an excellent criticism of the predominant Anglo-Saxon "rights" talk discounting all so-called
   "positive rights" and the corresponding policies to downplay or neglect all International or European Covenants on Economic, Social, and Cultural Rights.
14 Carens 1987: 252. See Carens 1989, p.2 and 1992; Beitz 1979, 1985, 1991; Walzer
   1983: 55 and 1992: 96f.; Schuck/Smith 1985: 2; Pogge 1989: 247; Dummet 1992:
   171; Brubaker 1992: 31f; Anderson 1983: 59.
15 If one accepts, for the sake of argument, a Rawlsian framework, this alone would
   challenge Rawls' own conclusions: the first thing the parties in the original position,
   meeting behind the veil of ignorance, 'would do would be to challenge the rules under which Rawls requires them to operate. Although they do not know whether their
   own society is rich or poor, they can presumably know that, if they live in the 20th
   century, there will be a minority of rich societies and a majority in which there is
   undernourishment or malnutrition. Surely then, the arguments which are said to lead

the participants in the original position to insist on maximizing the wealth of the worst-off within any given community would even more strongly lead to an insistence that what this minimum is should not depend capriciously upon the good luck of being born into a rich society or the ill luck of being born into a poor one.' 'There is no conceivable internal redistribution of income that would make a noticeable improvement to the nutrition of the worst-fed in India or resourceless African states. Surely, viewing things from the "original position" one would at all costs wish to avoid this kind of poverty if one turned out to live in a poor state' (Barry 1973: 129), particularly if one would avoid "high risk" strategies and "play safe" as is assumed by Rawls to close the indeterminacy of "rational choice" in his original position.

16 Again arguing from within a Rawlsian framework the distribution of natural resources 'is a purer case of something's being arbitrary from a moral point of view than the distribution of talents. Not only can one not be said to deserve the resources under one's feet; the other grounds on which one might assert an initial claim to talents, are absent as well' (Beitz 1985: 291; see first: Beitz 1979 Part III). It is important to note that this argument is independent from assumptions about 'self-sufficiency of national schemes of co-operation'.

17 Barry (1989: 452); not only must the inheritance itself be justly acquired (and transmitted), as Locke and Nozick would require, the claims 'that those now alive can make to special advantages derived from the efforts of their ancestors' attenuate with time.

18 1995: 184. See 1989: 17f, 27 and 1992: 56 for his concept of negative responsibility. See Singer (1993: 230f.) for a short utilitarian version.

19 The *normative claim* that we are responsible not only for the direct consequences of our individual actions but also for the policies and actions of our organizations and for the basic structure of our national and international institutions as well as for the working of global systems is refuted by absolute individualists like Hayek.

20 Obviously, the existing institutions could also be negatively legitimated either by claiming that they are the only possible ones or that they are the only feasible ones, because all alternatives would leave the worst off even worse off. This conservative "status-quo-realism" seems to be a very implausible last refuge, poorly masking the unwillingness to accept that "ought implies costs".

21 Let me shortly summarize two of them: Henry Shue (1980) argues that universal *basic rights* to security and subsistence have to be guaranteed against standard threats which are not ineradicable nor 'outside the control of society' (p. 25; statement 8). Extreme poverty is systemic or inherent in the structure of our global economic order (pp. 40 ff., 112f, 124 ff., 170 ff.) and we are morally responsible for this situation (expansive interpretation of no-harm principle, statement 6). Among our duties to avoid deprivation, to protect from deprivation and to aid the deprived figures prominently the duty to design, built and maintain 'institutions and practices that protect people's subsistence' (p. 45, statement 7).

In his *contractarian* 'theory of justice' (1971) Rawls has defended and developed a quite inegalitarian 'law of peoples' (1993). Pogge has shown that this is at odds with crucial elements of his own theory. His internal critique has demonstrated (i) that from the three possible interpretations of the "original position" ((1) one global setting (G) in which individuals decide principles of global and domestic justice in one and the same run; (2) in a second session, individuals from different states decide principles of global justice (R1); (3) parties to the second session are representatives of states (R2)) strong internal arguments favor G, the single, global version and that an international application of the difference principle would have more radical egalitarian consequences than R1 and R2 with the procedurally built in priority for compatriots (see Pogge 1989: 244 ff.). (ii) But even if people would agree to

Rawl's own preference for R2 the parties would have good internal reasons to disagree with Rawls' own inegalitarian conclusions (see Pogge 1994). Most Rawlsian critiques of Rawls agree with statement 7, particularly that principles of international justice should be used to design alternative institutions to prevent gross and systemic inequalities (see Beitz, Barry, Pogge) and on statement 8. However, there is some *prima facie* disagreement about statement 6. The common presumption by all Rawlsians is: 'where there is no social co-operation, there are no benefits of co-operation, and hence no problem of compensation for relative disadvantage. (This is why a world of self-sufficient national societies is not subject to something like a global difference principle)' (Beitz, 1985: 292). The crucial question, then, is what counts as a relevant scheme of co-operation. Beitz, summarizing 'facts, by now part of the conventional wisdom of international relations' (297) like the progressive removal of restrictions on international trade and investment, the rise of an international division of labour, the enormous impact of transnational corporations, the effects of international monetary, financial and trade institutions, concludes that we live in 'a world in which national boundaries can no longer be regarded as the outer limit of social co-operation' (296). Barry, to the contrary, thinks that Rawls is broadly right in denying that the whole world constitutes a single co-operative partnership in the required sense: 'trade, however multilateral, does not constitute a co-operative scheme of the relevant kind' and UN organizations, IMF, World Bank clearly fall short of relationships of mutual dependence found within 'societies' (1989: 445 ff..). In my view, Barry uses a very simplistic neo-classical fable of trade, markets and prizes on world-markets which all are more institutionalized and regulated than he assumes. Particularly, he neglects the role of "background institutions" like international law, private property of natural resources and means of production, sanctioning these practices of interdependency, even if they in themselves would not constitute schemes of co-operation. I think that Pogge is right that even a restricted interpretation of such schemes has to transcend the (nation) state level. However that may be, this disagreement is less far reaching if one realizes that Barry only wanted to show that one should read Rawls' theory not as 'justice as reciprocity' but as 'equal rights', and that he himself argues for a much stronger international scheme of co-operation to correct the 'scandalous immorality' of the present system.

22 The 'underlying principle is that each person has an equal prima facie claim to a share of the total available resources but departures from this initial standard could be justified (analogous to the operation of the difference principle) if resulting inequalities were to the greatest benefit of those least advantaged' (Beitz, 1985: 293).

23 This approach, again, can be shared by different theoretical traditions: Beitz has tried to show that a *Rawlsian* approach would require a 'resource distribution principle... (that) would function in international society as the difference principle functions in domestic society' (1985: 293). Perhaps such an argument would fit better into a *Dworkinian* theory of equality, which is more endowment-insensitive than Rawls' theory (see Pogge's critical remarks vs. Beitz, 1989: 250 ff.) and includes a mechanism to insure against natural handicaps which can easily be extended to disadvantages in the distribution of natural resources and which is independent of the difference principle. Within a *libertarian* conception of justice, fairly unlimited property rights and inheritance of natural resources (by states or individuals) would only be morally legitimate, if the original appropriation would fulfill the Lockean proviso that "enough and as good as" would be left for others, which could only be overruled if all would be better off under new rules, which is evidently not the case (see Steiner 1992, Perry 1995: 100f). The second requirement for morally legitimate property, that the transmission itself has to be just (without force and fraud) is also, evidently, not met with regard to natural resources.

24 See also the minimal recommendations for US Foreign Policy by Shue (1980: 155
    ff.) which follow from the first approach, and Singer's proposal of 10% of personal
    income (1993: 241f, 246) which highlights the point that our institutional responsi-
    bility, rightly stressed by theories of a necessary division of moral obligations,
    should never completely replace our individual responsibilities.

25 These however would all have the obvious disadvantage of being morally arbitrary.

26 From UN interventions in Cambodia, Somalia, Haiti, ex-Yugoslavia, Iraq to the
    moral legitimation to wage war (Luban 1985 and, much more carefully, Beitz 1985.
    See Walzer's excellent response 1985).

27 See Piore/Sabel 1984. See Hirst/Thompson 1996.

28 See Beitz 1979, 1985, 1991; Pogge 1989, 1992; Bader 1995 and 1996a. Ruggie
    1993.

29 Those who like hierarchies and lexical orderings may call that a "secondary" or
    "derived moral obligation". Political projects commonly have more than just one
    priority and, as far as I can see, are the same people and organizations who are in
    favour of much tougher and stronger efforts to tackle poverty and global inequality
    and, at the same time, criticize restrictive first admission policies.

30 Prematurely in my 1995: 216; more carefully: Beitz p. 247f; Bauböck 1994.

31 See for a similar strategy: Beitz 1979 and 1985; Shue 1980, Part II; Pogge 1989:
    259 ff..

32 See Beitz 1991: 246 ff. for a brief sketch of four ways to respond to the "dilemma of
    sovereignty and morality", of "sectional values" and "globally impartial view": (1)
    deny that moral principles matter at all in foreign affairs (Hobbesian political real-
    ism); (2) deny that sectional values should matter at all (Tolstoy's extreme cos-
    mopolitanism); (3) acknowledge the abstract possibility of conflict, but deny that
    there is any practical problem (Sidgwick); (4) deny that morality as correctly under-
    stood requires a cosmopolitan view (communitarianism).

33 See Beitz 1991: 246, 248 'we should hesitate before discarding sectional loyalties or
    local norms as no more than disguised self-interest or inherited myth'. Pogge 1994:
    221.

34 See also: Singer 1970: 23 ff.; 1993: 232 ff., 249, 252 ff..; Goodin 1988: 666.

35 This weakness is shared by Singer (see 1993: 233), Goodin and most utilitarians.
    See critically: Perry 1995: 99f. See more generally: Scheffler 1995.

36 See below. See Bauböck 1994, ch. 12, part. pp. 314 ff.. Bauböck (1996, points 4 and
    5). See Bader 1996: 'Most "communitarian" legitimations of particularist obliga-
    tions would not go so far to denounce any moral obligations towards "foreigners".
    But there is considerable space on the scale ranging from a complete separation of
    "Binnenmoral und Außenmoral" to a flat world without any special moral ties and
    obligations (most "cosmopolitans" would not go as far as that).'

37 See my criticism of Walzer in this regard: Bader 1995. See Margalit/Raz 1990.

38 See Goodin 1988: 665. See Bader (1996b): 'If one accepts that compatriots in mod-
    ern states are mostly strangers and that liberal public morality is a morality of
    strangers, the argument in favor of compatriots and in favor of the "nearer" circles
    of external strangers looses much of its "premodern" appeal and should be de-em-
    phasized to put it into its proper dimension.'

39 See Beitz 1985: 305 versus too 'psychological ties'. See Somers 1993 and Bader
    1995a (p. 158, note 44) for the difficult "transplantation" of loyalties from "local" to
    "national". Furthermore, these multilayered political loyalties have to compete with
    many other loyalties (see Shue 1980: 137).

40 See Bauböck1995b; see my short discussion in 1996c.

41 See Barry 1989, p.314. See for the limited claims from legitimate expectations:
    Kymlicka 1995: 116 ff..

42 See Bauböck 1994: 313 ff.. Seidman 1995.

43 See Goodin 1988: 667 ff.; and 1996: we may not take their property for public purposes, we cannot conscript them, we cannot tax them in the same way, we have to
treat them "in accordance with certain rules and principles of international law" etc.
The special obligations of compatriots are a much more mixed blessing 'than ordinary philosophical thinking on special duties leads us to expect'.

44 I think that Walzer, to whom I'm alluding here, does agree with regard to security
(see 1977, 1985, 1994) though his position is much more ambivalent with regard to
subsistence. See Baier 1995: 150 ff.: 'a realistic morality will take the natural network of ties as the place to start, but not as the place to finish', and immigration
policies have to be 'both caring and just if they are to be morally acceptable'.

45 See Shue 1980: 139. Bauböck 1996b, starting from a more historically situated and
moderate version of universalism, comes to quite similar conclusions: 'a reasonable
standard of universal morality' requires 'much more than any present state is willing
to do': 'mutual aid in cases of emergency, provision for survival for individuals and,
most importantly, foreign and economic policies which enable other societies to develop their own comprehensive systems of democratic citizenship.' See also: Tamir
(1993: 158 ff.). Goodin's conclusions from his utilitarian treatment of boundaries
and citizenship as merely instrumental devices for fixing derivative special responsibilities can, of course, be much more outspoken and radical.

46 Versus Tushnet 1995: 153. See my plea for rooted cosmopolitanism: Bader 1996c.
See also Beitz 1991: 246.

47 Still, these special relations should not allow 'loopholes in moralities', neither retro-
spectively nor in the design of institutions. Double standards for compatriots and
foreigners are acceptable only if minimal constraints of basic justice are met (Pogge
1992: 89f; see p. 93-5 for examples and correcting and strengthening steps. See
1989: 262).

48 See comments and replies by Pogge, Bauböck, Bader. See Bauböck's defence
against the objection that such an approach 'seems to dilute global obligations by
extending the area of special obligations beyond national ones'. 'Why should one
provide moral justification for actions which do not improve the situation of the
worst-off, but of those lucky enough to be able to raise special claims towards particular states?... I think that we have to balance special against universal obligations
and find ways how to meet both. The latter retain their pressing moral force when
the former have been met, but the former should not be sacrificed by concentrating
all efforts on meeting the latter' (Bauböck (1996) point 7).

49 See excellent: Shue 1980, 1988, Goodin 1988, O'Neill (1991: 278, 285-87, 295)
and Bauböck 1994. O'Neill holds that the disappearance of unallocated, imperfect
obligations within a rights framework forces us to replace the language of rights by
'an account of obligations among finite, needy beings' (1991: 296) combining a
Kantian theory of obligations with a Marxian theory of needs. Now I think that one
has to accept the challenge to fill the gap between rights and obligations, but
O'Neill's conclusion is hasty. Theories of rights, instead, can be complemented by
complex theories of duties and designs for their adequate assignment or allocation
among individuals, organizations, states, intergovernmental or international organizations. A short comparison between Shue's and Bauböck's approach reveals interesting differences: Shue is arguing for universal human rights to security and subsistence whereas Bauböck is arguing for citizenship rights (see for the importance
of this difference: Goodin 1988, 1996a; Ferrajoli 1994; Bader 1996a). Within the
first approach states have to be conceived of as "mediating institutions" and the corresponding duties do not "naturally" fall upon the state.

50 All three approaches, referred to in section I, share this common assumption and allow, therefore, overruling of sovereignty in certain respects.

51 This design should blow up the misleading but widespread dichotomy between "either" a global state "or" the existing system. A global state would be neither feasible nor desirable from a democratic point of view (see Bader 1996a): (i) it is a strategy to *replace* the multitude of states by one world state, the many constitutions by one world constitution, the many exclusionary citizenships by one universal citizenship. As such it is not "feasible", and it reproduces discredited legal myths of absolute, unitary, and indivisible state sovereignty on the higher level of the world state. (ii) It would, therefore, reproduce all, or at least most old problems within the new world state because sovereign powers would have to be delegated downwards; (iii) from a democratic point of view it is quite unattractive, even if it were feasible: historical experience tells us that "the higher up" and "the farther away" the more difficult is democratic participation (and, by the way, the more inefficient are systems of governance). States, of course, have to play an important role in guaranteeing minimal standards of security and it is dangerous to strengthen smaller "national" or "ethnic" units opposed to states without, at the same time, creating stronger supra-state and global institutions. This is not only obvious in cases of the breakdown of multi-national empires and multi-nation states like the ex-Soviet-Union and ex-Yugoslavia but also in Italy. The conditions for legitimate secession are only rarely fulfilled (see Buchanan, Hannum). More and more authors have therefore tried to design a model of overlapping political units (from local to global), of multi-layered, delegated and limited sovereignties, and of multi-layered political loyalties. Such a model should be tested in the usual way: is it "feasible"? Doesn't it lead to counterproductive consequences which would leave us worse-off than with the existing system? But such criticism, welcome as it is, should and can not serve as an all too easy excuse for giving up such endeavours in favour of the *status quo*.

52 'Different from universal obligations not to interfere with negative liberties, food must be provided by specific agents. But if a local structure of obligations such as those of kin, neighborhood, regional administration and the state has broken down or is no longer willing or capable of maintaining adequate levels of provision, who will then be responsible for complying with the obligation? We might think that it then turns into a universal one so that everybody with sufficient resources would be obliged to take action to secure the right. But this is no answer to the question of how to get food to the single starving family. The problem obviously requires an allocation of obligations with international institutions and organizations' (Bauböck 1994: 309, excellently summarizing Shue's & O'Neill's exposition of the problem).

53 I also agree with Bauböck's plea for institutional solutions instead of moral pedagogy. Let me add two critical remarks: (i) in his book, one often finds an uneasy mix of normative and empirical/historical statements: "can" states be seen to fulfill (always to certain degrees only!) or "should" they fulfill this role? Empirically, the 'reconciliation of special and general obligations' (Bauböck, 1996, point 9) on a national level is very questionable. (ii) A similar development of allocating imperfectly allocated obligations is taking place at a supra-national level. Bauböck rightly points at the 'lack of a strong central agency' and the 'lack of democratic arrangements', but - in analogy to the development of modern states - first came central agencies, then came democratization. Why should it be different for the EU, for the UN?

54 See 1994: 316 ff. for refugees and asylum seekers. See Coleman/Harding 1995: 20 ff. for the empirical recognition of 'special historical ties'.

55 See Bader 1989: 332f; see Pogge 1989: 261f and 1992, Bauböck 1994 and 1996b, Coleman/Harding 1995: 52: 35f.

56 See Bauböck 1994 and 1996, point 11: 'reform of the Security Council composition and decision making rules, a global court of human rights with similar powers as the

Strasbourg court, a strengthening of the powers of certain UN-organizations in relation to member states (e.g. a power for the UNHCR to work out systems of burden sharing..) and a much more prominent role for global NGO's like Amnesty International would be essential pieces of reform'. See also Shue 1988: 703.

57 I suppress a longer discussion of another problem commonly invoked, that only states can help to solve the problem of *motivational compliance*. At first sight, an appeal to state-centred identities and loyalties seems to be rather counterproductive when the problem is to strengthen compliance to imperfectly allocated global duties. Commonly, the reference to "national commitment", necessary to solve motivation problems, serves as a device to get rid of global obligations or to keep them at a harmless distance. Attempts to appeal to the 'moral usefulness of the (nation)state' as a source of loyalty and commitment remain ambivalent even if they 'aim at the progressive expansion, but not the abolition, of existing solidarities' (Walzer 1995: 249). They may only help to alleviate the problem if they de-emphasize the ethnic pre-political base and strengthen the trans- or international civil pre-political base (trans- or international old and new social movements, NGOs) and, at the same time try to develop and implement stronger global institutions.

58 Not only by T.H. Marshall the progressive "internal" inclusion is linked with arguments for external exclusion.

59 See Sidwick, Shue, Carens, Bauböck, Walzer, Weiner, Whitaker. It is a delicate subject, which should be much more carefully spelled out and addressed than I do in this sketch.

60 Here, I disagree with the completely instrumental conception of democracy by v. Parijs (1996: 110f.) who otherwise rightly elaborates the tension between democracy and justice, particularly in the case of migration (see Bader 1995: 221f.) and asks for 'democratic engineering' on a global scale, for the design 'of true democratic institutions beyond the national level' (p. 116) to make 'our world a little more just, or at least a little less massively unjust, than it is today' (p. 114).

61 See Bader 1995: 212, stressing all fields and levels of democracy, not only "polities"; see Walzer 1985a: 236.

62 States are not the same as democratic polities. Even if states are democratic, the "liberal" side of liberal democratic constitutions still should trump an otherwise unlimited legitimacy of exclusion which is so characteristic for theories and practices of republican democracy (see critically: Bauböck 1994; see Pogge's case 2 in 1992: 88f; see Bader 1995; v. Parijs 1996).

63 See also Bauböck p.190 and 201f. Membership in a democratic world state - replacing existing political units - would have to be all-inclusive and automatic and would, therefore, 'eliminate altogether choice and consent as criteria for determining membership, i.e. those very aspects that allow the *demos* to be seen as an association.' (Bauböck 1994: 186); see 1996a.

64 See Bauböck 1994: 202; 1996a. See for a defence of some inevitable ascriptive elements of *jus sanguinis* and *jus soli* for the determination of involuntary, 'passive' state-membership: Bauböck, 1994: ch. 2: 'Attributed Membership'.

65 See for the systematic interdependence of political and thicker, ethnic cultures: Bader 1996c. Thicker 'ethics of citizenship' (Bauböck 1996b) can, indeed, be morally permissible and legitimate, "if" (see above; see Bader 1996c (§ 2.2.4.3) for further restrictions). See Zolberg 1997 for the examples of 19th century Catholic Irish immigrants in the US.

66 See Castles/Miller 1993, Castles 1997. See Bader 1996d.

67 'Such rights do not exist in a state of nature and they would be endangered in a global state. Only democratic polities in a world of many states are a relatively safe place where rights can be claimed as well as enjoyed. The rights of citizenship equalize individuals as members of a polity and limit the extent and effects of social

and economic inequalities. Any redistributive system which tries to keep internal inequalities smaller than those in its environment cannot keep access completely open for further participants... free movement would certainly not lead to a global redistribution of those social rights that depend on the state's capacity to regulate territorial labor markets and employment conditions' (Bauböck, 1994: 331; see 1995b: 21); see Walzer's Response (1995) and my reply. See Føllesdal 1995. Walzer, Bauböck and Føllesdal agree 'that state borders affect the standing of foreigners' claims to equal shares' (Føllesdal, 1996: 5).

68 See critically: Føllesdal, 1995: 9, 17; see Beitz 1985: 302-5, 308.

69 Democratic socialists and radical democrats clearly ask for more socio-economic equality (see Cunningham 1987 for many) than most well-known egalitarian liberals (see Føllesdal, following Rawls).

70 Bracketing outright elitism (Huntington), it still is an open question "how much socio-economic equality" representative democracy "requires". Recent neo-liberal policies have shown that "domestic minima" can be considerably reduced and, obviously, that relative economic inequalities are mushrooming domestically as well as internationally.

71 See Føllesdal, 1995: 22: 'An important task in working towards a legitimate world order is therefore to develop indicators of living standards, so that we as citizens can check whether justice is served: respecting legitimate claims to benefits, as well as claims to control our own fate'.

72 Here I would agree that a reasonable standard of minimal universal morality would require 'much less than a truly democratic state would consider to be necessary in order to flatten social inequality between citizens' (Bauböck 1996b). However, I would question the very general and context-free conclusion that one would have to opt for a 'far much higher minimum internally' and that, therefore, democracy would practically legitimate closure of 'internal redistribution systems to outsiders' (Bader 1996b).

73 See v. Parijs 1992: 164: Local equalization 'can be justified even by reference to those with least real freedom in the world. For it demonstrates that a strongly redistributive economy is more than a fancy dream, and it thereby provides a tangible model both for redistributive strategies in each country and for an admittedly very remote first-best fully individualized transfer system on a world scale.' In his 1996 article, v. Parijs seems to have changed his mind.

74 See Bader 1996c, balancing my earlier treatment in 1995: 229 ff.

75 See Bader 1995: 217 ff.; see also: Perry 1995: 117-21; See for weak versus strong perfectionism: Kymlicka 1989, 1990.

76 See Kymlicka, Rickards, Bauböck, Buchanan, Hannum. See Bader 1995c and 1996d. See Perry (1995 § II) for a short discussion of three arguments for exclusion: the perfectionist argument, the argument from stability, and the argument from autonomy.

77 See Walzer 1995 and Bader 1995a.

78 See Bader/Benschop 1989 and Bader 1995c for a critique of all pseudo-exactness in quantifications in empirical studies of inequalities as well as in normative theories of complex equality.

79 This should not be misread as an unconditional surrender to any outcome of democratic procedures in a Habermasian way: our moral outcome-tests may be weaker than we wished them to be, they still impose limits to the morally tolerable; the "outcomes" of democratic decisions with regard to global poverty and first admission in all "rich democracies of the North" are clearly intolerable, in my view.

3 The 'Nature' of Nationality

Verena Stolcke

> 'Man was born free, but everywhere he is in chains.'
> (J.J. Rousseau, 1762)

INTRODUCTION

Citizenship is the quintessence of the modern individual's political emancipation and equality in the eyes of the law. Citizenship as the bundle of
civil rights enjoyed by free and formally equal citizens became bounded,
however, almost from the start in the emerging bourgeois world dividing
into territorial nation-states which vied for dominance. The acquisition of
citizenship rights became conditioned by specific legal rules, the so-
called nationality laws, which codified the formal requirements which
individuals must meet to be entitled to become citizens of concrete states.
As a consequence, citizenship rights became the exclusive privilege of
those who were recognized as nationals of a particular state to the exclusion of the nationals of any other state so constituted.

Of the three constitutive elements of the modern state, a territory, a
government, a people, circumscribing the 'people' proved to be the most
controversial issue (Lichter 1955). A territory without a people, a government without a clearly bounded community to be governed, makes no
sense. Hence, bounding the citizenry, that is determining the conditions
for becoming a member of a state, acquired a logic of its own as a fundamental constitutive political dilemma in the formative period of the modern territorial nation-states.

There are three analytically distinct dimensions to membership in a nation-state, one regarding an individual's legal status within a polity which
warrants the unqualified enjoyment of civil, political and social rights.
Second, this political status is formally grounded in a prior legal relationship entered into by the individual and a state (Keller & Trautmann 1914:
32; *Staatslexikon* - Recht, Wirtschaft, Gesellschaft 1962: 570).[1] And
third, belonging to the nation-state has, moreover, often been taken to be
'ascribed' by an inner, subjective sense of shared national identity.

In this chapter I will retrace the manner in which nationality, understood as the possession of certain legally stipulated qualifications which make of individuals members of a nation-state and which, in turn condition citizenship, was conceptualized in the process of nineteenth-century nation-building in Germany, France and Britain.

Persistent economic crisis and deepening social exclusions recently have endowed citizenship with new political prominence. The uncertainties surrounding European political integration coupled with the alleged threat of so-called extra-communitarian immigration have provoked a heightened concern over national identity, unity and sovereignty. Citizenship and 'national identity' occupy a central place in contemporary political agendas, in academic debate and in research. The constitutive role *nationality* has played in modern nation-building has, however, received surprisingly little analytical attention in the social sciences (e.g. Hobsbawm 1990, Wallerstein & Balibar 1988, Finkelkraut 1987, Anderson 1983).[2] This is so because, as I will argue, nationality became generally *naturalized* throughout the formative period of the modern nation-state. Citizenship and nationality became subsumed into one indistinct status inherent to rather then acquired by the modern individual thereby simultaneously becoming almost self-evident.

Illustrative of this taken-for-grantedness of nationality is the conceptual difficulty of separating out the formal legal requirements for acquiring citizenship from the substantive civil, political and social rights thereby obtained manifest in the semantic ambiguity that surrounds the two concepts. While Brubaker, for example, defines citizenship as "a legal institution regulating membership in the state, not a set of participatory practices or a set of specifically civic attitudes" (1992: 51) Silverman insists that "...nationality is essential for the acquisition of certain rights when citizenship is likened to nationality." (1992: 160-61). In most contemporary dictionaries the two terms connote indistinctly the conditions *for* and *of* membership in a nation-state. Nationality and citizenship are taken interchangeably to signify nominal and substantive membership in a state, often thought to be, moreover, grounded in some shared subjective 'national-ethnic' feeling of identity (e.g. Ritter 1986: 285).[3]

Because it is self-evident, for the ordinary citizen nationality laws are not unlike the small print on the back of insurance policies, rarely read and largely ignored. The question why a person possesses French, British or German nationality usually elicits a blank look or, in the best of circumstances, a hesitant and vague allusion to the fact of the individual in question (or her/his parents) having been born in the respective country. Even among academics, safe experts in international private law or immigration policy this question usually prompts comments on nationalism and national identity.

The indistinct usage of the terms nationality and citizenship tends to disguise the constitutive role of nationality for citizenship and national identity. In actual fact, neither are these terms synonymous nor can they be conflated in the nation-state in a phenomenological sense even if all three phenomena are linked historically and ideologically.

In this chapter, instead of addressing the theme of citizenship or the dramatically fashionable topic of 'nationalism' in their immediacy, I will examine this more elusive aspect of both, namely *nationality*, at once more *basic*, in fact so basic to our conception of belonging and self that it has, as it were, become second nature so that we are often scarcely aware of it.

As Gellner wrote, in a world of nation-states, "a man (sic) must have a *nationality* as he must have a nose and two ears". If noses and ears like 'nationality' are intrinsic attributes of human beings they obviously need not be explained (Gellner 1983: 6, my emphasis). But Gellner here refers, of course, to national identity as a subjective sense of belonging rather than to *nationality* as the legal requisites for acquiring state membership. This is just one example of the conceptual slippage I referred to above. There is more to this than a mere game with words. The etymological and semantic confusions surrounding nationality, citizenship and national identity are but one manifestation of intersecting political imperatives and ideological assumptions that informed nineteenth-century endeavours to unequivocally circumscribe the citizenry of contending states in a divided though interdependent bourgeois world.

To capture the meaning of key political concepts they need to be situated in their historical contexts. Europe is the cradle of the democratic territorial nation-state. But some nation-states more than others set the rules of the modern nationality game. Throughout the nineteenth century access to membership in a state became defined in, moreover, apparently disparate ways. The conventional distinction drawn between the German model of the *Kulturnation* and the French concept of the *Staatsnation* (Meinecke 1919), no less than the ideal type contrasts between the republican, the ethno-national and the liberal tradition need to be transcended, however, to rescue significant underlying historical commonalities in the manner in which the 'people' of the new nation-states became circumscribed legally as well as ideologically. Hence, rather than analysing demonstrable imperfections in the democratic implementation of nationality and citizenship, I will focus on the contradictions and ensuing limitations that were intrinsic to their very origins and marked their later development.[4]

The ideological conflation of nationality, citizenship and national identity no less than the contemporary nationalist resurgence are rooted in a fundamental contradiction that dates back to the early phase in European nation-building which the modern nationality laws were designed to overcome (Stolcke 1995, Bader 1995b).

The growth of capitalism and of competing national bourgeoisies, the dissolution of traditional bonds of political allegiance and the resulting freedom of movement of the populations endowed the question of national belonging with new urgency. The nineteenth century saw the emergence of a multiplicity of bounded territorial states contending for sovereignty and dominance. Traditional communities did not, however, necessarily coincide with the territorial states as modern polities. A clear regulation of membership in the emerging states, the focus of loyalty of its inhabitants and the source of expanding civil rights and duties but also of disdain of all strangers, became thus imperative.

An unqualified cosmopolitan spirit inspired the new republican order for which the French revolutionaries fought which was to become the model of the modern democratic nation-state. Democratic revolutionary thought advocated for a universalist, voluntarist idea of citizenship founded in consent born of free will. Yet, as Kamenka has rightly noted, "... in establishing the institutions of popular sovereignty, it is necessary to define what is the populace: self-government required a community that is the self." (Kamenka 1976:14; see also Cranston 1988:101, Hobsbawm 1990: 19). Citizenship rights extolling individual freedom and hence choice, in theory also of nationality, replaced the old notion of the subject of the *Ancien Régime* founded on traditional vertical allegiances and primordial loyalties. The revolutionary cosmopolitan doctrine of the new territorial state peopled by free, self-determining citizens would have made any legal circumscription of 'the people' in the last instance superfluous.

Political reality was, however, another, namely the division of that new world into contending nation-states each claiming the right to control its own population and to exclude all others. Hence, one of the crucial functions of the modern state became the regulation of peoples' movement across frontiers. Modern nationality laws were intended to overcome the contradiction between this original cosmopolitan, democratic and voluntarist ideal of citizenship and the imperative boundedness of the polity.

Nationality laws fulfill a bounding function not unlike that of kinship principles in so-called 'tribal' societies. Both sets of rules play the structural role of setting the personnel boundaries of meaningful socio-political groups, be it a 'tribe' or a modern nation-state. Both have in common that despite the often 'bloody' metaphors that are invoked which purvey an image of permanence of the social groups so constituted, these rules are nonetheless the outcome of positive historical conventions. But there is also a notable difference in this respect between 'tribal' societies and modern states. As anthropologists know only too well, in 'tribal' societies kinship principles define group membership with its attendant rights and duties unequivocally. In the modern world supposedly peopled by free and formally equal individuals, ascription of nationality and hence of the enjoyment of civil, political and social rights constitutes, by contrast, an evident paradox. In effect, while democratic liberalism was and is committed to individual freedom and equality so that the moral, political and legal claims of the individual transcend those of the community and the state (Goldberg 1993: 4-5), the emancipatory idea of citizenship was born, nevertheless, bounded by exclusive nationality laws which, moreover, became progressively naturalized throughout the nineteenth century. As Huxley and Haddon, referring to the principle of national self-determination, noted pointedly in the thirties "the desire for freedom from sovereign domination...is very far from the desire for freedom itself with which it is often confused..." (Huxley, Haddon and Carr-Saunders 1939: 18).

Aside from creating a formal legal bond between an individual and a concrete state at a given point in time, nationality laws also regulate the reproduction of a national community over time. Not only are nationality laws historical phenomena embedded in specific contexts and hence open to change. They also configure *national reproduction*, that is the manner in which membership in a state is ensured over time in often gendered ways. In addition to excluding foreigners from the community of nationals, as I will show, nationality laws also introduced formal inequalities among nationals which affected women in particular.

NATIONALITY AND FRENCH UNIVERSALIST REPUBLICANISM

Nationality referring to the conditions individuals have to fulfill in order to claim the status of citizenship dates back to the French Revolution and the ensuing struggle for popular sovereignty. According to Rousseau, since man (sic) is free and master of himself, nobody may, under whatever pretext, subject him without his consent. To safeguard individual freedom from subjection to others in society, the general will needed to be the collective expression of individual wills. Here are the first elements of the modern idea of democratic citizenship thereafter consecrated in the *Déclaration des Droits de l'Homme et du Citoyen* (1789), a declaration of the rights of men (sic) as citizens. Sovereignty resided in the 'nation' composed of freely consenting man.[5] This universalist republican democratic ideal of the sovereign nation-state replaced the free and formally equal citizen for the subject of the *Ancien Régime*, though it shared with absolutism a belief in unified sovereignty. Political thinkers were well aware at the time of the difficulties involved in bounding the community of sovereign individuals capable of entering into a social contract. They developed several compromise solutions ranging from the universalist republican, the liberal territorial, the organic communitarian models of the state to the idea of a world state as, for example, Hegel and Kant proposed. All, except the last model, were beset by the same contradiction between an ideal of individual self-determination and the necessary boundedness of 'the people'.

Instead of allowing for progressively greater freedom of movement of individuals between states, emerging nation-states set about codifying nationality by legally drawing a boundary around the citizenry and thereby conditioning the acquisition of citizenship rights. Two contrasting nationality doctrines were drawn upon to bound the citizenry of particular states: the conservative, exclusive principle of *jus sanguinis* (the law of blood) which gave nationality an almost ontological quality since it made state membership dependent on a shared cultural heritage transmitted by descent typical of the *Kulturnation* conventionally associated with Germany and the more inclusive *jus soli* (the law of soil) which made nationality dependent on birth in the territory of a state, characteristic of the *Staatsnation* typical of France (Meinecke 1919, Kohn 1948).[6] A comparative historical analysis of developing nationality laws will, nonetheless, reveal this disparity between the German and the French 'national' traditions more apparent than real.

France was the first modern state to codify nationality. Revolutionary cosmopolitanism conferred citizenship in the Republic on anyone who desired to become a citizen. In those politically turbulent times revolutionary constitutions aimed less at circumscribing the 'nation' than at ensuring citizenship rights to all inhabitants. The Constitution of 1791, those of 1789 and 1793, consecrated the pre-revolutionary principle of birth in the territory and secondarily *naturalization* (note the term!) as grounds for becoming *citoyens francaises* entitled to full civil rights. The Constitution of 1793 went even further by admitting *the will to become French*.[7] In sharp contrast with early revolutionary cosmopolitanism in the context of the restoration, the Napoleonic Code of 1804 decreed *descent from a Frenchman* (sic) as the foremost nationality rule, children of foreigners born on French soil being entitled to French citizenship if they so willed. As the Napoleonic wars covered Europe, *jus sanguinis* was deemed fundamental to warrant loyalty on the part of the armed forces (Weiss 1907: 47 ff.).[8]

With the articulation of a social ideology of freedom and equality and the dissolution of feudal structures which had defined women's roles, the Revolution also catalysed women's consciousness and activity. The most outspoken manifesto of feminist claims is Olympe de Gouges' *Déclaration des Droits des Femmes et de Citoyennes* of 1791, a radical critique of the limitations of revolutionary rhetoric, which while combating class oppression and claiming to represent universal principles in fact was oblivious of women's subordination. The new 'nation' excluded them from equal enjoyment of liberty and equality on the assumption that women by their nature belonged to the family which was a natural rather than social institution. Because they were therefore dependent on their menfolk, women could only be *citoyennes passives*. Olympe de Gouges' 'paranoia reformatoria', her vehement feminist attacks on the revolutionaries and in particular on Robespierre, earned her the guillotine in 1793, shortly after all women's clubs and associations were declared illegal by the National Convention (Diamond 1990).

With the Napoleonic Code of 1804 women became more powerless than they had been before the Revolution. Aside from other disqualifications, henceforth a women's nationality was made dependent on that of her husband (Crozier 1934).[9]

Law reflects political-economic circumstances and interests overpinned by ideological meanings situated in contemporary contexts of knowledge. Under the second Republic French nationality law combined descent and territorial principles. In 1851, when demand for qualified labour became acute, a new law declared children of Frenchborn fathers French at a time when a first census was taken which distinguished *étrangers*, aliens, from nationals.

The concept *étranger* has been coined during the French Revolution to designate political enemies and traitors to the revolutionary cause - the French nobility plotting against the *patriotes* and the British suspected of conspiring to reimpose monarchical rule in Paris. The imputation to the *étranger* of disloyalty to the nation was to prove a powerful solvent in times of war (Wahnich 1966).[10]

In 1889, in the aftermath of the Franco-Prussian war and the foundation of the German Empire, the third French Republic enacted its first genuine, independent nationality code, the *Code de la Nationalité*. This Code drew a sharp line between nationals and *étrangers*. By contrast with Germany where immigrants had been extensively naturalized, foreigners of Belgian, Polish, Italian and Portuguese procedence had a large presence in France. This Code stipulated descent from a French father and, in the case of illegitimate children, from the mother, as the foremost condition conferring French nationality; in addition, individuals born and resident in France could become French through naturalization. Compulsory military service was introduced simultaneously.

The relative prominence given to *jus soli* in the French nationality code of 1889 has often been interpreted as a liberal inclusive solution though Noiriel has recently disagreed with this view (Brubaker 1992, Noiriel 1988: 83). In effect, this combination of descent and birth-place rules can also be seen as a clever compromise struck for military and ideological reasons in the context of the confrontation with Germany over Alsace-Lorraine, which drew on both the original voluntarist and the later organicist conception of the Republic which, though contradictory, were intrinsic in the French notion of the nation-state almost from the start.

National identity is historical and relational (Sahlins 1989). Hence military confrontations between states have had a powerful effect in quickening sentiments of national belonging and boundedness among all sectors of the population. During the bombardment of Paris in the Franco-Prussian war, Haddon, the anthropologist, notes, the National History Museum suffered some damage through shells. Soon afterwards the director, the eminent conservative craniologist Quatrefages, published a pamphlet on *La Race Prussiènne* (1871) where he argued that Prussians were not Teutonic but mere Barbarians with a hatred for a culture they were incapable of appreciating. Being descended from the Finns who were classified with the Lapps, Prussians were in fact alien intruders into Europe. Professor Virchow of Berlin irately countered this view (Haddon 1910: 27).

Renan's classical contemporary essay "Que'est-ce qu'une nation?" dates from the same period. This essay is emblematic of the intrinsic tension between democratic republican and communitarian views of the nation. Liberal advocates of an idea of the 'nation' suited to modern democratic individualism usually draw on Renan's celebrated metaphor, "The existence of a nation is a plebiscite of every day". They tend to overlook, however, that Renan simultaneously invoked another culturalist argument to resolve the problem of how to circumscribe the 'people' entitled to partake in this plebiscite, namely "the shared possession of a rich heritage of memories...The nation, the same as the individual, is the realization of an extended past of endeavors, of sacrifice and of devotion. *The cult of the ancestors is among all the most legitimate, the ancestors have made us what we are...*" (Renan 1992: 54).

In 1893, presumably under the impact of the Dreyfuss affair and spreading racist nationalism of which the trial was only one example, *jus sanguinis* gained further ground in France, which had proved to be an especially fertile breeding ground of nineteenthcentury scientific racism. But race and nation were by now used interchangeably all over the continent. This reform gave preference, as in 1889, to *jus sanguinis* even in the case of children born of French fathers abroad, and restricted access to French nationality of children born to foreigners. As the French jurist Weiss declared in 1907, individuals need to belong "to a more or less tight group...like the family." Social relationships are necessary for social life, "and it is in nationality that they find their form and their *natural* regulation."[11] Family, people and nation are thus organically linked by an 'essential' bond and this had particular consequences for women. This organicist conception also poses a new important question, namely why republican universalist mythology, despite the progressive naturalization of nationality proved nonetheless so resilient.

In the course of the nineteenth century then, as nationality became an independent object of legislation in France, regulation shifted from the birth-place principle to that of descent, women in the process being denied independent nationality.

OF GERMAN BLOOD AND SOIL

Let me now look at the German case. German states soon followed the French example by dissolving territorial bonds of allegiance. For the sake of brevity I will focus on Prussia though Prussia may be regarded as being representative of the other German states. The Prussian law 'On the acquisition and loss of the condition of Prussian subject and the admission to foreign civil service' of 1842 is usually taken to be the first genuine modern nationality law (Lichter 1955: 1 ff.).[12] This law replaced the pre-constitutional *Untertanenrecht* (the law of subjecthood) which defined the subjects' allegiance to the monarch or lord by domicile and limited personal movement and choice of occupation without, however, excluding aliens provided they complied with fiscal obligations. "A Prussian is anyone", Gaus wrote in 1832, "who has the desire to be Prussian" (quoted in Koselleck 1967: 60). The 1842 law, by contrast, made the status of Prussian subject dependent on descent from a Prussian father, on admission by legitimation, by naturalization and, in the case of women, on marriage to a Prussian subject. Subjects absent from Prussia for over ten years lost their nationality (Lichter 1955: 519-26). Finally, the foundation of the *Norddeutscher Bund* produced the law on acquisition and loss of nationality of 1870 which became the first law of its kind of the German Empire and confirmed *jus sanguinis* as the foremost principle conferring German nationality, now denominated *Staatsangehörigkeit* (literally state membership).[13]

In the dynamic interplay between nation-states during the formative period, economic-political and demographic practicalities compounded with ideological assumptions informing notions of national identity and belonging fashioned the conceptualization of nationality as the pre-requisite of citizenship. Primary criteria conferring nationality need, however, to be distinguished from subsidiary procedures so as to disentangle intersecting practical reasons from ideological logics.

By the eighties, similarities between French and German nationality law clearly outweighed differences. In both states *patrilineal jus sanguinis* was the foremost rule conferring state membership. Subsidiary criteria contrasted more markedly. In France birth place qualified the descent rule while the German Empire allowed for nationality by legitimation or naturalization by an act of state. Primary nationality rules reflect the more profound moral meanings with which the nation was endowed. Subsidiary criteria were typically more flexible, being the domain where demographic, economic and political reasons of state could be and were played out.

The priority given to *the bond of blood* stood in striking contradiction to modern individualism. Civil rights had been conquered by the French Revolution whereas political rights, that is, the right to participate in the exercise of political power as a member of the community or as a voter - though with the notable exception of women - were acquired in the course of the nineteenth century (Marshall 1965). Inevitable territorial conflicts made it imperative to firmly bound and bond the 'community-nation' but this occurred to the obvious detriment of revolutionary liberal democratic universalist ideals.[14]

THE BRITISH SUBJECT OF THE CROWN

If we now look across the Channel, in Britain, the cradle of modern individualism and liberalism, we cannot find any clear-cut nationality or citizenship at least until after WW II. Britain had no single document-constitution or basic law and its constitutional theory did not envisage some British nation, or a sovereign people (Dummett & Nichol 1990: 2). The United Kingdom's 'national' history, instead, is that of a territory encompassing a diversity of peoples sharing a vertical bond of indelible allegiance to the Crown and its Parliament as *natural-born British subjects* who owed loyalty to the King and were entitled to his protection. The Naturalization Acts of 1844 and 1870 introduced a gender qualification of perpetual allegiance to the Crown when a woman's nationality was made dependent on that of her husband, so that her bond of allegiance was automatically severed upon marriage to an alien. Unconditional *jus soli* was, however, maintained.[15]

So far I have shown that toward the end of the nineteenth century not only in Prussia and later in the German Empire but also in France, and contrary to the French cosmopolitan republican spirit of the revolution, nationality had progressively become 'naturalized', as the growing prominence attached to ascription of nationality demonstrates. In the light of this argument the British case poses special questions.

In the 1880s, French advocates of *jus sanguinis* had already rejected British unconditional *jus soli* because of its alleged feudal connotations and its inclusiveness which conflicted, so they thought - as it turned out rightly - with the more exclusive concept of citizenship as a substantial, enduring rather than accidental bond with France (Brubaker 1992: 90).[16] Nevertheless, Colley has recently shown that though Britain may have lacked a constitutionally enshrined notion of popular sovereignty in the French sense, during the eighteenth century a British nationalism developed, forged mainly by a succession of wars with France, even though Great Britain never experienced a major invasion from without (Colley 1994: 1-7). And there is an added peculiarity. By contrast with the substantial migrations between continental states, the British Isles had exchanged hardly any migrants with the continent since the seventeenth century (Page Moch 1997).

Indelible allegiance to the King was clearly at odds with the modern liberal ideal of the free and equal individual in yet another sense. Indissoluble subjecthood contradicted adhesion based on free consent. Dummett and Nicol attribute this British peculiarity to the English revolution stopping short of individuals' consent and active political participation (Dummett & Nichol 1990: 88). In 1870 the Crown abolished, however, indelible allegiance in the case of British men abroad and wives of aliens, allowing them to renounce British subjecthood. The Commission's argument was revealingly that indelible allegiance "conflicted with liberalism and individualism, the freedom of action which is now recognized as the most conducive to the general good as well as individual happiness and prosperity." Thereafter, freedom of action was to be restricted only in the case of "persons having a disability, namely infants, lunatics, idiots or married women" (Dummett & Nichol 1990: 88). And in 1886 a court ruled that allegiance was to the Crown, not to the person of the monarch but it maintained the *jus soli* rule.[17] Only the Conservatives' *British Nationality Act* of 1981, at last, severely curtailed unconditional *jus soli* to deal with the 'colonial vengeance' transforming Commonwealth immigrants into aliens. As Europe is at pains to become a supra-national polity, a European continental style nation-state paradoxically rises out of the ashes of the British Empire.

The prominence of *jus sanguinis* on the continent became exclusive in an instrumental no less than an ideological sense. Though decried as feudal, British *jus soli* created a people open to newcomers provided immigrants had children born on British soil. As the anatomist Sir Arthur Keith, however, argued in the immediate aftermath of the First World War, "In the course of centuries statesmanship has succeeded in raising up in the minds of all the inhabitants of the British Isles - all save in the greater part of Ireland - a new and wider sense of nationality, a spirit of British nationality" because, contrary to "ancient belief", in "physical type (that is, race) the inhabitants of the British Isles are the most uniform of all the large nationalities of Europe." (Keith 1919: 22).

For analytical purposes I have distinguished nationality as the legal regulation of access to citizenship from subjective notions of national identity and unity. But changing laws of nationality and citizenship as legal conventions cannot be detached from ideological-political conceptions of belonging which they reflect and enforce.

On occasion, for example, German authors have justified the adoption of descent (*Abstammung*) in lieu of birthplace in such pragmatic terms as recruitment to compulsory military service said to require a simpler and more reliable principle of enlistment than domicile offered (Rehm 1892: 230). Still, because of its distinctness and independence from the parents nationality by birthplace in reality poses far fewer difficulties than nationality by descent for the latter requires that the nationality of the father, that of the grandfather and so forth be so determined as well. Presumption of descent has therefore been drawn on at times to overcome insoluble 'genealogical' uncertainties (Makarov 1947: 316, Strupp 1925, vol. 2: 589). Still, these largely rhetorical arguments for nationality laws have to do above all with historically situated notions of belonging, exclusion and difference.

The contradictory prominence the 'law of blood' progressively gained on the Continent and belatedly in Great Britain is not a matter of mere political-economic expediency. It is intimately linked with the essential and primordialist notion of the nation which evolved throughout the nineteenth century. As the nation-state became a self-evident reality and nationality was derived from a moral fact, it came to be taken for granted, as the Russian philosopher Solovyev aptly put it in 1897, 'as an inner, inseparable property of the person' (quoted in Kamenka 1976: 9).[18] Instead of being recognized as a formal legal condition founded in a legal bond entered into by an individual and a particular state in accordance with specific legal rules that were codified in the formative process of the modern nation-state, nationality came to be understood as an almost 'natural' quality of the person in the sense so well captured by Norbert Elias' 'national habitus' (Elias 1991). That is, rather than an outcome of modern state-formation, nationality was thus construed as the very foundation of the nation-state as state-membership became the formal expression of national identity. Hence, we now literally carry the nation-state imprinted in our hearts and minds. Crucial in nurturing this essentialist conception of nationality are the fears, real or imaginary, of foreign intervention in the polity from without in an unequal world of warring nation-states, of states at once 'open' and 'closed' (Anderson 1983: 129, Huxley, Haddon and Carr-Saunders 1939: 25). It is also for these essential reasons that citizenship rights, the symbol of the modern individual's political emancipation and formal equality, almost from the moment they had been achieved, became exclusive.

A MAN AND HIS WIFE ARE ONE, AND HE IS THE ONE

There is, however, yet another at least equally far-reaching contradiction embedded in the modern nation-state, namely women's dependent nationality. Not only did nationality and with it citizenship acquire an exclusive reality of its own but both became properly the domain of men. In spite of the universalist claims of citizenship, women were not incorporated in the modern state as citizens in their own right like most men, but on account of a social bond they entertained with a man as head of household who was thus constituted into her representative (Pateman 1986). When in 1797 Kant distinguished between active and passive citizens, he also assigned women to the latter category. For "It is only the ability to give consent which qualifies the citizen; yet, the former presupposes the individual's independence among his people [*Volk*], forming not merely part of the community but being a member of it, that is, that out of his free will he desire in community with others to be an active part of it. But this latter quality requires that the active citizen be distinguished from the passive citizen, even though the latter concept may appear to contradict the very definition of the citizen. The following examples may serve to overcome this difficulty: the apprentice of a merchant, or of an artesan, the servant..., the minor...*all women and in general everybody who is obliged to earn his living (food and protection) not by his own enterprise but under the orders of others (except the state), lacks the personality of a citizen [bürgerliche Persönlichkeit] and his existence is as it were only inherent.*" (Kant 1977: 432-3, my translation and emphasis). Women's exclusion from the exercise of purportedly universal civil and political rights is amply documented (Vogel 1991). The suffragettes' struggle for women's franchise partly 'corrected' this inequity. Aside from disenfranchisement, all three countries contemplated in this chapter in the nineteenth century also denied women independent nationality. Because of the conventional subsumption of nationality into citizenship, the gendered 'nature' of nationality has passed largely unnoticed.[19]

France and Germany no less than Britain in the nineteenth century became 'fatherlands' in the most literal sense. A woman's nationality was submerged into that of her father or husband by a double *patrilineal 'matrix'*. Married women took their husband's nationality and it was, therefore, the latter who transmitted *his* nationality to a woman's children, save when these were illegitimate, that is when no man as legal father could or would lay claim to them so that they received their mother's nationality as it were, by default.[20]

The underlying philosophy of family unity and the presumption that upon marriage a woman transferred her rights to her husband as household head, was, of course, not new (Vogel 1991). In pre-constitutional

German law women came under the tutelage of their husbands as regarded community membership. As a German jurist explained the *Ge-
schlechtsvormundschaft* (the tutelage of women by fathers or husbands),
"The special character of the rights of parents and children, of the power
of the father, of conjugal relationships and of the husband's dominance in
the household in contemporary law still rests largely on that more profound concept of the family and that special moral force which the spirit
of the German people attribute *to this natural bond*." (Quoted in Gerhard-
Teuscher 1986: 117). In nineteenth-century Britain the wife's legal individuality was 'submerged into that of the husband in accordance with the
so-called 'principle of identical nationality' which followed the English
common law norm that "A man and his wife are one, and he is the one"
(Bhabha, Klug & Shutter 1985: 10-14). In France, married women's earlier dependent community membership was incorporated into the
Napoleonic Code and thence into the Civil Code.

Women's dependent nationality should come as no surprise. If membership in the modern nation-state became an almost 'natural' quality of
the person in a world of bounded territorial states, the nation, its boundaries and loyalties needed to be guarded. This could be achieved by
denying women as the 'bearers of the nation' independent capacity to
decide upon their own and their offsprings' belonging. Yet, it needs
stressing that nationality, be it dependent or independent, always imposes
constraints on choice of belonging. While independent nationality for
married women may liberate them from their conjugal bond in this respect, not so from the bond with a concrete fatherland. A Nazi woman
lawyer therefore insisted in 1934, "We national-socialist women wage the
same struggle (for independent nationality) but for other reasons; being
German by blood we do not want to lose of necessity our belonging to the
fatherland through marriage to a foreigner." (Endemann 1934: 331-2).[21]

A brief comparison of the manner in which married women's nationality developed in the Americas by contrast with Europe is enlightening in
this respect. In the second half of the nineteenth century the women's
movement in Britain began challenging their dependent nationality as
they mobilized for the right to vote, though initially with little success
(Dummett and Nichol 1992: 8990). Early in this century international
women organizations campaigned more forcefully for married women's
independent nationality. At the International Women Congress held in
Paris in 1900 participants formally demanded a revision of nationality
law in this respect. In 1923 the International Women's Suffrage Alliance
submitted a draft convention demanding independent nationality. In the
aftermath of the First World War the campaign received a new impulse
when the Council of the League of Nations set up a special experts' commission whose agenda gave first priority to the codification of national-

ity. For women the outcome was nonetheless disheartening. Concerned primarily with statelessness and double nationality, a problem which acquired particular urgency with shifting state frontiers produced by the war, the Commission merely issued a provision designed to prevent women's statelessness or double nationality in the case of the husband's naturalization in another state or marriage and its later dissolution. The broader claim of nationality independent of the husband's and the right of women to transmit their own nationality was not contemplated.

This unresponsiveness to women's political claims foreshadowed later developments. At the World Conference for the Codification of International Law of 1930 held in The Hague women's nationality again occupied a central place on the Nationality Committees' agenda. Chile's delegation had submitted a far-reaching draft convention which had been approved at the earlier Havana meeting of the Inter-American Commission of Women. International women's organizations had simultaneously submitted a Memorandum demanding equal nationality rights for women. Nonetheless, the Convention voted by the Conference's Plenary solely contemplated cases of legal conflict over nationality caused by marriage between nationals of different states but relegated women's claims for equal treatment to a lukewarm recommendation of no practical consequence. And the following year the Conference's member states decided by majority vote that no further changes in nationality law were feasible at that stage (Bhaba, Klug and Shutter 1985, Societé des Nations 1932).

European women, in effect, conquered independent nationality only in the sixties (United Nations 1950, United Nations 1962). In the Americas women's nationality rights from the thirties onward developed, however, quite differently.

The Panamerican Union at its seventh conference held in Montevideo in 1933, ruled that "There will be no distinction based on sex as regards nationality, in legislation or in practice." (Brown Scott 1934: 219). Thereafter, women in the American republics progressively acquired the right to gain, hold and transmit nationality to their children equal to that of men (Shapiro 1984).

European countries have conventionally styled themselves as emigration countries despite evidence to the contrary. The Americas as the classical haven of European immigration are familiar. For exclusivist European states women's independent nationality would have meant that, should they marry a foreigner, they would have brought undesirable alien bastards into the 'national family' or lose their own 'blood'. In the young American republics nationality was from the beginning based on unconditional *jus soli*, immigrants being traditionally regarded as potential citizens. This responded to the dominant ideal of peopling and thereby 'whitening' their vast, allegedly empty territories to the obvious detriment of the 'first nations' who were contradictorily transformed into second rate citizens or entirely deprived of citizenship rights. In this ideological environment, women's independent nationality had the advantage that children born not only of male but also of female immigrants, ideally of European procedence, became an unequivocal part of the new nation by severing bonds with their countries of origin.

In their widely publicized condemnation of Nazi racist thought of the thirties, *We Europeans*, the distinguished physical anthropologist Haddon and the biologist Huxley, had emphasized "*the contrast between family and nation, since*", as they argued, "the family is an ancient biological factor, while the *nation-state* is a modern conception and product, the result of peculiar social and economic circumstances." (Huxley, Haddon, Carr-Saunders 1939: 15). They were only partly right. Notions of family relatedness are, of course, no less historically and culturally construed than the nation-state. Nonetheless, once the nation-state became 'naturalized' its linkage with the similarly biologized family indeed became 'exclusively' crucial.

CONCLUSION

When the French Revolution of 1789 overthrew the *Ancien Régime* and asserted the principle of popular sovereignty as the basis for the new political order in Europe it was ushering in a radically new world. The fiercely anti-Jacobin French priest Barruel, author of the term nationalism, lucidly foreshadowed subsequent national developments. "At the moment in which men combined in nations", Barruel wrote in 1798, "they ceased to recognize one another under a common name. *Nationalism*, or the love of nation [*l'amour national*], took the place of the love of mankind in general [*l'amour général*]...It became a virtue to extend one's territories at the expense of those who did not belong to one's empire. It became permissible, in order to achieve this, to despise strangers, to deceive them, to injure them. This virtue was called *Patriotism*...and if this is so, why not define this love yet more narrowly?...Thus, one saw *Patriotism* giving birth to *Localism* (Particularism) or the spirit of family, and finally to *Egoism*." (Quoted in Kamenka 1976: 8). As the presumption gained ground "of the nation and the nation-state as the *ideal, natural or normal form* of international political organization, as the focus of men's (sic) loyalties and indispensable framework for all social, cultural and economic activities...", (Kamenka 1976: 6) nationality simultaneously became generally naturalized on the Continent. Britain, so as to protect its newfound national identity and unity from immigration from the Commonwealth followed suit more recently.

A brief reference to recent 'national' events in France may serve to illustrate the resilience of the paradoxical 'nature' of nationality I have examined above. As may be recalled, in September of 1991 Giscard D'Estaing expressed profound alarm over France's 'invasion by immigrants', calling for the return to the traditional concept of the 'droit de sang'. A public outcry and a heated controversy followed between advocates of *jus sanguinis* as the foremost principle of access to French nationality and universalist republicans who attempted to disguise this juridical reality by exalting the subsidiary criterion of *jus soli*.[22] The latter lost. In 1993 the new conservative government's reform of the *Code de la Nationalité* once more curtailed the *jus soli* rule thereby endowing *jus sanguinis* with added prominence.

I guess it is for all the above reasons - boundaries, exclusions and deadly wars - that between the two great European wars Virginia Woolf proclaimed: "As a woman I have no country, as a woman I want no country, as a woman my country is the whole world." This is, of course, an impossible cosmopolitan dream in these times. Although it is nowadays commonplace to prophesy the end of the nation-state, the powerful ideological logic of the nation-state in reality appears to be far from fading away. Instead, progressively tighter nationality laws control the freedom of movement in particular of certain peoples despite or precisely because of ever more intense globalized economic competition.

Notes

[1] Modern legal theory conceives of nationality as a legal bond: "on the one side of this bond (there is) one single, concrete subject, the individual state, and on the other each individual *Staatsangehörige*, i.e. an individual whose condition as member of the state must be determined." (Makarov 1947: 22).

[2] The analysis of nationality laws has been the special province of students of immigration.

[3] Ritter defines 'nation' and 'nationality' as "related terms of group classification and identity. 'Nationality', usually the narrower and less ambiguous of the two, refers to group consciousness based on a variable range of shared cultural traits -for example, language, historic traditions, social conventions, or values." (Ritter 1986: 285).

[4] I want to thank Rainer Bauböck and Hans Ulrich Jessurun d'Oliveira in particular for their useful and challenging comments on my original paper which have helped me to, I hope, make my own ideas clearer. This chapter is a shortened version of that paper.

[5] The *Déclaration des Droits de l'Homme et du Citoyen* of 1789 proclaimed that 'Each people have the right to organise and to change the forms of their government. A people does not have the right to interfere in the government of others. Undertakings against the freedom of a people are attacks against all peoples." Nowhere is there a definition of who the 'people' are.

[6] Kohn aptly described the voluntarist spirit which inspired the struggle for popular sovereignty in revolutionary France. Aside from some objective factors (a common language, a territory) "the most essential element is a living and corporate will. Na-

tionality is formed by the decision to form a nationality. Thus the French nationality was born of the enthusiastic manifestation of will in 1789." (Kohn 1948: 15). Brubaker is an adherent of Meinecke's classical distinction (Brubaker 1992).

7   These laws explicitly identified nationality as the pre-condition for acquiring citizenship rights. The constitution of 1791 distinguished, however, the 'citoyen actif' who enjoyed full civic and political rights from the 'citoyen passif' whose rights were subsumed under those of a 'citoyen actif' (Makarov 1947: 107, Weiss 1907: 45).

8   D. Louchak argued at the time that under prevailing demographic circumstances France could well forego those citizens who would have been French had *jus soli* prevailed (Weiss 1907: 80).

9   The Napoleonic Code contained two articles on married women's nationality. Article 12 established that an alien woman who married a French citizen must thereby acquire French nationality. Article 19 required a French woman who married an alien to give up her French nationality (Crozier 1934: 129).

10   Since "Each people do and must enjoy the sovereignty of their territory; this is one of the principles of the rights of people which may be considered beyond dispute. From this derive two terms: *patrie* and *étranger* where one is the cause and the other the effect" (Block, 1863, vol. 1: 982).

11   As Weiss elaborated, "If society, to constitute itself and function normally, needs the contribution of all individuals, man himself needs the help of his fellow men to fully satisfy his appetites and desires. He must thus, and this is a law of nature, belong to a more or less tight group within which he can exercise his faculties. His inherent weakness forces him to attach himself to a superior and collective social force which will serve as support and refuge...like the family. Social relationships are necessary for social life, and it is in nationality that they find their form and their natural regulation." (Weiss 1907: 20-21 and 54 ff.).

12   By contrast with the notion of subjecthood which prevailed in Prussia, Saxony, Baden and the Great Duchies of Mecklenburg-Strelitz and Sachsen Weimar, Bavarian law spoke of *Indigenat* (the status of being indigenous).

13   This is the *Gesetz über die Erwerbung und den Verlust der Bundes- und Staatsangehörigkeit*; this law confirmed the nationality rules in effect in the German states. According to *jus sanguinis* German nationality was acquired by descent from a German father, by legitimation, by marriage to a German national or by state concession (Keller and Trautmann 1914: 4-5). It is worth noting that German political language distinguishes neatly 'nationality' (*Staatsangehörigkeit*) from citizenship (*Staatsbürgerschaft*).

14   The intense political debate between French and German political historians over the principle of national self-determination following the Franco-Prussian war of 1870 hightlights once again the difficulties of reconciling the democratic right to self-determination of all peoples with a world of competing nation-states. The exchange between the German historian Theodor Mommsen and the French legal historian Fustel de Coulange is often cited as further evidence of contrast between the French and the German 'national' traditions. Fustel de Coulange's reply to Mommsen's claim regarding Alsace-Lourraine is worth quoting: "We want not conquest but revindication; we want what is ours, neither more, nor less." Fustel de Coulange replied, "You invoke the principle of nationality but you understand it differently from all the rest of Europe. According to you that principle authorizes a powerful state to appropriate a province by force under the sole condition of declaring that that province is inhabited by the same race as that state. According to Europe and common sense, this merely authorizes a province or a population to not obey a foreign master in spite of itself...I am astonished that a historian like you pretends to ignore that it is neither race, nor language which are the foundations of nationality...

Men feel in their hearts that they are one people because they constitute a community of ideas, of interests, of affections, of memories and hopes. It is this which makes a fatherland [*patrie*]. This is what makes people want to march together, to work together, to fight together, to live and die for each other. It is the *'patrie'* which we love. Alsace may be German by race or by language; but nationality and the sentiment of patriotism make it French. And do you know what makes it French? It is not Louis XIV, it is our revolution of 1789. Since that moment Alsace has shared our destiny; she has lived our life. All what we think, she thinks; all what we feel, she feels. She has shared our victories and our adversities, our glories and our faults, all our joys and our pains." (Quoted in Weil 1938: 20-21). Fustel de Coulange's, like Renan's culturalist nationalism, was certainly anathema to contemporary race theorists, but it equally contradicted universalist republican voluntarism.

15 In response to nationality and loyalty disputes provoked by the independence of the United States, *jus sanguinis* had been adopted in the special case of children born of British fathers abroad and was later extended to second generation descendants without, however, becoming hereditary in perpetuity.

16 The distinguished Dutch jurist François Laurent in 1880 wrote similarly "That the Anglo-Americans should maintain their common law, well, that is their problem; nobody will envy them a law that is uncertain, indigestible and impregnated with feudalism. It is not to the Middle Ages that modern peoples should look for their ideal of liberty and equality." (Quoted in Jessurun d'Oliveira 1989: 826).

17 At issue in Britain by the end of the century was the question whether a common nationality should be shared indistinctly by all inhabitants of the British Empire rather than the rule conferring nationality itself. The Nationality and Status of Aliens Act of 1914, in effect, extended allegiance to the Crown to the entire Empire (Hampe 1951: 9ff, Bhabba, Klug, and Shutter 1985, chap. 1).

18 "Let it be granted", Solovyev wrote, "that the immediate object of the moral relation is the individual person. But one of the essential peculiarities of that person - the direct continuation and expansion of his individual character - is his nationality (in the positive sense of character, type and creative power). This is not merely a physical, but also a psychological and moral fact." (Quoted in Kamenka 1976: 9).

19 Jessurun d'Oliveira (1996) objected that independent nationality as a connecting factor for women's rights as citizens was of little practical relevance for them. Women were not subject to obligatory military service; they shared with other disprivileged social groups the exclusion from voting rights and an even larger proportion of men and women than nowadays were not married in the nineteenth century in view of widepread 'free marriage' among the poor. Independent nationality constrains, as I have argued, unqualified choice of belonging and formal legal equality is, of course, no guarantee of *de facto* equality. Yet, the point here is that women's dependent nationality contradicted universalist claims in an additional way which not only needs to be made visible but requires an explanation.

20 Social reproduction has been analysed from a variety of perspectives. Attention focused mainly on gender hierarchy structuring family relations in connection with the economy and the polity. Most studies examine women's specific exclusions in labour laws and family law in the Welfare State. Citizenship has been subjected to feminist scrutiny but the regulation and codification of 'national reproduction' has scarcely been addressed. For women's nationality see (Bhabha, Klug and Shutter 1985, Shapiro 1984, Yuval Davis 1980, Cohen 1985, MacKinnon 1982). For historical sources see Nickel 1915, Endemann 1934, Beck 1933, Aubertin 1939, Collard, 1895, Lournoy Jr. 1924, Crozier 1934, Maguire 1920, Delitz 1954, Rauchberg 1969.

21 In 1939 Aubertin argued similarly that "The state, especially the one which attaches importance to the racial unity and spiritual community of its people [*völkische*

Gesinnungsgemeinschaft] must have an interest in avoiding that undesirable foreign women who may threaten political security be forced upon it by marriage to nationals without undergoing the assessment customary in the case of naturalisation." (Aubertin 1939: 56).

22 See *Le Monde* (23 to 26 September 1991); *Die Zeit* (26 September 1991).

4 Segmented Macrosystems, Networking Individuals, Cultural Change: Balancing Processes and Interactive Change in Migration*

Dirk Hoerder

Until a decade ago, scholarship has dealt with migration in terms of disruption (Vecoli 1964). Under present-day immigration pressures on countries in the Atlantic economies, politicians and conservative voters demand restrictionist policies. Continuities of culture and migration flows, however, characterize intra-European migrations as Moch (1992) has emphasized and Nugent (1992) has pointed to the continuity in the demographic transition.

I will first argue that migration is a balancing process, a process of redistribution of human resources according to the interests of those involved, whether migrants or persisters, and according to the interests of the sending and receiving societies. Since forced migrations, whether slave transports or streams of refugees, are not in the interests of the migrants, the question of the scope of the argument has to be raised. Taking Italian and Chinese worldwide migrations as examples, Gabaccia (forthcoming) suggests intermediate, semi-voluntary stages. The concept of balancing processes may be extended by taking uneven power relationships into account: Slave and forced labour balance supply with demand in the interest of the stronger side only. Similarly, present-day migrations from poverty areas attempt to balance unequal distribution of goods and economic power, but are stopped by entry barriers of powerful states. Only

---

* Parts of this essay were read at the symposia *Migration and Settlement in a Historical Perspective*, Wassenaar, Sept 1993 and *Interethnic Relations and Social Incorporation in Europe and North America*, Toronto, Oct 1994.

81

by day-to-day resistance, by militancy to change labour regimes, or by clandestine entry can migrants try to balance interests (Nonini 1993). Furthermore, I will argue that the world systems approach and an analysis of individual migrants' behaviour can be related to each other beyond abstract push and pull forces if larger systems are discussed on a meso-level in terms of segmentation of labour markets and regions and if individual actions are considered in terms of local networks and family economies.

Secondly, I will argue that incorporation of migrants by the receiving society, the process of acculturation from their point of view, is not simply one of diversity and fragmentation as opponents of multicultural societies argue, but that it is an interactive process within unequal power relationships, that changes both the receiving and the immigrant cultures (Bodnar 1985). Opponents of immigration who fear for their culture, have undergone cultural change since 1945 themselves. Fear of cultural change assumes a static, pure culture without interactive development. It emphasizes loss rather than increase of options. Taking Canada as an example, I argue that a deconstruction of old ethnic power relationships has opened options for construction of a new society.

MIGRATIONS AS BALANCING PROCESSES: THE MATERIAL AND THE EMOTIONAL

Migration, whether circular or permanent, permits a matching of human resources with perceived opportunities. In circular processes, seasonal migrants in agriculture and multi-annual industrial migrants temporarily venture into a different location, into a different economic stage of development, and into different concepts of time. Circular migration may also bring back different persons, e.g. in marriage migration or in exchange of commercial or intellectual elites between cities. If circulation becomes unbalanced, brain drain occurs or sex ratios no longer match. Circular migration may also be career migration, as in the case of artisans or of younger sons of merchants. It increases opportunities for choice, whether of marriage partners, or of jobs, or of forms of income. It permits better information, acquisition of new skills, establishment of regional or international networks. Permanent out-migration connects areas with a relative demographic surplus to comparatively 'understaffed' agricultural or industrial segments in distant areas. In some cases, areas of out-migration are replenished by in-migration from different sources: labour or land is in demand, but at prices that the out-migrating part of the population is considering unsuitable. Out-migration may become inadvertently permanent, as when men or women leave temporarily but postpone return until death. It may thus develop out of circular migration.

In an approach that I call an extended economist one, because benefits and costs are weighed both by societies and by individuals, out-migration - viewed from a top-down perspective - is a reallocation of human resources in regional, national and international economies by administrative decree, via market forces or via a combination of both. Among the administrative regulations are governmental inducements, such as bonuses, tax rebates, homestead laws; coercion such as deportation, involuntary contract labour, forced labour; and prohibitions, e.g. of slavery. Market forces include comparative levels of wages or total income, job opportunities, and travel costs.

The concept of family economies, and the inclusion of non-measurable emotional and spiritual factors into the balancing process, permit a reformulation of the economist approach that includes human agency and individual interests in the decision-influencing factors (Tilly/Scott 1978, 12). Family economies combine the income-generating capabilities of all family members with the whole of the reproductive needs - e.g. care for dependents - and consumption patterns as to achieve the best possible results according to traditional norms for the family and its standing in the community. Allocation of resources depends on the respective stage of the family cycle as well as on the stages in individual life-courses. Allocation of time, labour power and skills of all has to be negotiated in terms of benefits for each: maximization of income or of leisure, child/elderly-care or out-work, education or wage-work for children, traditional networking or individualist separation from the community. An in-migrating new member of a family, a bride, was judged by the family in terms of labour power, status of her family and, of course, child-bearing capability. Only after this family-wide assessment, the two prospective partners could (try to) demur because of emotional incompatibility.

The extended economist approach considers individuals as making conscious choices about perceived opportunities concerning life-courses, levels of subsistence, and interests in personal improvement. The framework includes a conglomerate of traditional cultural norms and practices, of actual emotional and spiritual needs, and of economic rationales. The non-material sphere, emotional and spiritual well-being, and the sphere of material security are linked. Immigrant women workers in the United States wanted 'bread and roses, too'. A methodological problem results: loss of relationships, sadness, and home-sickness, which I prefer to call network-deprivation, for happiness and social contacts cannot be measured by one scale as wages and cost of living may be. They enter individual calculations and decision-making as subjectively weighed factors. Furthermore, decisions about migration are being made so as to satisfy the interests of those who remain as well as of those who leave.

Economic gains of migration influence status in the culture of origin. They may be used to increase land holdings because land provides status. They may be used for ostentatious consumption, the American houses or gold watches. Loss of status may arise from working conditions or cultural norms in the host society that induce migrants, male or female, to transform themselves to such a degree as to become unacceptable to fellow-villagers and non-migrating kin.

Both economic slumps in material status at home or in the receiving society with the resulting decrease in earning opportunities and emotional 'slumps' in family relations, influence the timing of departures, thus demonstrating the intricate link between economic and emotional factors. The macro-economic aspect is well-known, recessions in receiving countries are followed, with a time lag caused by information flows, by a decrease of in-migration. Similarly, the changes in intra-familial relationships at the time or the death of a parent, especially a mother, or arrival of a new parent by remarriage, especially a stepmother, causes increased out-migration. At a time when all emotional relationships within the family unit have to be rearranged, latent migratory potential is actuated, departure is more easy, less costly (Kaztauskis 1904; Gabaccia 1988, 80; Diner 1983, 31).

The extended economist approach, by including all socio-cultural aspects, furthermore, helps understand acculturation processes. Migrants have to come to terms with the receiving society to such a degree as to be able to fulfill their goals. Quick insertion (assimilation), demanded by a number of receiving societies, may thus be in the interest of the newcomers - unless the pursuit of their economic goals becomes personally more costly than return. Arrival without funds demanded an immediate 'functioning' in the new labour markets and work places in order to survive. In terms of loss of quality of life, goal-achievement by migration may appear to be overpriced to a degree that benefits are negligible. Then decisions for leaving are postponed, return migration occurs, migration patterns may be changed (Hoerder 1995; Harzig, forthcoming). This insertion occurs in a situation of unequal bargaining power. Newcomers usually can demand little for their labour. Only after an economic foothold has been established will mass strikes or other struggles for improved conditions be undertaken. Most of the early bargaining, in fact, concerns the migrant only: he or she has to decide how much of the old-culture customs, values and habits to trade for new job and income opportunities.

Understood in this way as combining measurable material benefits or losses with objectively non-quantifiable but subjectively well weighable emotional and spiritual benefits or losses, the extended economist approach is no longer concerned merely with the achievement of an improved balance between demographic and economic structures over space. It includes the family economy and its networks, i.e. the whole human side.

NETWORKS OF INDIVIDUALS AND SEGMENTED STRUCTURES: THE MESO-LEVEL

Migration, once conceived of as a singular event (the flight of the Huguenots), is now regarded as a process (proletarian mass migration). The macro-level (world) systems approach is frequently not related to micro-level life course analysis. Neither world economy nor global pool of (cheap and docile) labour explain the diversity of labour migrations. I propose to deal with a meso-level, segments of larger systems and networks of individuals. The worldwide systems approach has to be tailored to be applicable to local circumstances or to specific groups. Networks of families, larger kin groups and neighbourhoods integrate individuals into local units, societal segments. For particular family economies, particular village or neighbourhood groups, for members of specific crafts and commercially active families, migration provides spatial options in other parts of the world (Green, forthcoming).

The concept of economic segmentation postulates three levels, primary or growing, secondary or stagnating, and tertiary or marginal sectors in national systems, divided into different branches. Capital and skill connections concern sectors and branches (Kerr 1977: Gordon et al. 1982). Thus Manchester's cloth manufacture was related to and in competition with those in Bombay, New England, and Lodz. It was connected to cotton plantation labour in the American South, Egypt or Uganda. Migrating investors often imported skilled labour from their society of origin. Cloth manufacturers from Saxony, investing in Passaic, N J, established a community of skilled German workers (Beckert 1995). Particular skills and expertise cannot simply be transferred to other segments (Hodson/Kaufman 1982; Licht 1982).

Therefore, migrating men and women do not move into one single reserve labour pool but into a specific labour market segment of the receiving society. Masons do not compete with tailors, seamstresses not with pastry cooks. Marginal farmers, seeking employment in winter, move into lumbering but not into skilled cabinet making. Competition between workers is not between each and every immigrant and each and every native-born worker. Rather competition occurs within segments or when workers of one segment enter another because of lack of jobs, because of higher wages, or because of deliberate employer hiring practices. Competition becomes particularly acrimonious when the entering group differs in the price of its labour, when it undercuts wages (Piore 1979;

Bonacich 1972). Among immigrant workers of different cultural backgrounds an 'ethnocultural or segmented class formation' process takes place which is characterized by 'relations between the generations of immigrant workers and the various ethnic working-class communities', by interaction across boundaries (Barrett 1992: 999).

The choice of destination depended on migration patterns, i.e. networks of friends, kin, and fellow-villagers. Moves were worldwide but within networks. These channelled migrants into particular labor market segments, particular regions, particular communities of countrymen or even fellow villagers. Communities are meso-level segments established from the bottom up interacting with segmented labour markets, meso-level units established from the top down. Selection of who was advised to follow in immigrant letters, at least in the initial stage of community formation, was determined by earning capacities more than by affectionate ties. The emphasis on earning capacities included as non-economic aspect the building of a secure foothold which permitted residential and emotional stability and mutual support in times of crises.

Specific villages might be connected to different labor market segments in different parts of the world depending on the gender and the stage of the life cycle of the migrants. All of them faced different cultural systems to which they had to acculturate, by which they were offered certain, often restricted ways of incorporation (Hoerder 1995).

To summarize: Individuals depart from meso-level units, families and communities, according to interests - or frictions - in them. The 'objective' economic and social push and pull factors are operationalized by families, 'subjectively' charting the best course for survival or improvement. A balancing of interests within a gendered division of labour established family economies which took into account - depending on societally determined gender-specific power distribution in families - the interests of all family members. The intra-familial negotiations combine material and emotional well-being.

INCORPORATION AND ACCULTURATION AS INTERACTIVE CHANGE

Cultural persistence in rapidly changing societies places emphasis on conserving over developing trends or, to overstate the case, on the static over the dynamic. Migration, on the other hand, implies a fourfold rapid cultural change, between national or local cultures, across time (e.g. from agrarian to industrial time), across stages of economic development (e.g. from rural to urban), and, finally, between different forms of family relations and gender roles. While emphasis will be on national cultures, it has to be stressed that most immigrants arrive with a particular regional specification of their nation of origin and that they arrive into a particular region of the receiving society. Secondly, they are never confronted with one binding set of values and beliefs of a monolithic receiving society since it is internally heterogeneous and stratified. Working-class immigrants, for example, will have to come to terms with that particular class only or a craft specification of it. Acculturation is also gender-specific (Eisenstadt 1951; Goldlust/Richmond 1974; Hoerder 1995).

I will be concerned here with the subjective side of cultural retention. Maintaining a culture implies a consensus within the respective group (internally differentiated by region, class, gender and time of arrival) about what is to be maintained - the culture has to be defined. Since culture as a whole way of life - in Raymond Williams' terms - is a lived and therefore constantly changing complex of values, beliefs and patterns of action, it is necessary to select a fixed point in time for definition purposes. Within ethnography some scholars have attempted to do so, searching for the 'original' or 'pure' character of a group. But this was politics more than scholarship: Is not the debate about ethnic culture in Canada, Germany, and elsewhere still beset by the question of its fixed or ever-changing character? Spokespersons of ethnic groups in immigration countries still seem to be looking for the pure, the original, the definable. Rather than taking culture as a process, as everyday material and spiritual life, they refer to the culture of origin, to their cultural heritage from before migration. Of course, the term 'heritage' again implies a definite point in time, the testator's relinquishing of his 'goods and valuables' (Isajiw 1977; Juteau 1979; Goldstein/Bienvenue 1980).

To understand the concept of ethnic - as opposed to pre-migration - cultures and to evaluate the possibilities of cultural maintenance, I propose to distinguish between 'experienced' and 'reported' cultural reality, i.e. between the cultural surroundings in which people live and which they experience, and the culture about which they are informed by reports from friends or by newspapers. Potential migrants experience their culture of origin while hearing reports about a culture of destination. By migration, the experience–report relationship is reversed. After arrival, migrants do not usually experience the mainstream culture, but move into an ethnic enclave. From then on, information about the culture of origin comes via reports. This is the fixed point in time ('mental stop') from which culture will later be defined: Messages about the culture of origin will be decoded and judged in terms of its particular character at the time of departure ('frozen in time'). Selected aspects will be incorporated according to the interests of immigrant individuals, local communities, or the whole of an ethnic group in the new society. The resulting image is no mirror image of the old society.

Interaction in the new society and pressures for adaptation lead to a change in behavioural patterns while ethnic organizations still publicly and ritually proclaim retention of the old traits. A second distinction, between practised and perceived ethnic culture, emerges. Some changes are obvious: at least in urban areas, rural in-migrants' initial cultural development is not characterized by retention but by shedding certain aspects of his/her behavioural patterns to escape ridicule by the hegemonic culture. Outward signs such as specific ways of dressing are discarded, while non-visible characteristics, e.g. eating habits at home, are retained. Fast adaptation also occurs regarding work patterns in order to secure job and income and to become economically self-supporting. Only after this quick insertion does a slower process of deliberate acculturation begin (Harzig forthcoming).

When an ethnic community or its older members feel that the process of acculturation is going too far, active intervention may occur. Demands for restoration of the old ways are raised, e.g. for teaching the ancestral language to the children. Poles in Cleveland, for example, upon community demand opened classes to teach children the Polish language - but no parents sent their children: consciousness was still tied to old values but practices had changed. Perceived ethnic culture differed from practised ethnic culture. The changes resulted from both exigencies in the receiving society and from the economic and social interests of the migrants themselves.

Since acculturation, particularly the imperceptibly slow changes that lead to the rift between perceived and practised culture occur within family life, the secluded atmosphere of private ethnic homes may be the arena in which changes are negotiated. Since this is the traditional female sphere it seems reasonable to conclude that women were more deeply involved in the process of acculturation than has usually been admitted. This interpretation is supported by a comparison to the public sphere, the male-dominated ethnic organizations that explicitly intend to preserve ethnic specifics.

The intermediate culture between old society and new, the ethnic culture, has recently been called an 'invented culture'. I prefer to avoid the term 'invention' because it implies an imposed, intentional change. Rather, according to Conzen et al. (1990) it allows for the appearance, metamorphosis, disappearance, and reappearance of ethnicities. What does occur is the transposing of a lived multifaceted ethnic culture into a verbalized, conceptualized whole, a process of increasing self-awareness that occurs when interaction between different ethnic groups increases whether through cooperation, coexistence or conflict along ethnic boundaries. Thus, the ethnic culture that immigrant groups seek to maintain is not the culture of origin. It is a combination of the specific local form of the culture of origin at the time of departure modified by the experience of the migrants in the new society. This dynamic ethno-Canadian (or ethno-American or ethno-German etc.) culture is heterogeneous and varies according to class, social status and gender.

To return to the image of a cultural inheritance: once the testator, the old culture, relinquishes control, it may no longer influence the decisions the inheritors make about the transmitted valuables. The inheritors appropriate valuables and their usage to themselves. Such ethnic cultures are distinctively Canadian (in our example), neither copies of the culture of origin nor copies of English- or French-Canadian cultures. This impression is reinforced by a reading of immigrant autobiographies. Fredelle Bruser Maynard, who is keenly aware of being Jewish and thus different from Canadians, does not understand the Jewish stories of her immigrant father. Laura Salverson realized that for her father the cultural heritage was changing - unnoticed by him. 'By now he had come to idealize the easy-going life' in Iceland, 'willfully setting aside the prods of less sweet memory.' In fact Maynard noted that any growing, physically, mentally, emotionally, implies a distancing from one`s roots. Historians agree (Hoerder, research in progress).

In addition, the intentional introduction of visible signs of ethnicity, its construction, is connected to interaction with the dominant culture and with other ethnic cultures. Magyar ethnic feeling developed more rapidly in North America because of the better means of expression and the need to establish an ethnic distinctiveness to the neighbours across the street from Slovakia, Poland or Romania (Puskas 1994). So, probably, does Kurdish ethnic politics in present-day Western European states. H. Arnold Barton noted that 'much - if not most - of what has come to be Swedish-American tradition did not come over with the mass of the emigrants.' Most visible, assumedly typical, 'traditions' developed after the end of mass migration. 'They were consciously and deliberately introduced into Swedish America by a small cultural elite' which was tied to the recently emerging national Swedish cultural tradition, a tradition alien to the 'farming and working classes from which most of the emigrants came' (Barton 1993, 132). In a highly differentiated empirical study of the retention of ethnic identity among nine ethnic groups in Toronto Isajiw argued that retention is a selective process in a dynamic group development that follows no general patterns (Isajiw 1981).

ETHNIC IDENTITIES IN A PLURALITY OF CULTURES

Let us now approach the plurality of ethnic groups from the interests of the receiving society and the migrants themselves. Canada - and other states encouraging immigration or temporary in-migration - want able-bodied persons whose labour increases the gross national product. Sifton, Secretary of the Interior in the 1890s, called farmers with stout wives (they, too, had to work) and many children. He wanted family working units. Cultural concerns entered on a secondary level via the 'preferred nation'-clauses. This basic economic interest demands that the incoming (wo)manpower fit into the new society to a degree that profitable labour is possible (objective side).

While this interest- and revenue-oriented approach is often criticized as non-humanitarian, it is at this point that government and migrants' interests meet. Labour migrants and settlers - with few exceptions - did not come as missionaries to propagate their old-world ways of living (unless they met 'Indians') but to improve their economic standard of living. In result work patterns and (visible) forms of behaviour were changed to suit the new environment (subjective side). In a dialectic approach, the newcomers also try to change the environment to suit their needs and premigration values. The process of coming to terms with the new society is dependent on the openness of the receiving society, the relative position of an ethnic group within it, and the size and internal structure of the group itself. Several options for the formation of ethnic group identities exist: strict retention of pre-migration cultural characteristics, cooperation with other groups to the detriment of ethnic specifics, diversification, homogenization, boundary maintenance as alternative or supplementary ways to join the culture of the receiving society (Vallee et al. 1957; Sarna 1978; Breton et al. 1980; Breton et al.,1990).

Self-segregation, i.e. intentional and dogmatic cultural maintenance, has been practised by groups which for reasons beyond ethnicity did not intend to acculturate, ethno-religious groups or political refugees intending to return. Cooperation or merging of one ethnic group with others has received little attention. In the initial period after arrival, receiving society populations, for lack of better knowledge, tend to lump together similar peoples ('ascribed' common character). In Canada, numerous East European groups became 'the Galicians', different groups from Asia 'the Orientals'. For different reasons, such a generic approach may be shared by the newcomers. Ethnic specifics recede temporarily into the background to share common approaches, facilities, and political leverage with related groups. A Scandinavism developed among North European groups in the United States (Danielson 1985). Distinct cultures from Eastern Europe cooperated, as in Cleveland, for example, Poles did with the earlier settled Czechs and Croats with the earlier arrived Slovenes (Walaszek 1991). In this phase ethnic boundaries lose their importance because of a need for mutual support, churches are built jointly by more than one group, votes are cast for jointly selected ethnic candidates. Similarities of experience and each group's weak societal position cause groups to cooperate.

In a later phase, when groups have reached a numerical size sufficient to support their own separate institutions, when they are economically ready to rely on their own resources, a process of differentiation begins. Boundaries become more important. The distinctive ethnic identity modified by intervening experience was reestablished, a process of ethnic homogenization turned Swabians, Mecklenburgers, Westphalians into Germans, Toscani and Lombardi into North Italians, or German, Russian and Austrian citizens of Polish ethnicity into Poles again. Once these changes are being accepted, group responses may be decided upon consciously. When no kids showed up in the above-mentioned Polish-language classes, the ethnic press began to insert English-language children's corners into its daily or weekly issues. This is the next phase of acculturation, the development of a hyphenated culture, an ethno-Canadian one. Ethnics begin to move out of the ethnic language into the hegemonic one, out of the ethnic enclave into suburbs.

Finally, and usually over generations ethnic cultures become almost indistinguishable from mainstream society, unless the ethnics belonged to a 'visible minority' or were locked into hierarchical economic positions ('vertical mosaic'). Ethnic culture and identity are replaced by a consciousness of and perhaps pride in ethnic origins ('roots'). Enclave culture is replaced by a Canadian everyday culture combined with cultural symbols visibly displayed: symbolic or flag-waving ethnicity. Practices have disappeared, highly visible and because of their strangeness supposedly 'authentic' signs of folk culture are held up for people of other backgrounds to view: coloured Easter eggs, quilts, embroidery work. Folk-dances are recreated, ceremonial dresses paraded. Symbolic ethnicity occurs when immigrants have been acculturated behaviourally and structurally. If Canadian society is considered homogenous within each of the two charter group territories, identificational acculturation would be the next step (Hughes 1948; Gans 1979; Breton 1985). However, if Canadian society is considered culturally pluralist, then symbolic ethnicity denotes the final stage of acculturation. The symbols assume an importance which they did not have in the ethnic enclave and which they do not have in the modern version of the society of origin and perhaps never had there. Retention of culture in the sense of clinging to it is gone, a distanced respect for the different ways of ancestors remains. This private, personal respect is made public in a homogenized mass society.

In view of the everchanging character of culture and of interests, it seems highly doubtful, whether any long-term benefits arise from cultural retention beyond the need to adjust at a self-determined pace in order to re-form ethnic identity in a way that avoids personal psychic disruption.

We now have to ask, who benefits from adherence to ethnic traditions? Several social groups, in fact, have a stake in unchanged ethnic culture.

A clear economic interest is that of small storekeepers catering exclusively to the needs of their group, and of ethnic entrepreneurs employing group members. The viability of their businesses and the opportunity to earn a livelihood depends on the continuity of the demand for ethnic specialties. Storekeepers, however, cannot prevent the move of their clients out of the enclave and usually they are no vocal defenders of ethnicity. Only when ethnic business finds niches in the new economy supplying or servicing customers beyond the ethnic community, e.g. truck farming in the vicinity of larger cities, they are able to survive without reference to a group culture of clients though they continue to rely on ethnic affinities to defend their niche against others. A second group with a clear economic interest is the ethnic intelligentsia: Priests, journalists, and teachers are dependent on addressing parishioners, readers, pupils fluent in their own language. Once an ethnic leadership assumes a function of brokers, once it attempts to enter the politics of the majority society, compromises have to be negotiated on the strength of the ethnic vote as a bloc. Both entrepreneurs and intellectuals, will themselves opt for changes when they want to expand their business or influence beyond the ethnic boundaries. Cases in point are brewers and politicians who cater to a larger public.

A different reason for cultural retention is the structural factor of rejection of the newcomers by the receiving society or the inadequacy of the receiving society's institutions. If, as in the United States, no social security system exists, ethnically-based mutual help organizations are indispensable. If, as in the case of the turn-of-the-century Poles in Germany or of 'Orientals' in Canada, the receiving society accepts nothing but the migrants' labour power and embarks on a process of cultural repression, the immigrants have to organize ethnically to defend their identities. A 'secondary minority formation' occurs, in which a group, ready to acculturate however reluctantly is forced back into recreating its waning ethnic affiliation and institutions (Klessmann 1985; Glettler 1985).

A similar secondary minority formation may be the result of inducements rather than repression. Given the interest of ethnic leaders in maintaining their clientele and position, a guarding of remnants of ethnic culture may occur from the top down. Ethnicity no longer is a whole way of life. It is kept alive, in a sense, artificially. If support from governmental or other institutions can be received by means of ethnic organization such organization will occur. Ethnic leaders become conservative forces slowing down or reversing a dynamic development in order to receive funding and to maintain status. Ethnic culture or what is left of it may become clientele culture with certain spokespersons acting as gatekeepers for access to multiculturalism programmes. The intention of a multiculturalism policy to support practised group cultures in the context of the receiving societies is turned into support for organizational structures separate from everyday culture.

A re-examination of the two most important terms of the current debate about multicultural policies in Canada (and elsewhere), 'mosaic' and 'multicultural', may explain some of the present concerns. Most Canadians prefer to live in the Canadian mosaic rather than under Anglo-conformity. But pieces of a mosaic are glued or cemented into a defined space. An 'ethnic' who cannot move out of his or her assigned slot has reason to complain. Culture, whether an ethnic, Anglo, or French past or a Canadian present, is always in motion. Over the course of Canadian history the contributions of newcomers of many origins can be readily discerned. In the past, these contributions appear to be fixed, multi-cultural. In the present, the multiple parts influence each other and change constantly, society is inter-cultural. Peoples are a culturally interactive whole of multiple groups engaged in actively structured courses of development.

Those who want to retain their Canadian culture in its present form and those who cling to their pre-migration culture do so with equally valid reasons. But by living together, they interact, negotiate forms of living, develop new identities. Retention is a slowdown of changes to permit both a withering of older identities without psychological damage and the development of new identities without demands for unconditional surrender. New cultures need as much respect as the host-society expects from the newcomers for its ways.

In consequence of far-reaching changes economic and societal changes in anglophone and in francophone Canada, a new view of the national past emerged, a view not induced by either immigration or multicultural policies. The two self-styled 'founding groups,' were deconstructed and came to be seen as heterogeneous. The assumedly homogenous Anglophones were transformed into immigrants of English, Irish, Welsh and Scottish background with even some faint recognition of a Cornish or other component. The Francophones no longer consist of one single cluster defending its culture within the relatively recent and artificial boundaries of the province of Quebec but of immigrants to early new France, of Acadians, of later French and French-Belgian newcomers, and of Francophones in Ontario, Manitoba or elsewhere, of Mètis and most recently Haitians. Because French on the one hand, and English, Scots, United Empire Loyalists on the other came early, they were able to form the institutions of society, to shape the political discourse, to take leadership in business.

Some of the criticism of multiculturalism hinges on the relationship of Euro-Canadians to the cultural heritage and the rights of what are called visible minorities or 'non-white' groups – Native Canadians, Afro-Canadians, Caribbean-Canadians and Asian-Canadians– all groups internally as heterogeneous as Euro-Canadians. 'Race', a concept with no scientific basis, was constructed to justify the domination of 'whites' over 'non-whites' using color of skin as criterion. But mixed marriages increase, more and more Canadians are of multicolored ancestry. Would a child of Euro-Asian parentage alternate its answers when asked about its 'race'? In German history people were designated according to ancestry as 'quarter-Jews' or 'half-Jews'. In the US census, the 'one drop' rule still applies: one black parent generations down the line makes a person non-white, an absurdity that merely reflects racism and power relationships. Recent congressional hearings indicate that this may be changed before the next census.

In Canada, in 1981, a category 'multiple origin' was introduced into the census-forms. It was marked by 11 per cent of the respondents in 1981, by 29 per cent in 1991. A 1988 Statistics Canada trial run of a form with a mark-in box for Canadian ethnic origin and one for Canadian ethnic identity showed that the former was marked by 36 per cent of the respondents, the latter by 53 per cent. Canada is less diverse than it appears to some. Most inhabitants of Canada today consider themselves Canadian citizens with a Canadian identity and with multiple cultural backgrounds (Reitz/Breton 1994; Priest 1990; Boyd 1994).

Euro-Canadian groups' discrimination against and opposition to newcomers of different religions, colors of skin, or alphabet, has led to the designation of 'visible minorities' as target groups for equalization policies and affirmative action programmes. These policies jointly with every-day multicultural forms of living have been successful to a degree, that in fact some 'residents' of these categories do no longer place themselves there. Chinese-origin people consider themselves Canadian, not a visible minority, as a study at York University has shown (Grayson 1994). Claims that this particular policy is wrong, gloss over racism among sections of Canadian society that demanded remedial political action. Anglo-Canadians had to learn in the sixties they alone were not Canada, now Euro-Canadians have to accept that Canadian identity is more than the sum of European cultures of origin.

Diversity and fragmentation ascribed to immigrants, in reality reflects a generational conflict among Canadians whether native or foreign-born, as a study at the University of Calgary indicates. As concerns political behaviour and choices older Canadians and older immigrants act alike, so do younger Canadians and younger immigrants. Diversity is generational not ethno-cultural. Young Canadians seem to pay considerably less attention to one, two or many Canadas than today's older politicians, as other opinion polls show (Frideres 1994). Ethno-cultural groups have become interest groups, similar to those based on economic status, employer organizations and unions, or, more recently recognized, based on gender.

Two issues of cultural diversity need specific attention. Equality of men and women has become more important a value to many than culturally-determined gender hierarchies. In consequence, newcomers with traditional gender hierarchies will undergo pressures to move towards gender equality. Ethno-cultural heritage takes second rank to human equality. Secondly, equal treatment of non-Christian religions is less well established even though Churches and state have long since been separated. Equality of creeds - and of people declaring no religion - will necessitate changes in the future. Intolerant expressions of religion, whether a fundamentalist Christian Right or a doctrinaire Islam (or an expansive Orthodox Christianity), merit no place in society since they violate concepts of individual freedom and mutual respect. Human rights take precedence over customs of ethnicity and religion.

The present Canadianness is a result of the far-reaching changes in Canadian society in the 1960s and after. Multicultural policies have been one aspect of these changes. For newcomers they have facilitated entry into the society, for established residents they have created options beyond conformity to Anglo- or Franco-models. Depending on length of stay and degree of acculturation men and women will decide for themselves, whether to consider themselves intercultural Canadian, hyphenated ethnic, or recent newcomer. The new Canadian identity is as much a result of the 1960s changes as of a deliberate policy of cultural respect for otherness. It will continue to receive input from present and future immigrants. Like the Australian, Brazilian or United States variants, it may serve as an example for those states which consider themselves monocultural or based on blood lineage, for states that have not yet found humane ways to accept newcomers into their societies. The next generation, young people of many backgrounds, represent this new identity as some studies show. Jointly, changes and increased options have brought about a new identity, the multi-cultural Canadians.

5 Multicultural Citizenship: The Challenge of Pluralism in Canada

Danielle Juteau

Multiculturalism has often been presented as a politics involving the recognition of identity (Taylor 1994 [1992]: 26-27) and the accommodation of cultural differences (Kymlicka 1995:10). While this interpretation is not false, it remains incomplete, and in my view much more is at stake. I would like to suggest that a comprehensive understanding of multiculturalism in Canada requires that the normative, philosophical, and sometimes culturalist perspectives adopted in much of the recent work on citizenship be complemented by a sociological approach.

I am not trying to assess the inherent conflict or the possible reconciliation between liberalism and pluralism (Mouffe 1996; Weinstock 1996), nor do I endeavor to determine whether the demands of ethnic or national groups are compatible with liberal principles of individual freedom and social justice (Kymlicka 1995).[1] Rather, I propose to scrutinize the impact of the power relations constitutive of majorities and minorities[2] on the process of inclusion in a society in which citizenship, in/equality, and pluralism have become indissociable.

First, I consider distinct forms of pluralism as well as their interrelations. I then explore the specific challenges posed by the institutionalization of citizenship rights in a society which adheres to the pluralist solution. I then go on to examine recent debates concerning multiculturalism in Canada. These, as we will discover, are in great part fostered by differentiated conceptions of full societal membership, founded more on power differences than on cultural ones. While multiculturalism as policy has dealt with some of the challenges it faces, I argue that Canada will have to rethink its present politics of recognition and broaden its scope.

THE PROCESS OF INCLUSION

Inclusion and forms of pluralism

Equality is not a given, an uncontested value and goal that can be understood ahistorically. It is adopted and actualized, defined and redefined, through constant struggle and not, as pointed out by Bader, through "some transcending universalizing logic of argumentation or some evolutionary necessity" (1995c:13). In the Canadian context, it is closely related to inclusion, the process through which excluded groups attain full citizenship. Inclusion differs from assimilation inasmuch as it produces an increasingly pluralistic social structure[3] allowing for the maintenance of distinctive identities (Parsons 1967: 464). [4]

This process can be envisaged in terms of the horizontal and vertical extension of citizenship rights. The horizontal dimension involves the acquisition of citizenship status and its extension to new populations, slaves, women, non-property owners, immigrants, etc., while the vertical one refers to the institutionalization of the legal, political and social components of citizenship. It is only when all components of citizenship have been institutionalized that we can speak of full membership and equality. Inasmuch as citizenship is multilayered and multiple (Bader 1995: 212), these processes do not occur in a linear fashion.

The extension of citizenship rights in Canada cannot be understood without reference to its existing pluralism. Pluralism has several interrelated dimensions — political, normative, structural and cultural (Schermerhorn 1970; van den Berghe 1967). While political scientists often use the term 'pluralism' to refer to the presence of the cross-cutting alle-giances found in a society, I focus here on the other three components as they are used in the literature on racialized and ethnic relations. Normative pluralism refers to the conception held by various ethnic and national groups with respect to the ultimate objectives of their interrelation. It can entail the acceptance of structural pluralism as a value and as a desirable end-state. Structural pluralism presupposes a social structure characterized by institutional duplication, that is, by the compartmentalization of the social structure into analogous, parallel and non-complementary segments (van den Berghe 1967: 270).[5] Structural pluralism thus differs from the structural differentiation between the economic, political, and cultural spheres occurring in modern societies. While structural pluralism can rest on factors other than cultural difference (eg., segregation, apartheid), it often results from demands formulated by minority groups seeking control over their own institutions. One of the central questions for sociologists lies in understanding the complex interactions between normative, structural, and cultural pluralism.

Cultural pluralism is equated by these authors with cultural differences tied to the presence of different ethnic groups. It is important here to clearly differentiate between cultural and ethnic groups, for the latter's demands usually involve distinct aims. While cultural pluralism can be based on the presence not only of ethnic groups but of social classes and other subgroups, such as generations and sexual categories, ethnic groups cannot be reduced to their cultural dimensions. In order to avoid the confusion posed by the indiscriminate usage of these concepts, a confusion also plaguing the Canadian Multiculturalism policy, in which the terms 'cultural pluralism' and 'multiculturalism' usually refer to ethnic pluralism and multi-ethnicity, I will replace the term 'cultural pluralism' by 'ethnic pluralism'.

The difference is important. Ethnic groups[6] often include economic, political, and social institutions and can be examined in terms of the scope of their institutional completeness (Breton 1964). What is critical is control over their boundaries, which can include institutional as well as cultural dimensions. As pointed out by Barth (1969), boundaries can be maintained while cultural content changes. I am not arguing here that the relation between boundary and content is arbitrary, only that boundary maintenance should be differentiated from cultural maintenance.

The organizational capacity (Breton 1974) of dominant and subordinate groups, i.e., their capacity to mobilize resources in view of a concerted action, varies. It rests in great part on the type of relationship constitutive of minorities; immigration, whether voluntary or involuntary, leads to demands quite distinct from those rooted in slavery and colonialism. It is also related to values and conceptions of what is desirable and acceptable; for instance, the fact that colonialism is seen as unjust becomes a resource, a tool for fighting against oppression, and its condemnation can be used to legitimize redress. Organizational capacity influences the importance accorded by minorities to material and ideal interests, as well as the goals they pursue, such as control over: the economy and the state, institutions like schools and social services, values and norms. While some collectivities fight to obtain funding for Heritage languages, some seek control over their educational system (Francophones in Ontario), and others want their own state (*Québécois* of French-Canadian ethnicity).[7] Thus the pursuit of distinct goals cannot be explained in terms of cultural differences; it is indissociable from social relations and can be examined in terms of levels of organizational capacity.

Differentiated levels of power thus become the basis for a dynamic understanding of ethnic and national diversity in Canada. Consequently, the demand for recognition includes many forms: the maintenance of cultural traits, boundary maintenance coupled with changing cultural contents, different types of control over boundaries, ranging from isolation to political independence. The latter can be pursued as a means of transforming a collectivity or of ensuring its stability. Such claims must be understood in terms broader than the somewhat static and essentialist view based on *différance*. In the present chapter, they will be examined in terms of debates and issues surrounding the ideological field as well as the institutionalization of the legal, political and social components of citizenship. Although these components are empirically interrelated and constantly

interacting, each will constitute, for clarity's sake, the object of a specific
locus of empirical inquiry.

CITIZENSHIP RIGHTS AND THE CHALLENGE OF PLURALISM

Assimilationism or normative pluralism?

The struggle over the desired end-states, such as homogeneity or pluralism, a nation-state should espouse represents the first level of analysis.
Esman (1975) identifies four models. Institutionalized domination excludes any possibility of equality and maintains dominated groups in a
state of subordination. It is usually linked to an ethnic conception of the
national collectivity, where ethnicity is defined in terms of blood and
'real' common ancestry. The assimilationist model offers the chance for
equality to those who opt to work in the dominant society, as is the case
in France. Syncretic integration recognizes the equality of citizens and
ethnic identities while searching to define new national symbols, such as
in some nation-states in post-colonial Africa. Balanced pluralism accepts
the legitimacy of multiple ethnic collectivities and solidarities and fosters
structural pluralism; there is an attempt to resolve competition for resources by way of structured processes of negotiation between ethnic and
national groups.

Balanced pluralism thus competes with other forms of nation-ness such
as the assimilationist (France) and the ethnic (Germany) models, as well
as with institutionalized dominance (former South Africa). It differs radically from plural societies, those typically non-egalitarian societies
founded on colonization and the domination of one group by another
(Furnivall 1948; M.G. Smith 1965). The choice of a model is embedded
in specific historical processes and relations and remains a site of struggle. One could identify the links between various national models and the
horizontal extension of citizenship rights and conditions of naturalization.
We could then explore, as have for instance Bader (1995a), Brubaker
(1989), Hoerder and Juteau (1995), Schnapper (1991), and Stockle (1996)
the relationship between *jus sanguinis, jus soli,* and other conditions of
naturalization in countries adhering to different models.

Pluralism and the rights of citizenship

The institutionalization of the legal and political components of citizenship runs into specific problems in a pluralist context, particularly in situations of structural pluralism. How are religious, educational, linguistic,
and other fundamental rights of diverse collectivities actualized and guaranteed? The protection of civil rights often takes the form of either legal-
cultural or territorial autonomy. The former rests upon a personal principle and the second on a territorial one (Esman 1975). But structural plu-

ralism is not only actualized in macro-structures such as federalism. It is also found in parallel school systems based, for example, on confessionality. Furthermore, the pluralist conception of a society criticizes the orthodox model of democratic decision-making, i.e., majority government, because it corresponds in fact to government by the majority segment (Nordlinger 1972). In effect, the structuration of politics in terms of the majority condemns minorities to the status of permanent minorities (Esman 1975). Some of Esman's suggested solutions include proportionality, mutual veto, compromise, concessions, and the depoliticization of certain issues. This is where the current debate over group representation fits in (Bauböck 1995; Kymlicka 1995).

The vertical extension of the social rights of citizenship has also engendered strong controversies over the measures necessary to actualize them. Inclusion requires more than the institutionalization of legal rights and political participation. In other words, civil and political rights are empty if opportunity is not equalized, if remediable handicaps linked to status position continue to prevail. How opportunity is equalized remains at center-stage.

The new balance between citizenship and democracy (liberty and equality) requires taking into account formal rights and substantive rights, that is, equal rights and equal practices (Hall and Held 1990). Turner (1986) distinguishes equality of opportunity, which can lead to inequality of consequences, from equality of results. No consensus has been reached over the fact that equality of results is more just than equality of opportunity, nor on the means necessary to attain these results. One thinks here of the struggle against structural or systemic discrimination, particularly with regard to the role played by employment equity and affirmative action programmes (Bader 1995c). The question of differentiated citizenship as posed by Young (1989 1990) has thus become crucial. Equality sometimes requires taking group differences into account, and not treating people in an identical way.

The politics of recognition
The institutionalization of the rights of citizenship encounters new obstacles in ethnically pluralist settings, the most important and complex of which have to do with the politics of recognition. In his celebrated article, Taylor (1994) opposes two forms of liberalism,[8] the first one calling for equal treatment regardless of differences while the second demands the recognition and protection of particularism. These two forms of liberalism are often in opposition to one another. While the former remains inhospitable to difference, the latter seeks to "accomodate what the members of distinct societies really aspire to, which is survival" (1994: 62). While I appreciate Taylor's rejection of the first model, I have problems

accepting the second one when it is presented as accommodating the goal of survival pursued by members of distinct societies. For survival constitutes the tip of the iceberg, and much more is at stake.

This analysis is problematic for many reasons. It posits two types of groups, distinct and separate. Members from some groups, clinging to collective goals and cultural survival, are opposed to individuals from other groups who "... cut loose in the name of some individual goal of self-development" (58). Some groups would pursue the goals of cultural survival and boundary maintenance while others would not. Some groups would seek to produce members identifying with the community, while others would not. Some groups are particularistic in their outlook and goals while others are universalistic. Some societies are distinct while others are not. It does not question this dichotomization and does not seek the factors underlying its construction. Although this approach recognizes difference, it does not transcend 'chauvinist' universalism.[9] It does not ask why some groups choose universalism while others endorse particularism and it treats as separate and distinct two principles, namely the principle of universalism and the principle of difference, which are actually inseparable, indissociable.

It is here that emphasizing the social relations constitutive of differentiated collectivities reveals its usefulness. Ethnic groups are not equal; some possess majority status, and others minority status. Furthermore, as Guillaumin (1972) reminds us, the majority defines itself as incarnating the norm while defining minorities as specific. In other words, universalist and particularistic claims are not only interrelated, but the former engenders the latter. It does seem that it is majority groups who typically advocate the universalist orientation and the difference-blind principle of the politics of equal dignity. This is not surprising since the dominant institutions of a society are not ethnically neutral and re/produce the majority's boundaries and identity. Its claim to universalism masks the reproduction of its own particularism and distinctiveness. Meanwhile, minorities are obliged to adopt 'alien' cultural and institutional forms in the name of the superiority of universalism over specificity.

This focus on social relations helps us understand why conceptions of what is desirable and acceptable are subject to change. For, as our examination of the Canadian case will indicate, it is the very transformation of these relations that underlies its changing dynamic. We will also see why multiculturalism must transcend essentialist claims for the recognition of an unproblematized difference and take into account the power relations constitutive of the groups it seeks to recognize.

THE CHALLENGE OF ETHNIC PLURALISM IN CANADA

Anglo-conformity

Canada is a relatively young country, built on two distinct processes of conquest and colonization followed by the arrival of a steady flow of immigrants. It is involved in a fragile and never-ending process of nation-building. While the colonizers called themselves the founding peoples, the founding peoples were called Indians and Natives, and all others were called immigrants and/or 'ethnics.' Each of the two 'founding' peoples clung to its respective vision of a homogeneous nation; by excluding or by trying to assimilate the Aboriginals and by keeping, as much as possible, the French fact within Quebec. Because of their different positions within the system of ethnic social relations, their strategies differed. French-Canadians developed an organicist and ethnic model of the national community. Common ancestry and history (the Conquest) became central elements defining the boundaries of the nation, separating those who were included from those who were excluded. English Canada developed a national model akin to that of the French *Staatsnation,* the state actively pursuing its goal of nation-building. In most parts of Canada, this process was fairly successful (Breton 1984: 127-128). Oriented toward the construction and imposition of a British model of identity and symbolic system, it allowed for the hegemony of Nativism, Anglo-conformity, and assimilationism. Clearly, then, the existing Canadian mosaic was not planned, although the relations between the conquered French and the British have continuously been marked by debates over the type of society to be constructed. The recognition of French-Canadian language and religion in the 1774 Quebec Act, and the separation of Lower and Upper Canada, each with its own legislature in 1791, and the passing of the British North America Act in 1867 after decades of bitter political strife are examples of increasing levels of structural pluralism. Canada is a federation of provinces, each of which possesses a provincial government with jurisdiction over culture, education and social services. It is interesting to note that contemporary debates over the future of Canada are linked to conflicting interpretations of what Confederation actually meant, whether it was an agreement between two nations or between provinces. During the century following Confederation, the two 'founding' nations did not blend into one another, but the French fact was increasingly, though not completely, relegated to Quebec.

Challenging the vision of homogeneity

The combined effect of three simultaneous yet autonomous factors — the increasing rate of immigration after World War II, the rise of *Québécois* nationalism, and the political emergence of First Nations — would soon challenge this specific process of nation-building.

The modernization, expansion and bureaucratization of the Quebec State apparatus in the post World War II period gave rise to the development of the *Québécois* social identity. The ensuing transition from 'we' the French-Canadians to 'we' the *Québécois* represented a change in group identity and group boundaries, and saw the emergence of new criteria of inclusion and exclusion. This shift to a territorial basis of identification is indissociable from the emergence of new political aspirations and projects for the French-Canadians in Quebec, such as renewed federalism, binationalism, special status, Associate States, independence, sovereignty and association. The passage from the French-Canadian to the *Québécois* nation had a direct impact on the forms of pluralism demanded in the political sphere. As the territorial basis of the community shifted from Canada to Quebec, the former's demands for cultural maintenance were replaced by a focus on territorial control, including sovereignty.

In this case, the demands voiced by Quebec had little to do with cultural maintenance. What was at stake was control over one's community in order to transform it. Demands for structural pluralism should not be equated with a desire to preserve specific cultural traits. Thus, it cannot be argued that structural pluralism should be evaluated in terms of the right to maintain a specific culture or the presumption of the equal value of cultures. The issue is more one of boundary-maintenance than of cultural maintenance.

The Canadian case illustrates the transformation of dominant ideologies concerning nation-building and forms of nation-ness. Assimilation in this country became extremely contested in the sixties, as not only French-Canadians, but also Aboriginals[10] and 'ethnics' presented competing views about what Canada should be. To the internal factors briefly reviewed here, external forces such as decolonization and desegregation added themselves, as well as the growing rejection of economic, political and cultural imperialism. Movements of decolonization questioned the legitimacy of assimilationism (Fanon 1952), inamuch as this ideology, as well as that of universalism, is defined by dominant groups, who in fact, impose their specificity onto others.

A new package

In the debate which followed the creation of the Royal Commission on Bilingualism and Biculturalism in 1963, a gradual shift of emphasis took place, going from an equal partnership between the founding peoples to equality between two languages and two cultures. Solutions involving a major restructuring of the central political institutions were left behind;

projects aiming at the recognition, at the political level, of two nations, such as special status and associate States were gradually phased out. Equal partnership was now to be defined in linguistic and cultural terms as the issue was redefined in terms of the equality between two languages and two cultural groups. There would be no binationalism in Canada. The 'Official Languages Act,' adopted in 1969, recognizes the equal status of two languages, French and English, and not of two nations. Current debates in the House of Commons over the type of recognition to be accorded to Quebec still revolve around this issue. Demands for the recognition of a 'distinct society' are interpreted in different manners, ranging from a minimalist perspective, a question of *distinction*, to a maximalist option linked to Associate States. This controversy is far from over: while some English-Canadians reject the minimalist position, some *Québécois* remain unhappy with the maximalist one.

In the context of this redefinition of Canada, another voice, identified as the third force, emerged. For the most part, it included descendants of immigrants other than French and British. It has often been pointed out that the almost five million Canadians who did not belong to the two 'founding' peoples were outraged at being left on the sidelines (Gray 1989: 19). Members of these groups contested the development of a bilingual and bicultural image of Canada which excluded them from the redefinition and the restructuring of Canada's cultural-symbolic order (Breton 1984:134). The policy of multiculturalism, which replaced the original idea of biculturalism, did not emerge 'naturally', nor was it the application of a principle defining the just society. It was the outcome of changing social relations between ethnic and national collectivities in Canada fostered by changes in the world system.

In his speech to the House of Commons on October 8, 1971, the Prime Minister of Canada declared that cultural pluralism within a bilingual framework constituted the essence of the Canadian identity. Though there are two official languages, he said, there is no official culture, and no ethnic group should take precedence over any other.[11]

Multiculturalism, as an ideology and a set of policies and practices, can thus be viewed as a terrain of struggle opposing interrelated, yet differentiated and hierarchized ethnic and national groups. Their changing relations affect material and symbolic interests, collective identities and group boundaries, as well as state policies and discourses. The adoption of the multiculturalism policy implied that the existing ethnic pluralism was recognized as a desirable state and goal. Pluralism had replaced assimilationism. This policy received both applause and harsh criticisms, the latter voiced in large measure by Francophone and Anglophone intellectuals. For some observers the Canadian state was proposing the noblest of ideals; for others it was playing a cynical game. This policy, it was often repeated, occludes the existence of First Nations, denies the national status of the French, separates culture from language, encourages a static and folkloric view of culture, and remains silent about the political and economic inequalities besieging the groups in question (Moodley 1983: 320-321). Multiculturalism, so it seemed, was blind to the power relations which had engendered it. In addition, the term 'multicultural,' not 'multiethnic', was retained, once again leaving room for ambiguity, as we will soon discover.

Multiculturalism on the move
Breton (1984) has convincingly argued that the policy set out to recognize ideational rather than material interests. The key issue was the recognition of the contribution of immigrant groups to nation-building in Canada, the valorization of their heritage and the legitimation of their right to preserve their culture. There is no doubt that at this first stage the policy emphasized prestige and ethnic honour. These interests are nonetheless very real and the policy altered the image of Canadian society. To be a Canadian, it was hoped, could be compatible with other ethnic-type identities it encompassed.

Pressures exerted by both new and former immigrant groups, academics and other social actors did bear fruit. Since the 1980s, multiculturalism has embraced social issues, and the programmes linked to this ideology have diversified and multiplied. First, heritage language retention was recognized as important to cultural maintenance; the funds allotted to heritage languages increased to almost 20% of the budget between 1981 and 1984 (Stasiulis 1985:9). Second, there has been a shift to combat racism. A national anti-racist programme was established in 1981 and a 'race relations' unit was set up within the multiculturalism Directorate.[12] The 'visible' minorities, who are excluded from both the symbolic and the material order, did not recognize themselves in a white multicultural policy oriented towards the restructuring of ideational interests. They commented on the fact that 'visible' minorities were actually invisible in all areas of power. A 'special committee on the participation of Visible Minorities' consulted with the public in 1983 and presented its report *Equality Now!* in 1984. Many important recommendations pertaining to social integration, employment, public policy, justice, media and education were made; and the need for action dealing with both the concrete and symbolic dimensions is expressed (Stasiulis 1985: 15 ff.) Although the Multicultural Directorate's Race Relations Unit has been criticized for its consistently conciliatory and cautious approach, it has nonetheless responded to real concerns expressed by members of the 'visible' minorities. Third, a multiplicity of programs has been developed in various areas, particularly in education. Since education in Canada is under provincial jurisdiction, it must be examined in terms of ten differ-ent provinces, something which is beyond the scope of this chapter. But most provinces have tackled the issue of multicultural education and de-veloped a myriad of programmes.

In short, we have seen a shift in multicultural practices, or perhaps I should say, an enlargement, as material aspects have been tackled in ad-dition to symbolic ones. Exclusion is also defined in economic terms, and the institutionalization of the social component of citizenship is seen in some circles as necessitating affirmative action programmes. This re-thinking of multiculturalism was accompanied by a move to increase its political and administrative strength. Multiculturalism and equality rights were enshrined in the 1982 Constitution Act as part of the Canadian Charter of Rights and Freedoms. In Section 27, it is affirmed that "This Charter will be interpreted in a manner consistent with the preservation and enhancement of the multicultural heritage of Canadians."

In addition to the Charter, the Employment Equity Act was passed in 1986. But, constitutionally speaking, multiculturalism still remained mar-ginal. It was not included as a fundamental characteristic of Canada in the 1987 Meech Lake Accord. It was finally described as a fundamental characteristic of Canadian society when the Canadian Multiculturalism Act was passed by unanimous consent in the House of Commons on July 21, 1988. This Act incorporates a new Multiculturalism policy based on three principles: multiculturalism is a central feature of Canadian citizen-ship; every Canadian has the freedom to choose to enjoy, enhance and share his or her heritage; the federal government has the responsibility to promote multiculturalism throughout its departments and agencies (Mul-ticulturalism Canada 1989: 17). Multiculturalism as ideology and policy had reached its peak, and a separate Department of Multiculturalism and Citizenship was established in 1991.

THE LIMITS OF CANADIAN MULTICULTURALISM

Multiculturalism in question

This policy has undergone constant transformations since its inception in 1971 so as to address some of the criticisms voiced by its opponents. The inclusion of other collective identities within our 'own' ethnic and /or na-tional boundaries redefines more than boundaries. It changes our way of thinking about boundaries.[13] This is why multiculturalism can no longer be defined as a policy oriented towards the others, to the 'ethnics'. Sooner or later, it is bound to transform the dominant group, its bound-aries, practices and conceptions of the desirable society. As mainstream culture becomes 'multiculturalized' (Moodley 1983: 327), the dominant view of what constitutes a 'real' Canadian, but also a 'real' English-Canadian, will be modified.

Yet, multiculturalism is presently the object of criticisms (Pietrantonio, Juteau and McAndrew 1995; Abu-Laban and Stasiulis 1992), voiced by politicians, writers and other public *personae* in English-Canada, and by most politicians, editorialists, and academics in Québec.

It is viewed as responsible for ghettoizing communities, for disuniting Canada, for creating too much heterogeneity, for encouraging discrimination through racial labelling, for the support given by 'ethnics' in Quebec to the No side (against independence), for essentializing the dynamics of Canadian society, for creating and selling illusions (Bissoondath 1994).

While some groups advocate a return to a White Canada, or at least, to low immigration rates and assimilationist policies, others are asking multiculturalism to erase and eject all traces of the naturalism and essentialism that it still carries. Yet these numerous critics are often put on the same footing. The distinction between the multiculturalism of 1971 and its more recent practices such as antiracism is not always made. The intent of the policy, its underlying goals, its successes and failures, are often reformulated according to political creed. This behaviour is striking in Quebec[14] where the slightest positive remark about multiculturalism is often construed as an uncritical endorsement of a static federalism, an acceptance of Trudeau's rejection of binationalism in Canada, and a commitment to the formation and reproduction of ghettos based on the essentialization of the 'Other' (Harel 1996; Micone 1996).

Listening to these critics, one gets the feeling that, prior to multiculturalism, Canada was a haven of peace, devoid of racism, discrimination, ethnic inequalities and ghettos. They forget that the essentialization and naturalization of ethnic groups preceded multiculturalism as a policy. They also seem to have forgotten the 'Speak White' comments thrown at French-Canadians in Toronto of the 1950s, insults such as 'Wops' and 'Bohunks', the strong feeling that there were too many Jews in Canada, discriminatory immigration policies and the vertical mosaic (Porter 1965), etc.

National unity in Canada has been problematic from the birth of this country, as any history book reminds us. French-Canadian and *Québécois* nationalisms are rooted in social relations, not in governmental policies. Furthermore, if multiculturalism cannot abolish social inequalities, it is surely misguided to claim that it creates them.[15] This is tantamount to attributing to multiculturalism the phenomena that clearly precede it. One cannot help but remark that lurking behind these criticisms there seems to be the idea that the counter-models or the old models were and would be better. They evoke a nostalgia for a golden age in which majority/minority relations appeared to be much simpler, which is essentially the same nostalgia that one finds in the longing for those gender relations, which were apparently much more harmonious before the arrival of feminism (Pietrantonio, Juteau and McAndrew 1996). Finally, as certain cynics have argued, if multiculturalism had ghettoized groups and maintained inequalities, it would not be as contested as it is today.

Rethinking multiculturalism
What is 'wrong' with multiculturalism is not so much to be found in what it does; for it marks a passage from an assimilationist liberalism to cultural pluralism. It marks another step towards inclusion in the sense that some of the groups formerly excluded from the material and/or symbolic order acquired greater opportunity for achievement without loss of identity.

In hindsight, one can also see that multiculturalism served as a mobilizing ideology for a heightened participation in public institutions. It allowed for the definition of a more inclusive discourse on the participation of minoritized groups within the political community (Stasiulis 1992) and fostered the erosion of the myth of national homogeneity founded on nature or on culture. Former conceptions of Canada have been altered and its Waspish core challenged. The acceptance of ethnic pluralism opens up a space for public debate, as exemplified in the critique of the folklorizing and essentializing aspects of multuculturalism, and the growing emphasis on material as well as on ideational interests. No such debate is imaginable in France, for example, where multiculturalism is often equated with racism or at least with naturalism (Schnapper 1994).

MULTICULTURAL AND MULTINATIONAL CITIZENSHIP

My – probably unfair – suggestion is that the problem with multiculturalism lies in what it cannot do. We have seen that the policy has extended beyond cultural recognition, embracing a more constructivist approach to ethnic identities and to combatting economic, political, and social inequalities. But multiculturalism in Canada deals with demands formulated by ethnic groups, those formed through migration, and is incapable of responding to the demands voiced by collectivities defining themselves in national terms, such as First Nations and the *Québécois* which construct themselves mainly in terms of colonialism. Their claims focus less on the recognition of diversity *per se* than on increased control over their boundaries, that is, over economic, political and socio-cultural institutions. There is a considerable difference between adapting the Canadian justice system to Aboriginal realities and creating an autonomous judiciary system controlled by Aboriginals. The latter involves structural pluralism — institutional separateness and duplication.

Cultural and structural pluralism thus constitute two different means of taking ethnic pluralism into account. Choosing one over the other is tied more to the respective positions of the groups than to their respective 'core' values. As pointed out by Kymlicka (1995), differentiated groups can make differentiated claims even when they share common ideals and values. Adherence to common values cannot insure harmony because they are specified differently according to the situation of groups. What differentiates the First Nations and the *Québécois* from other ethnic groups in Canada is that they possess different statuses, linked to what Schermerhorn calls the initial sequence of interaction (1970). While the former were essentially constructed through colonialism, the latter were defined mainly through migration.[16] The difference in the relations constructing them has an impact on their respective claims. Groups that are constituted through colonialism usually seek enhanced forms of structural pluralism in order to exert control over and within their boundaries. I am not saying here that they possess a different right, only that they do make different claims based partly on their definition of what is just and unjust. Such definitions, of course, are socially constructed. Furthermore, it is important here not to fall in a reductionist dichotomization of nation versus ethnic groups; for the levels of organizational capacity are multiple as are the types of national ethnic diversity. The official language minorities also possess specific goals and claims.

Aboriginal collectivities want more than the recognition of their difference and the adaptation of Canadian society to their specificity. At the centre of their claims is a demand for indigenous self-government. Although extremely slow, this process is moving ahead. Their demands do not include separation; as such, they force us to rethink Canada, but do not threaten to 'break' it.

Quebec is defined by many as the site of a collectivity constituted through specific historical experiences. Arguing that its language, legal and educational systems, symbols and identity are distinct, a majority of *Québécois* supports the claim that Quebec constitutes a distinct society. Many Canadians are uneasy with this demand, because they fear it extends beyond the symbolic level, entailing more power and control.[17] A rapprochement seems difficult. Actually, the situation is more complicated than ever. Binationalism in Canada is a thing of the past, as outdated as the hoolahoop. The former sympathy that Quebec and other nationalisms encountered in the sixties is weakening in the face of the recent growth of ethnic nationalisms. Aboriginals in Canada are also claiming national status and call themselves First Nations, thus challenging the two nations concept. Multiculturalism has empowered ethnic groups and made binationalism and/or special status seem less legitimate.

How then can the challenges posed by demands for increased structural pluralism be met?

New solutions are required. Multiculturalism cannot deal with claims voiced by national collectivities, and, as Will Kymlicka has reminded me, it should not be expected to.[18] But I am arguing that the problem resides in presenting multiculturalism as *the* solution to Canada's unity problems. Demands formulated by formerly colonized collectivities are not and cannot be covered by multiculturalism. It has to be unequivocally presented as such, and its limits must be clearly spelled out. The 1971 policy on multiculturalism complemented the Official Languages Act adopted in 1969. As it has become obvious in recent years, official bilingualism has proven to be an inadequate solution to the 'Quebec' question, and must be supplemented. One of the proposed avenues lies in multinationalism, as presented by some English-Canadian and *Québécois* intellectuals.[19] Their proposal is enticing, but whether it is politically feasible remains unanswered at present. I will rather examine this claim in terms of its underlying and implicit premises.

In my mind, building a multinational country could reinforce the capacity of Canada to redefine itself beyond the nation-state model. By accepting claims recognizing the right of the *Québécois* and the First Nations to exert more control over their boundaries, Canada would transcend the very national models it makes possible. The institutionalization of citizenship rights would no longer be reduced to the recognition of cultural pluralism, and would include multiple forms of structural pluralism, which would move the country further in the direction of inclusion. Finally, two other conditions must be met in order to transcend the old model of the nation-state. This emerging multinational State and its constituent parts should remain committed to multiculturalism (or interculturalism), if they are not to recreate small ethnically homogenous political units. And, it may well be useful to question the dichotomy the new multinational State would rest upon. This dichotomy opposes two types of groups, ethnic and national, the first based on immigration and the second on conquest. Although useful, these categories oversimplify the situation and mask the diversity of ethnic and national collectivities in Canada, which include for example, the Acadians and official language minorities, which also seek some form of control over their institutions. Maybe the most useful way to think our way out of the impasse is to recognize that Canada comprises a great diversity of ethnic and national collectivities, pursuing distinct goals with regards to boundary-maintenance and common goals vis-à-vis their recognition.

Notes

1 These important questions have been more than adequately addressed by leading political theorists and philosophers in Canada and elsewhere.

2 The concept of minority is used here in its sociological and not its mathematical sense. A minority is a group possessing less power, a subordinate status.

3 As it has been pointed out (Juteau 1993; Kymlicka 1995), Marshall (1949) was the first to study the development of citizenship in an historical perspective. Despite its critics, his analysis of the links between citizenship and equality remains the necessary starting point for any research in the area. Parsons further refined this analysis by examining inclusion, a "process through which previously excluded groups attain full citizenship or membership in the societal community" (1967: 428).

4 Contrary to Kymlicka's affirmation (1995), citizenship as a focus of analysis makes a comeback before the eighties, with Talcott Parsons' (1967) analysis of the struggle for equality between Blacks and Whites in the United States in terms of full citizenship for the "Negro" American.

5 In Canada, for example, there are ten provincial governments and two official languages, as well as, in Quebec, a quadruple network of schools laden with Catholic or Protestant school boards (Proulx 1993).

6 Ethnic groups are based on the subjective belief in common ancestry, real or putative. I am aware of the dangers of using the concept of ethnicity lightly (Juteau 1983 and 1996). Nonetheless, when ethnicity is apprehended as a construct, it remains a very useful tool for understanding what is at stake in many of the conflicts traversing contemporary societies. The defining characteristic of an ethnic group is the "...subjective belief in a community of origin because of similarities of external habitus or of customs or both, or because of memories of colonization or migration; this belief must be important for the propagation of communalization; whether a community of blood actually exists or not" (Weber 1971: 416). The relations underlying the construction and transformation of ethnic groups and boundaries include colonization, migration and slavery. They determine their respective statuses and goals, explaining the existence of projects as diverse as assimilation, cultural survival, boundary-maintenance inside the existing political system, and sovereignty.

7 The difference between ethnic groups and national communities lies precisely in their respective goals and political projects. While both constitute what Bauer called communities of history and culture, what is specific to the nation, what it uniformly refers to, is "the idea of a powerful political community of people," a state which may already exist or may be desired. The concept of nation seems to refer to a specific kind of pathos linked to political power; and the more power is emphasized, the closer the link between nation and state appears to be (Weber 1978: 397-8).

8 These two models rest upon two values and political orientations, each claiming to be derived from the principle of universal equality and the notion of equal respect which coexist, but not without difficulty, in several societies.

9 I borrow this expression from V. Bader (1995c), who uses it in his critique of 'benign' versions of state-neutrality.

10 Their strong negative reaction to the White paper in 1969, "from the White paper to Red power," marks their rejection of an assimilationist perspective based on a politics of equality.

11 House of Commons Debate, Official Report, Vol. 115, No. 187, 3rd Session, 28th Parliament, October 8, 1971. In the initial statement in the House of Commons in 1971, four policy objectives were spelled out: cultural retention, cultural sharing, official language acquisition, and the reduction of cultural barriers to equal opportunity (Stasiulis 1985: 2). These involve the principle of equality of status, the princi-

ple of sharing the Canadian culture, the free choice of life-styles and cultural traits, the concern for and protection of civil rights (Lessard et Crespo 1990:11).

[12] In Canada, the term "visible minority" was coined to designate non-whites. Although a definite improvement over the notion of "race," it nonetheless assumes strangely enough that whites are invisible. This is of course similar to the discourse opposing universalism to particularism rather than opposing the particularism of dominant groups to that of the subordinate ones.

[13] The anthropologist E. Roosens (1989) shows how some traits that Hurons in Quebec claim as specifically Huron and constitutive of their boundaries and essence are actually borrowed from the French-Canadians. I am convinced that this applies to all groups.

[14] Although Quebec has always been relatively hostile to multiculturalism in the Canadian context, it has articulated its own vision of pluralism. The leaders of the Quebec state, in a way similar to that of their Canadian counterparts, also began in the early 1980s to praise the merits of cultural diversity. Pluralism became a dominant State ideology and replaced the past-oriented and primordialist discourse held by traditional French-Canadian elites prior to the sixties. What is favoured in Quebec is interculturalism. One is not faced here with tolerating, accepting, or protecting minority cultures; at stake is the fostering of a dynamic interaction between the minorities and the majority.

[15] The difficulties also should be mentioned in rigorously comparing the pluralist model with the Jacobin model and its resistance to the use of ethnicity in any attempted statistical "performance" measure of integration.

[16] Of course, it can be rightly argued that migration is also a consequence of colonialism, but then one leaves the country where colonialism has been experienced. The situation of the *Québécois* (and of all French Canadians) is interesting since it is built on the dual status of colonizer and colonized.

[17] In my view, this is not false. In a document prepared by Paul Gérin-Lajoie, *Québec, une société distincte* (1967), the Quebec Liberal Party rejected separatism but called for a special status for Quebec. Here, the demand was for the power to preserve the collective personality of Quebec, notably, in the areas of arts and culture, education, immigration, social assistance and security, employment, economic development, fiscal policies, and public investments. This demand was based on an interpretation of the federal compact as being between the two founding peoples (Gagnon and Latouche: 79). Of course, this is precisely what many non-*Québécois* reject. The specific history of French Canada, which includes the Conquest, should not constitute the basis of differential treatment. My own analysis does not take sides with either position; but as a sociologist, I point out that the initial relation underlying the constitution of ethnic and national groups has an impact on their demands.

[18] When this chapter was originally presented as a paper at the conference organized by Veit Bader, Kymlicka, in his critique, convincingly argued that it would be dangerous to extend the meaning and scope of multiculturalism in Canada. His thoughtful comments have forced me to clarify my earlier position.

[19] P. Resnick (1994), A.-G.Gagnon and G. Laforest (1993) represent some, but not the only, examples.

6 Multicultural Citizenship: The Australian Experience*

Stephen Castles

Globalization has profound effects on culture and society, partly due to internationalization of communication and the mass media, but also because of growing international mobility of population. The populations of many countries are becoming more diverse, leading to shifts in national cultures and identities. This is likely to have major impacts on political institutions. Such issues are of key importance for Australia, where large-scale immigration since 1945 has led to profound demographic and cultural changes. As a relatively new nation, made up of settlers from all over the world as well as indigenous people, Australia has special problems in defining its culture and identity, and in devising appropriate political institutions. Our polity is based on the model of the nation-state as it emerged in Western Europe and North America from the 18th century, but does this really fit our situation on the eve of the 21st century?

The concept of the nation-state implies a close link between ethnicity and political identity. The *nation* is usually seen as a group of people who have a feeling of belonging together on the basis of shared language, culture, traditions and history – in other words an ethnic community. The *state* is seen as a structure with territorial boundaries that should coincide with ethnic ones, and which represents the political values of the nation (Gellner 1983). Such a concept of the nation-state implies ethnocultural homogenization of the population. This can be achieved positively through institutions (such as schools, administration, church, national ser-

---

* An earlier and longer version of this chapter was published by the Parliamentary Research Service, Canberra in 1996.

A central category for analysing the link between the nation and state in a democracy is *citizenship*. The central idea of this chapter is that the transformation of our society requires a new notion of *multicultural citizenship*. This may be characterized as *a system of rights and obligations which protects the integrity of the individual while recognizing that individuality is formed in a variety of social and cultural contexts.*

Growing ethnocultural diversity sharpens a basic dilemma of liberal democratic principles. These stipulate that all citizens are equal individuals and should be treated equally. State policies and services should therefore be based on the idea of universalism. However, the population actually consists of people belonging to a variety of social and cultural groups, with specific needs, interests and values. This makes equal treatment questionable, because it may maintain or cause unequal outcomes. How is a liberal-democratic political system to resolve this dilemma?

In fact modern states deal with this ambiguity through a range of economic, social and cultural policies. In Australia, it can be argued that recent policies on social justice and multiculturalism actually imply an underlying concept of citizenship much broader than the traditional liberal-democratic one. However, the policies have been based on restricted and short-term policy objectives, concerned with facilitating migrant settlement and avoiding community relations problems. It is now important to move more consciously towards a new notion of citizenship.

This chapter will start by looking at the ways in which various immigration countries have responded to the challenge of growing ethnocultural diversity. Then it will examine current political science debates on the dilemma of universalism and difference. Finally, we will examine multicultural policies in Australia, and some of their problems.

MODELS FOR MANAGING DIVERSITY

Mass labour migration and refugee movements have been significant in virtually all highly-developed countries since 1945. Since the late 1980s, migration flows have accelerated and become more complex. The existing immigration areas (Western Europe, North America and Australia) have been joined by newcomers (Southern Europe, Japan and the newly industrializing countries of Asia and Latin America). Current major international issues include immigration control, and how to respond to the presence of new minorities within society. Multiculturalism and citizenship have become hotly debated themes in many countries.

By 1993, there were 19 million foreign residents in European OECD countries, and 1.3 million in Japan. Foreign residents made up 8.5 per cent of the population in Germany, 18 per cent in Switzerland, 6.3 per cent in France and 1.1 per cent in Japan. The USA had 20 million foreign-born residents in 1991 (7.9 per cent of the total population), Canada had 4.3 million (15.6 per cent) and Australia had 4.1 million (22.7 per cent) (see Appendix Table).

Such statistics give only a partial indication of ethnic diversity. Figures on foreign residents leave out illegal entrants, as well as people who have become naturalized. The data also leave out members of ethnic minorities who are not immigrants or foreigners. For instance, the United Kingdom had 2 million foreign residents in 1993 (3.5 per cent of the population) but there were a further 2.6 million ethnic minority members (4.7 per cent of the population), most of whom had been born in the UK. In the USA, the 1990 Census showed an ethnic composition of 80 per cent white, 12 per cent black, 1 per cent American Indian, 3 per cent Asian and 4 per cent 'other race'. There were also 9 per cent Hispanics, who could be 'of any race'. In Canada 'ethno-cultural origin' cuts across classification by immigrant or non-immigrant: 34 per cent of the population are of British origin, 24 per cent French, 5 per cent British-French combined, and 38 per cent 'other' (mainly immigrant) origin (Castles and Miller 1993: 197–202). Finally, most European countries have older ethnic minorities, including Jews, Gypsies and regional groups (such as Basques in Spain, Corsicans in France).

Each country has developed its own responses to issues of ethnic diversity (Castles, 1995). However, for the purposes of cross-national comparison, it is possible make out three basic models: (1) differential exclusion, (2) assimilation, (3) pluralism.

No country fits these ideal-types exactly. In some countries there has been an evolution, starting with differential exclusion, progressing to attempts at complete and rapid assimilation, moving on to ideas of gradual integration, and finally leading to pluralist models (Australia is a case in point). Other countries, such as the United Kingdom and the Netherlands, are much more ambivalent, with strong elements of both assimilationism and pluralism. Policies of assimilation in specific areas (such as economic or social policy) may co-exist with pluralism in other areas (such as citizenship or cultural policy).

Differential exclusion

Differential exclusion may be characterized as a situation in which immigrants are incorporated into certain areas of society (above all the labour market) but denied access to others (such as welfare systems, citizenship and political participation). Membership of civil society (as workers, taxpayers, parents, etc.) does not confer a right to membership of the nation-state (as citizens). Exclusion may be effected through legal mechanisms (refusal of naturalization and sharp distinctions between the rights of citizens and non-citizens), or through informal practices (racism and discrimination). Immigrants become ethnic minorities, which are excluded from full participation in society. These minorities are usually socio-economically disadvantaged, implying a strong link between class and ethnic background. Patriarchal constructions of gender in both countries of origin and immigration countries lead to special forms of exclusion for migrant women. Gender is therefore linked to ethnic background and class as a factor of differentiation.

Differential exclusion is mainly to be found in countries where belonging to the nation is based on membership of a specific ethnic group. This 'ethnic' or 'folk' model is typical of Central and Eastern European countries where historical difficulties in forming nation-states led to an aggressive and exclusionary form of nationalism. A variant is found in countries like Switzerland and Belgium which have developed as nations with more than one 'founding group'. The historical arrangements developed to deal with this have led to delicate balances, that make it hard to incorporate new groups. Several newer immigration countries fit the ethnic model.

In Japan, historical isolation led to a high degree of cultural homogeneity (although with both indigenous and immigrant minorities). The move to a modern nation-state has been based on a notion of ethnic belonging, which finds it hard to accommodate new groups. Other Asian immigration countries are often recently emerged nations which have sought to build nation-states out of diverse groups in post-colonial situations. They find it hard to accept new forms of ethno-cultural difference.

Nations based on ethnic belonging are unwilling to accept immigrants and their children as members. Acceptance of new linguistic and cultural diversity is seen as a threat to national culture. The result of this approach is restrictive immigration policies, the ideology of not being countries of immigration even when mass immigration has taken place, the denial of civil and political rights to immigrants, and highly restrictive polices on citizenship for immigrants and their descendants. Immigration policies are based on the notion that admission of migrants is only a temporary expedient. Immigrants are kept mobile through restrictions on residence rights and prevention of family reunion.

The contradiction of the differential exclusion model is that denial of settlement has not prevented it from taking place. Countries like Germany, Austria and Switzerland now have large ethnic minority populations, which are politically excluded and socially marginalised. This contradicts the basic liberal-democratic principle that all members of civil society should also be members of the political community. Exclusion of minorities leads to a split society, serious social problems, growing levels of racist violence and a threat to democracy from the extreme right.

In Germany, the position of immigrants and their descendants has become a major political issue since reunification in 1990. Despite official policies, a form of 'de facto multiculturalism' is developing in education, social work and local politics. A major debate on citizenship for minorities is taking place in all political parties. The central theme is how to reconcile national identity and culture with the reality of a diverse population. Multiculturalism has become a major issue, which would have been unthinkable even ten years ago.

The assimilationist model
Assimilation is usually defined as the policy of incorporating migrants into society through a one-sided process of adaptation: immigrants are expected to give up their distinctive linguistic, cultural or social characteristics and become indistinguishable from the majority population. Immigrants can become citizens only if they give up their group identity. In some cases, the notion of assimilation has been replaced with that of integration, according to which adaptation is a more gradual process. Nonetheless, the final goal remains absorption into the dominant culture.

Assimilationist approaches are to be found in nations which base their sense of belonging both on membership in the political community and on sharing a common culture. Examples are France, Britain and the Netherlands, which combine (in varying ways) two sets of historical factors: first, ideas on racial superiority resulting from a colonial history; secondly, ideas on citizenship, civil rights and political participation which result from the democratic-nationalist movements of the 18th and 19th centuries. These three countries conferred citizenship status on their colonial subjects to bolster ideological control and cultural domination. This had the effect of facilitating migration from the former colonies as the empires crumbled after 1945. At first migrants were welcomed by governments as useful labour, but attitudes began to change as labour needs declined and urban conflicts emerged. From the 1960s, citizenship rules have gradually been altered to eliminate the special rights of colonised peoples.

The assimilationist model was the prevailing approach in the USA in the early part of this century, at a time of massive immigration and urbanisation. It was also the policy of several post-1945 immigration countries, including Canada and Australia. In some cases, assimilation policies have been abandoned over time, and replaced with pluralist policies. This happened in response to the recognition that recent immigrants were not assimilating, but were becoming concentrated into particular occupations and residential areas. This helped bring about the emergence of ethnic communities, which maintained their mother-tongues and established social, cultural and political associations.

Today, of all the highly-developed immigration countries, metropolitan France probably comes closest to assimilationism. According to the French 'Republican model' it is easy for immigrants and their children to become citizens, who are supposed to enjoy full rights. Although the 'Republican model' is meant to be concerned purely with individual equality, it is tacitly based on certain assumptions on language use, social behaviour, dress, secularism and political behaviour, summed up in the notion of *civisme* or civic virtues. The contradiction of this approach is that it appears to be purely political, yet it brings culture in through the back door. There is no room for cultural diversity or for formation of ethnic communities.

Two factors negate the 'Republican model'. The first is socio-economic marginalization: people of non-European origin are concentrated in the lower segments of the labour market, and experience high unemployment rates, especially for youth. Many are segregated in huge housing projects on the fringes of the cities, which have become ghettoes of disadvantage. The second factor is racism. Racist violence has increased sharply, and the attraction of racist ideologies is shown by the success of the extreme-right *Front National*, which commands up to 16 per cent of the vote in elections.

The result is a politicization of the situation of minorities, as shown by continuous debates on immigration and nationality law. There is something of a moral panic about the rise of Islam—now France's second religion. Recent events in Algeria have heightened fears of fundamentalism. Various forms of ethnic mobilization have become important, including strike movements by immigrant workers and riots against exclusion and police repression by minority youth. In recent years anti-racist movements like SOS-Racisme and France Plus have become the focus for political involvement by the *beurs* (youth of North African origins).

France is at a cross-roads: the assimilationist model of turning immigrants into citizens at the price of cultural conformity no longer works adequately. Many immigrants are no longer willing to accept assimilation when it brings neither social equality nor protection from racism. Organizations based on cultural identity are increasingly seen as the only way of combating racism and achieving a political voice. The answer for the right is to shift immigration and nationality policies towards a differential exclusion model. The left argues for maintenance of the *status quo*. For them, multiculturalism is unthinkable for France, for it would question the prevailing ideas on secularity and equality.

The pluralist model

Ethnocultural pluralism may be characterized as the acceptance of immigrant populations as ethnic communities which remain distinguishable from the majority population with regard to language, culture, and social organization over several generations. Pluralism implies that immigrants should be granted equal rights in all spheres of society, without being expected to give up their diversity, although usually with an expectation of conformity to certain key values. Here, membership of civil society, initiated through permission to immigrate, leads to full participation in the nation-state.

This model is to be found today in the 'classical immigration countries': the USA, Canada and Australia. The process of building new nations has led to the inclusionary principle that anyone allowed to be permanently resident on the territory should be offered citizenship. This goes together with encouragement of family reunion, naturalization and access to civil and political rights. For these countries pluralism appears as the best way of incorporating large groups of immigrants with diverse backgrounds. Moreover, the imperative of making immigrants into citizens reinforces the pressure for pluralist policies: when immigrants are voters, ethnic groups can gain political clout.

However, it should be noted that ethno-cultural pluralism is a fairly new approach, going back to the early part of the century in the USA, but only to the 1970s in Australia and Canada, and originating as a reaction to the failure of earlier policies of assimilation. Moreover, other forms of closure are to be found in these countries: until the 1960s, they all had racist immigration policies, which openly discriminated against non-Europeans. Today there is still selectivity on the basis of economic, social and humanitarian criteria (which may contain hidden bias against people with certain backgrounds). The real decision on who is to become a citizen falls at the time of deciding who to admit as a permanent resident.

Pluralism has two main variants. In the *laissez-faire* approach typical of the USA, difference is tolerated, but it is not seen as the role of the state to assist with settlement or to support the maintenance of ethnic cultures. The second variant of pluralism is explicit multicultural policies, which imply the willingness of the majority group to accept cultural difference, and to adapt national identity and institutional structures. Such policies exist in Canada, Australia and Sweden, while multicultural policies exist in specific sectors, such as education, in several other countries. The crucial factor is the role of the welfare state: cultural pluralism needs to be combined with policies designed to secure minimum economic and social standards for all if it is to lead to a reasonably equitable and peaceful society.

US society presents the paradox of a democratic political system which incorporates immigrants and other minorities as citizens, and yet is marked by extreme divisions based on class, race and ethnicity. The constitutional safeguards designed to ensure formal equality of rights for all citizens have not been sufficient to prevent formation of ghettoes and underclasses based on race and ethnicity. Three major factors explain this paradox: the extreme racism deriving from the enslavement of Afro-Americans up to 1865; the culture of violence resulting from the traditions of frontier society; and the tradition of individualism with its corollary of a minimalist social policy.

Canada has many similarities with Australia as a new nation with a strong tradition of state intervention in social affairs (Breton et al. 1990; Adelman et al. 1993). Sweden seems to be something of an anomaly, as a society which had a high degree of ethnic and cultural homogeneity until recently. Yet it has had large-scale settlement since 1945, and adopted multicultural policies very close to those of Australia and Canada. The reason lies in the state interventionist model of Swedish social democracy, which has used the same approaches to integrating immigrants into civil society and the state as were used earlier to integrate the working class (Hammar 1985). The Swedish model is an important indicator of the relevance of multicultural approaches in the European context.

The international debate on multiculturalism

This brief account of international responses to ethnic diversity indicates how important the issue has become. The differential exclusion model, as applied in former 'guestworker'-recruiting countries like Germany, seems highly problematic, for it attempts to deny the permanence of settlement and thus leads to socio-economic and political marginalization of immigrants and their descendants. The assimilationist model has been gradually abandoned or modified in most countries. Where it is still applied, as in France, it is running into serious difficulties due to the contradiction between the promise of individual equality and the reality of continued socio-economic exclusion and racism.

Pluralist models have their difficulties too. In the last two years, new governments in Canada and Australia have begun moving away from multicultural policies. Swedish multiculturalism is also currently under strain: refugee entries have been drastically cut in response to growing public hostility; generous policies on education, training, welfare and community funding for immigrants are being squeezed by the current fiscal crisis of the Swedish welfare state; and many immigrants are beginning to criticize the paternalism inherent in the official notion of ethnicity (Ålund and Schierup 1991).

Multiculturalism has become a major topic of debate even in countries which used to shun such ideas. However, the term is used in very different ways. In Europe, multiculturalism is generally seen as a model based on the long-term persistence within society of groups with different values and cultures. Multiculturalism is rejected by many because it is seen as a legitimation for separatism and fundamentalism, and therefore as a threat to modernity, secularism and gender equality. In the USA, on the other hand, multiculturalism focuses on the reinterpretation of US history and culture to recognize the contribution of groups traditionally excluded from the 'dominant canon': women, Afro-Americans, Native Americans, etc. (Goldberg 1994). In Australia, by contrast, multiculturalism is understood as a public policy designed to ensure the full socio-economic and political participation of all members of an increasingly diverse population.

DEMOCRACY AND DIFFERENCE

As the above discussion indicates, the relationship between immigration, citizenship and democracy is highly problematic. There appear to be four main issues. First, the *dilemma of formal inclusion* concerns access to citizenship. Failure to make immigrants into citizens undermines a basic principle of parliamentary democracy—that all members of civil society should have rights of political participation—but making them into citizens questions concepts of the nation based on ethnic belonging or cultural homogeneity. This remains a central issue in many European countries, but is not very important in Australia, where immigrants can obtain naturalization after two years, residence and where children born in the country to legally resident parents are automatically citizens.

The second dilemma concerns *substantial citizenship*—that is the rights and obligations connected with being a member of a national political community. Where immigrants are socio-economically marginalized and targets for racist violence, granting formal citizenship does not guarantee the full civil, political and social rights which constitute modern citizenship. Achieving full participation requires a range of policies and institutions concerned with combating racism and discrimination, and improving labour market status, access to welfare, education and housing. This issue is significant in all immigration countries, including Australia, and it is a major focus of multicultural policies.

The third dilemma is that of *recognition of collective cultural rights.* This arises because it often proves impossible to incorporate immigrants into society as individuals. In many cases, immigrants and their descendants cluster together, share a common socio-economic position, develop their own community structures, and seek to maintain their languages and cultures. Culture and ethnicity are vital resources in the settlement process. Immigrants cannot become full citizens unless the state and society are willing to accept the right to cultural difference not only for individuals but also for groups. Collective cultural rights are therefore a central part of multiculturalism. However, they are only meaningful if they are linked to social justice strategies. If cultural difference leads to social disadvantage (such as high unemployment, low incomes or poor housing) then we cannot speak of equality of respect for all cultural groups.

This leads on to the fourth dilemma, that of *the appropriateness of our political institutions*. As Canadian philosopher Charles Taylor (1994) has argued, political ideas and institutions are the expression of a certain range of cultures, and may be incompatible with other ranges. Even a doctrine like liberalism cannot claim complete neutrality. For instance its notion of the division between the public and the private is unacceptable to feminists. A multicultural society cannot expect the culturally-bound principles of the group dominant in earlier phases of its history to remain appropriate when new groups are included in the political process. For Australia this implies that it may be necessary to overhaul institutional structures which claim to be universalistic, but which are in fact based on British legal and constitutional traditions of the founding fathers of the Federation.

Liberal theories of citizenship have difficulty in dealing with collective difference (Bauböck 1994). Attempts to increase democracy have generally involved making citizenship rights available to ever-wider circles of the population. Suffrage in western countries applied initially only to male property-owners, but was later extended to the working class and then to women. In recent times, citizenship for indigenous and immigrant minorities has been seen as the key to greater equality. However, liberal citizenship tends to homogenize political identity: all citizens are supposed to have equal rights as citizens, whatever their actual economic and social positions (Pateman 1985). As women, indigenous people and immigrants have found, formal political equality may not overcome racism, economic disadvantage or social exclusion. Equality as citizens is not in itself sufficient to achieve real empowerment and change.

There are a number of solutions to this problem. The American feminist philosopher Iris Marion Young (1989) argues that full citizenship can only be achieved through recognition that people's primary social identity may not be as individual members of society but as members of a specific community. This implies the right for groups to remain different. Young therefore advocates a concept of *differentiated citizenship* with two main aspects. First, democracy must mean not only enfranchisement of all, but also mechanisms to secure participation of usually-excluded social groups in decision-making. This argument would legitimate special representative bodies for certain groups—a principle already embodied in Australia in the Aboriginal and Torres Strait Islander Commission. It could also justify veto rights on certain decisions by groups directly affected.

Second, universality implies that laws and policies should be blind to race, gender, ethnicity etc. The principle of equal treatment is based on the idea of generally applicable norms of behaviour and performance. But there are in fact no objective general norms: they are based on the experience of the groups who have the power to set them. Thus seemingly fair and objective standards may discriminate against those who are excluded—and indeed can serve as an ideological legitimation for that exclusion (Young 1989: 269–70). As Laksiri Jayasuriya has written: '...in a plural society, we discover that people's needs are unequal but equity policy dictates that we assume that needs are equal. Hence the paradox in a plural society ... that we cannot be egalitarian and equitable at the same time' (Jayasuriya 1993). Differential treatment is sometimes needed to achieve equity. The obvious examples here are affirmative action measures to improve the educational or occupational level of disadvantaged groups, or special services for groups with special needs.

Young's notion of *differentiated citizenship* is both useful and problematic. It does point the way to measures for increasing equity, but it could lead to a new type of fixation and homogenization of identity. If group rights are institutionalized, that must imply some mechanism for determining and registering group membership. But many people assigned to a group may not accept this as their principal source of political identity. Fixed group membership may be experienced as repressive, especially if it means binding people to groups with rigid values on gender, religion or social behaviour.

A second approach is that of Taylor, who takes as his starting point the need for *recognition.* He argues that our identity is shaped through recognition or its absence on the part of others. He sees liberal ideas on the equal worth of individuals as central to securing recognition in modern society. However, increasing cultural diversity and the emergence of multiculturalism lead to potentially contradictory discourses on two levels. On the one hand, the *politics of universalism* mean emphasizing the equal dignity of individuals through the equalization of rights and entitlements. On the other hand, the modern notion of identity has given rise to a *politics of difference*, based on recognition of the unique identity of a certain individual or group, and their distinctness from everyone else. The politics of universalism require norms of nondiscrimination which are blind to difference, while the politics of difference require special rights and treatment for certain groups, such as Aboriginal people.

The claims of individual rights and protection of collective identities seem irreconcilable, but Taylor sets out to bridge the gulf, using the example of Quebec's claims for special rights for the French language and culture. He argues that one can distinguish the fundamental rights (like *habeas corpus*) which should never be infringed, from rights that are important, but that can be revoked or restricted for reasons of public policy. On this basis, Quebeckers are justified in demanding special measures (such as priority for the French language in schools and public life) to secure the survival of their collective cultural identity, as long as they maintain fundamental liberal rights, and provide protection for minorities (Taylor 1994).

This approach may well be applicable in the case of Quebec, where a Francophone majority, which holds power at the level of the Province, is confronted by an Anglophone majority which holds power at the Federal level. But it is not clear how Taylor's approach would work in situations in which a powerful majority is faced by a range of minorities which lack political power. Taylor does not show us general mechanisms which would secure protection and equal rights for minorities, and empower them.

A third approach is that proposed by Jürgen Habermas (1994), who argues that Taylor is wrong in postulating a basic contradiction between individual rights and protection of collective identities. Rather, he says, there is an inherent connection between democracy and the constitutional state, in the sense that citizens can only be autonomous by collectively exercising their political rights within the law-making process. On this basis, the system of rights cannot be blind to unequal social conditions or cultural differences, because bearers of individual rights develop their individuality within varying social and cultural contexts. 'A correctly understood theory of rights requires a politics of recognition that protects the integrity of the individual in the life contexts in which his or her identity is formed' (Habermas 1994: 113). Democracy in a multicultural society therefore means guaranteeing social and cultural rights for everyone, rather than just for members of specific groups. However, as Habermas points out, this does not happen by itself, but rather as the result of social movements and political struggles.

The virtue of Habermas' formulation is that it removes the false contradiction between individual rights and group identities, by stressing that everyone is both an individual and a bearer of a collective identity. A democratic state must therefore guarantee rights at both levels. Combined with Habermas' emphasis on the legitimate role of political action in achieving change, and his notion that no political system can remain static in a changing world, this provides a valuable philosophical framework for a new notion of citizenship.

Principles of multicultural citizenship

On the basis of this discussion, it is possible to suggest some principles for *multicultural citizenship*. The aim must be to achieve full citizenship for everybody—not only for people of migrant origin, but also for members of hitherto disempowered groups: women, indigenous peoples, people with disabilities, gays and lesbians and so on. Recognition of group difference implies departing from the idea of all citizens as simply *equal individuals* and instead seeing them simultaneously as having *equal rights as individuals and different needs and wants as members of groups with specific characteristics and social situations.*

This gives rise to the following principles for multicultural citizenship:

1 *Taking equality of citizenship rights as a starting point.* It is essential to ensure that all members of society are formally included as citizens, and enjoy equal rights and equality before the law.
2 *Recognizing that formal equality of rights does not necessarily lead to equality of respect, resources, opportunities or welfare.* Formal equality can indeed mask and legitimize disadvantage and discrimination. Multicultural citizenship must be based on accepting group differences as legitimate, and not as disabilities or deviance.
3 *Establishing mechanisms for group representation and participation.* Despite formal equality as citizens, members of disadvantaged groups are often excluded from decision-making processes. Such groups need special institutional arrangements to secure full political participation. This means devising mechanisms to secure more democracy in more places (Davidson 1993: 8).
4 *Differential treatment for people with different characteristics, needs and wants.* Treating people equally, despite the fact that past conditions, laws, policies and practices have made them unequal in various ways, can only perpetuate inequality. Governments should provide laws, programmes and services to combat barriers based on gender, disability, origins, ethnicity, etc.

AUSTRALIAN MULTICULTURALISM

To what extent do multicultural policies in Australia correspond with this notion of multicultural citizenship? Multiculturalism was originally devised in the 1970s as a model to respond to the needs of a growing immigrant population after the failure of previous policies of assimilation. It does not provide an explicit model of citizenship and democracy, but, under the Australian Labor Party (ALP) Government from 1983–96 it developed into a set of policies that made a powerful implicit statement on these matters.

Multicultural principles and Australian citizenship
Multiculturalism was first officially embraced as a policy in Canada in 1971. In Australia, explicit multicultural policies were first introduced in

1973 by the ALP Government led by Gough Whitlam. In this early phase, it was based on rejection of assimilationism and policies for improving welfare and educational provision for mainly working-class migrants of European origin. The Liberal and Country Party Coalition, which governed from 1975 to 1982, continued multicultural policies, but modified them to emphasize: cultural pluralism, the role of ethnic organizations in provision of welfare services, and the value of multiculturalism for achieving social cohesion in an ethnically diverse society.

The central principle of this type of multiculturalism was the key role of the ethnic group, which was seen as having a relatively fixed and homogeneous cultural identity. Australian society appeared as a collection of ethnic communities united around a set of 'core values'. Critics of this 'ethnic group model' of multiculturalism argued that state funding policies might actually create the communities and leaderships that government wanted to work with, while ignoring diversity and tendencies to change within each group. Nonetheless, multiculturalism made an important new statement on substantial citizenship: that it was no longer necessary to be culturally assimilated to be an Australian citizen. You could be an Australian, even if you spoke another language and followed different cultural practices and life-styles (as long as these did not conflict with Australian law).

The ALP Government of 1983–96 again redefined multiculturalism, to fit in with other key policy goals such as economic deregulation, more efficient use of human resources, maintaining the social safety net and integrating Australia into the Asia-Pacific region. The shift was influenced by developments such as the shift from Europe to Asia as the main source of immigrants, increased emphasis on high skill levels as an entry criterion, and the labour market entry of second generation immigrants with much better education levels than their parents.

The Government moved away from the 'ethnic group approach' and developed what may be called 'a citizenship model of multiculturalism'. The new model was laid down in the *National Agenda for a Multicultural Australia* (OMA 1989). Multiculturalism was defined as a system of rights and freedoms, combined with such obligations as commitment to the nation, a duty to accept the Constitution and the rule of law, and the acceptance of basic principles such as tolerance and equality, English as the national language and equality of the sexes.

The document implicitly embodied an innovative concept of citizenship: it took for granted the three types of rights—civil, political and social rights—suggested in T.H. Marshall's classical analysis of citizenship in postwar Britain (Marshall 1964). It went on to add a new component: cultural rights. The *National Agenda* implied some of the principles of multicultural citizenship discussed above. Multiculturalism was not defined as cultural pluralism or minority rights, but in terms of the rights of *all citizens* in a democratic state. The *National Agenda* emphasized the recognition of *difference* as part of the state's task in securing *universality* in resource allocation. The programme was based on the recognition that some groups are disadvantaged by lack of language proficiency and education, together with discrimination based on race, ethnicity and gender. It was seen as the duty of the state to combat such disadvantage. There was an underlying understanding that cultural rights could not be fully realized unless they were linked to policies of social justice.

The new policy document issued by the National Multicultural Advisory Council (NMAC) towards the end of the period of ALP government, *Multicultural Australia: the Next Steps, Towards and Beyond 2000* (NMAC 1995) reiterated the 1989 statement, spelling out the principles in more detail and assessing the extent to which the policy initiatives had been successfully implemented.

A wealth of government policy documents could be cited as evidence that the principles and rhetoric of multiculturalism do, in many respects, correspond to the principles of multicultural citizenship suggested in the previous section of this chapter. But does this official rhetoric reflect fundamental changes? Some observers argue that multiculturalism is only a peripheral theme in the current debate on Australian identity and institutions. For instance, Alastair Davidson (1993:2) has shown that the current debate on whether Australia should become a republic has hardly addressed the need for constitutional change to reflect the diversity of the Australian population:

'Yet despite this disagreement about the British connection, both [sides] understand what it is to be Australian within the same parameters, those of a debate with the mother country. The myth of our foundation as heirs to the traditions of the English-speaking peoples carries with it an implicit notion of what it is to be a citizen. This notion excludes others more appropriate today.'

The move to a republic is seen by many as simply concerning the appointment of an Australian head of state, while all else remains unchanged. This one-sidedness is a continuation of 'the long silence about citizenship' (Davidson 1993: 3) which has prevailed since Federation. The lack of debate was originally based on the fact that Australians were British citizens until 1948, since then on the notion that there was no need for change and therefore little to discuss. In the last few years, citizenship has again become a public topic, with calls for better understanding of what it means to be a citizen through programmes of civics education. At the same time, citizenship campaigns have been carried out to persuade immigrants to get naturalized. But there has been little debate about the need for redefining citizenship itself.

This is linked to the fact that Australia—like Britain but unlike the USA, Canada and most European democracies—has no Bill of Rights to clearly stipulate what it means to be a citizen. In Canada, multicultural-ism and equality rights were integrated into the definition of citizenship through the 1982 Canadian Charter of Rights and Freedoms. This meant a recognition of collective identities and collective rights of specific groups as part of citizenship. In contrast the Australian approach is much more on the level of social policy: the special needs of ethnic groups are recog-nized, but the measures taken to deal with them are essentially concerned with welfare, education or services for individuals (Jayasuriya 1993: 2). The Australian approach is based on administration of social issues by the state, rather than active citizenship through collective participation in decision-making processes.

Official calls to rethink Australian identity in terms of cultural diversity and links to the Asia-Pacific region therefore seem to have little bearing on actual change in our political and economic institutions. Even within the debate on identity there is considerable ambiguity, as major recent public celebrations of Australianness have shown. The Bicentenary in 1988 acclaimed colonization and nation-building in terms which were un-acceptable to indigenous people, and which did little to include non-En-glish speaking background (NESB) people. Repeated celebrations of the fiftieth anniversary of various milestones in the Second World War evoked nationalist images of a people sustained in adversity by traditional Anglo-Australian values of discipline, stoicism and mateship. As David-son (1993: 3) has written: '... at the base of citizenship is a sense of na-tional identity as against others. In both the British and Australian litera-ture there is the theme of a warrior nation, of men and women who are ready to die for their country'.

Even on the level of political principles, multiculturalism therefore still seems far from being an effective model for Australian citizenship. How-ever, the problems become even more marked, if one contrasts rhetoric with actual social change.

Indigenous people and multiculturalism

A major problem is that multiculturalism has always been seen mainly as a strategy concerned with immigrants and their descendants. It is seldom linked to the needs of indigenous Australians. The *National Agenda* did refer to the situation of Aborigines and Torres Strait Islanders. Yet the policy initiatives which flowed from the document related mainly to im-migrants. Indigenous people were only included in certain general programmes, such as those concerning 'Access and Equity' (see below) and community relations.

This near absence of Aborigines and Torres Strait Islanders in multicultural policies reflects a dilemma: many indigenous people reject inclusion, as they feel it would make them seem like one ethnic group among others. Aboriginal spokespersons assert their special status, as the original inhabitants of the continent. In the late 1980s and early 1990s it became increasingly clear that Australia could never develop a coherent national identity unless it recognized the special position of indigenous people and the historical wrongs done to them. This realization found its expression in the Mabo verdict of 1992 and the Native Title Act of 1993, which overthrew the long-standing colonial legal doctrine of *terra nullius*, according to which indigenous peoples had never really possessed the land.

It is in this context that, in its last few years of office, the ALP Government made attempts to broaden multicultural policies to include indigenous people. In its work on the 1995 policy document, the National Multicultural Advisory Council liaised with Aboriginal spokespersons and with the Council for Aboriginal Reconciliation. *Multicultural Australia: the Next Steps* paid far more attention than the 1989 *National Agenda* to concerns of indigenous people. Yet there were still few concrete measures which could actually make multiculturalism relevant to Aboriginal people. The only way of overcoming this might be through much more vigorous anti-racist policies, as well as effective measures to overcome the disadvantage and exclusion of Aboriginal communities. Until such steps are taken, multiculturalism will be weakened by its lack of support from indigenous Australians.

Social justice and economic rationalism
There is a strong link between cultural rights and social justice. If members of certain ethnic groups can only maintain their culture at the price of social disadvantage (e. g. high unemployment and low socio-economic status) then we cannot speak of equal rights. This issue was clearly recognized in the *National Agenda, Multicultural Australia, Working Nation* (1994) and other policy statements, which laid down strategies to combat social disadvantage and remove labour market barriers. Several government departments introduced social justice strategies which target NESB immigrants, indigenous people, women and people with disabilities. Social justice in the *National Agenda* is concerned with fair distribution of economic resources; equal access to essential services such as housing, health-care and education; equal rights in civil, legal and industrial affairs; and equal opportunity for participation by all in personal development, community life and decision-making (OMA 1989: 19).

However, there was an unresolved tension between the principles of social justice and economic efficiency. The ALP Government pursued policies of deregulation and privatization of the economy, based on neo-classical theories of economic rationality. Such policies reduced the ability of the Government to intervene in economic matters to ensure social justice. The *National Agenda* tried to resolve the problem through the principle of 'economic efficiency', defined as 'the need to maintain, develop and utilize effectively the skills and talents of all Australians, regardless of background' (OMA 1989: vi). This principle underpinned policies designed to make efficient use of human resources through education, training and recognition of overseas qualifications. The Government also has stressed 'productive diversity': the notion that it is in the general interest to make efficient use of the skills and cultural capabilities of our diverse population.

The objectives laid down in Government social justice policies suggest indicators by which to judge their success. However, it is difficult to assess social justice policies due to 'lack of agreed benchmarks and patchy data on the many characteristics of our multicultural society' (NMAC 1995, vol. 2: 31).

One important area is participation in government. In 1991, only 6.7 per cent of legislators and government appointed officials at the three levels of government were of first or second-generation non-English speaking background, compared with their share in the population of about 25 per cent. The under-representation had actually got worse since 1986. The participation rate of indigenous Australians in government was 0.6 per cent, compared with a 1.6 per cent share in the population. NESB people were also under-represented in the Public Service and particularly in the Senior Executive Service, although the situation showed some improvement since 1989. Participation by NESB and indigenous people was low in many other important public positions, such as judges, magistrates, mediators and police officers. An examination of membership of government consultative bodies showed that NESB and indigenous people were well represented on bodies concerned with social and cultural issues, but significantly under-represented in other councils, such as those concerned with economic decision-making (NMAC 1995, vol. 2: 13–15).

Participation in senior management and union leaderships is another important indicator. NMAC found that NESB people made up only 6 per cent of directors and executives listed in major company handbooks. However, NESB people were over-represented among owners and operators of small businesses. A study of Victorian unions found that only 10 per cent of officials were NESB people, compared with 24 per cent of union members. Under-representation particularly affected more recent Asian immigrant groups (NMAC 1995, vol. 2: 15–16).

Another measure of social justice is unemployment levels. Indigenous people have chronically high unemployment. A recent major survey by the Australian Bureau of Statistics (ABS) noted an overall unemployment rate of 38 per cent in 1994. Moreover, many Aboriginal people are classified as not in the labour force, because they have given up looking for a job: the ABS survey found that 32 per cent of those not in the labour force wanted a job (ABS 1995: 45–7).

Unemployment rates tend to rise faster than average for NESB people in recessions, and their overall unemployment rates are higher. In June 1995, the unemployment rate for NESB people was 12.2 per cent, compared with 8.1 per cent for the total labour force. The rate for some groups was far higher: 25.1 per cent for Lebanese, 26.8 per cent for Vietnamese (BIMPR 1995: 48). These are not recently arrived groups; their unemployment rates have been high for many years, and labour market measures seem to have done little to improve the situation. Another government report has noted above-average unemployment rates for overseas-born youth from NES countries (HREOC 1993: 223).

Recognition of overseas skills and qualifications has long been seen as a crucial issue by ethnic communities. Despite some improvements in accreditation procedures, Australia is still far from a situation of equal opportunities for overseas-trained professionals and tradespeople in all occupations. Employers' reservations about overseas skills, and discrimination against people from certain countries influence employment chances for engineers (Hawthorne 1994). In 1991, the Human Rights and Equal Opportunities Commission (HREOC) concluded that there was compelling evidence that the medical registration system was discriminatory under the terms of the *Racial Discrimination Act* of 1975. A 1995 working party recommended a broad range of reform measures need to secure equal opportunities for overseas-trained people (NMAC 1995, vol. 2: 36–7), although there is little sign that these will be implemented.

The HREOC's 1994 *State of the Nation* report was concerned mainly with housing issues. It reported frequent racial harassment of public housing tenants in some areas, and also noted that housing authorities lacked effective strategies to deal with this. Perhaps as a result of the latter, over 80 per cent of tenants who had experienced harassment said they had not reported it. The report also noted 'the disjointed and haphazard approach to access and equity provision within the State Housing authorities' (HREOC 1994).

Multiculturalism has given rise to many measures designed to improve social justice for ethnic minorities in Australia. Some real progress has been achieved, and the picture is certainly much better than in countries which cling to exclusionary or assimilationist policies. However, in many key areas, progress has been painfully slow, and real socio-economic disadvantage persists for certain groups. Indigenous and NESB people are still far from equal with regard to participation in political and economic power.

Multiculturalism as bureaucratic practice

From the mid-1980s, both state and federal governments were concerned to move away from multicultural policies delivered by special agencies to special target groups. Multicultural policies were to become part of the mainstream of government service delivery. The key instrument for achieving this at the federal level was the Access and Equity Strategy, known as A&E. From 1989 to 1994 all Commonwealth departments and agencies were required to prepare A&E plans, and to report on their implementation annually. In 1992 a major evaluation of the A&E strategy reported improvements in language and information services. But the evaluation also noted many problems and deficiencies (OMA 1992). In 1994, NMAC noted further improvements, but also found areas of severe problems, including:

- delivery of services to indigenous Australians;
- consultation and participation policies, mechanisms and processes;
- services to small and remote area communities; and
- the collection and use of ethnicity data (NMAC 1995, vol. 2: 27–8).

Despite such concerns the general requirement for A&E plans was abolished in 1994. The preparation of triennial plans and of reports on their implementation was left to the discretion of individual agencies. Similarly, 1994 was the last year that Federal Government departments were required to report publicly on their equal opportunity programs. This requirement was abolished, although only 9 per cent of appointments to the Public Service were NESB people at the time (ACTU, 1995).

The bureaucratic response to racism reveals similar problems. The 1991 National Inquiry into Racist Violence showed a high incidence of racism, especially against indigenous people and Asian immigrants (HREOC 1991). Australia has no systematic monitoring of incidents of racist violence or discrimination—unlike the USA or Britain, which have established special reporting systems. Federal and state agencies set up to combat racial discrimination and vilification do not provide comprehensive information on the incidence of such practices—they merely respond to complaints.

HREOC received 458 complaints under the Federal Racial Discrimination Act in 1993/4 (ACTU 1995:5). But there is strong evidence that only a small percentages of such cases are actually reported (ACTU 1995: 10, 15). This is partly because of the complex and lengthy procedures faced by those who do complain, and partly because existing laws are weak and

rarely provide effective remedies. For example, the NSW Anti-Discrimi-
nation Board received 448 complaints on grounds of vilification over a
five-year period; of these three cases were eventually recommended for
prosecution, but not in fact proceeded with (ACTU 1995: 10). In the light
of this, people may feel that complaints are a waste of time.

The decline of ethnic politics

An important reason for stagnation in the development of multiculturalism is the relatively low level of political mobilization of ethnic communities. The higher level of activism among indigenous people may
help explain why their situation has been much more on the political
agenda in recent years.

One reason for the emergence of multiculturalism in the 1970s was the
realization by political parties that immigrants were making up increasing
proportions of the electorate. The introduction of social policies aimed
specifically at immigrants, first by the ALP and then by the Coalition
Government, put a premium on ethnic mobilization and formation of associations to speak in the name of immigrants. This caused some observers to imply that there was some sort of sinister 'ethnic lobby' which
was having an illegitimate influence on politics. Most political scientists,
on the other hand, argue that there is no monolithic 'ethnic vote' which
can be controlled by ethnic leaders to secure specific political outcomes.
Immigrants have not constituted a united political force, mainly because
the differences among them in terms of social position, interests and values are as great as among the Anglo-Australian population.

From the 1970s, leaders of ethnic associations were increasingly drawn
into government consultative bodies of various kinds. The state Ethnic
Community Councils and the Federation of Ethnic Communities Councils of Australia came to be predominantly funded by government.
Smaller associations representing specific ethnic groups also became dependent on government grants. Links between government and ethnic
communities was further encouraged by the fact that many second-generation immigrants made their careers in the Public Service: they often had
the ambiguous role of being both government officials and ethnic lobby-
ists. These tendencies are contradictory. On the one hand, the closeness
between ethnic communities and the government agencies was beneficial
in improving communication and sensitivity to needs. But it also led to a
process of creeping cooption, through which the ethnic associations became closely oriented towards bureaucratic goals and methods.

The overall result of this institutionalization of ethnic politics seems to
have been a depoliticization of ethnic associations and a reduction of
their political influence in the late 1980s and early 1990s. Old-style mobilization of ethnic groups still takes place around issues connected with

homeland politics. But major political actions connected with multicultural issues hardly occur any more. When a conservative government came to power in 1996, ethnic organizations lacked the ability to fight effectively against cuts in social rights for immigrants.

A shift away from multicultural citizenship?
On 2 March 1996 a Liberal-National Party Coalition was elected with a large majority. Prior to the election, the Coalition parties had promised to retain the social safety-net, but also to cut government expenditure and deregulate the labour market. Upon taking office, the new Government claimed that there was an unexpected $8 billion deficit, which made considerable reductions in expenditure vital. The August 1996 Budget contained cuts to many government services, including measures for the unemployed, health services, aged care and tertiary education.

During the March election, racism played an unexpected role, with several conservative candidates criticizing provision of special services for minorities. In one Queensland electorate, the Liberal Party Candidate, Ms Pauline Hanson, attacked services for Aboriginal people in such an extreme way that she was disendorsed as a candidate by her own party. Despite this, she won the seat, with one of the biggest anti-Labor swings in the country. This was widely taken as a signal that anti-minority discourses were now seen as acceptable by a large share of the population.

After the election, Government leaders and media commentators started to attack Aboriginal and migrant rights in a way that had not been seen in Australia for many years. Senator Herron, the Minister for Aboriginal Affairs publicly criticized the Aboriginal and Torres Strait Islander Commission for alleged poor management and corruption, and introduced strict measures to control this previously independent body. In August 1996 the Government announced cuts of $400 million to ATSIC's budget, which meant severe restrictions in the services provided to Aboriginal people, in fields such as health, employment, legal aid, culture and sport.

Major cuts were quickly introduced in the immigration and multicultural area. The immigration intake for 1996–97 was cut by 11 per cent. Fees for visas were increased drastically; for instance a Family Residence Visa went up from $415 to $1500. Costs for English language courses for new immigrants were more than doubled to $5000. At the same time, many occupational English courses were abolished. The largest cut was to be achieved by increasing the waiting period for eligibility for social security benefits like unemployment support from six months to two years for new entrants, which was expected to save $663 million. The very successful Bureau of Immigration, Multicultural and Population Research was abolished, reducing Australia's policy-oriented research capability in this area.

Perhaps the most important change in political terms was the abolition of the Office of Multicultural Affairs, which had previously been able to substantially influence core government policies from its location in the Department of Prime Minister and Cabinet. Some remnants of the Office were integrated into a (re-named) Department of Immigration and Multicultural Affairs (DIMA), but with very limited resources, and no political weight. This may be taken as a clear signal that the current Government does not see multicultural policy as an important area.

The election of a conservative Government with a neo-liberal agenda of small government, privatization and deregulation may herald a major shift away from the multicultural principles of its predecessor. The Government's social philosophy, while paying lip-service to multiculturalism, seems to be based on backward-looking and monocultural ideals, reminiscent of Australia in the 1950s. However, Australia in the 1990s is a very different society, marked by great cultural diversity, and the existence of many organizations representing the various ethnic communities. It remains to be seen whether current developments will lead to a re-emergence of ethnic politics, and to new demands for political and economic participation by minorities.

CONCLUSION

Is Australia on the way to a new form of multicultural citizenship, which could be a model for other democratic countries confronted by the dilemmas arising from globalization and growing ethnic diversity? Or has our model become stalled due to failure to tackle structural inequalities, loss of reform impetus in the treadmill of bureaucratic practice, and depoliticisation of protest potential?

Certainly Australia has come a long way since our racist world view began to be questioned in the 1960s. Assimilationism, for all its problems, did create a basis for change by providing formal access to citizenship for immigrants—something that has still not been achieved in many immigration countries. The 'ethnic group model' of multiculturalism in the 1970s did begin a process of rethinking identity which moved Australia's self-image away from the myth of ethno-cultural homogeneity—again, a step still to be taken in many places. The shift in the late 1980s towards a 'citizenship model' of multiculturalism made the vital link between cultural pluralism and social justice. This raised the fundamental dilemma of how to achieve the recognition of collective cultural rights within a universalistic democracy.

However, the development of multiculturalism has not been part of a conscious strategy for rethinking citizenship to make it appropriate for a culturally diverse nation on the eve of the 21st century. Rather, policies concerned with ethno-cultural diversity have essentially been top-down social policies. Multiculturalism has developed in an *ad hoc* way as a strategy for integrating immigrant communities into a basically unchanged society.

It is important to realize that cultural diversity is likely to bring about major changes in society. The impetus for change is unlikely to come from the those in power—it must be a result of social movements and political action. Active citizenship means constant participation by citizens in decision-making at all levels. The challenge is to bring about changes in representative mechanisms and bureaucratic structures to permit more democracy in more places, for both groups and individuals. This may lead to major shifts in political identity and institutions.

Appendix: Foreign or immigrant population in selected OECD countries

	Foreign population[1]			
	Thousands		% of total population	
	1983	1993[2]	1983	1993[3]
Austria	297	690	3.9	8.6
Belgium	891	921	9.0	9.1
Denmark	104	189	2.0	3.6
Finland	16	56	0.3	1.1
France	3 714	3 597	6.8	6.3
Germany4	4 535	6 878	7.4	8.5
Ireland	83	94	2.4	2.7
Italy	381	987	0.7	1.7
Japan	817	1 321	0.7	1.1
Luxembourg	96	125	26.3	31.1
Netherlands	552	780	3.8	5.1
Norway	95	162	2.3	3.8
Spain	210	430	0.5	1.1
Sweden	397	508	4.8	5.8
Switzerland	926	1 260	14.4	18.1
United Kingdom	1 601	2 001	2.8	3.5
TOTAL	14 715	19 999		

	Foreign-born population[5]			
	Thousands		% of total population	
	1981	1991	1981	
Australia	3 004	4 125	20.6	22.7
Canada	3 843	4 343	16.1	15.6
United States	14 080	19 767	4.7	71991.9

Source: OECD (1995) *Trends in International Migration Annual Report 1994* Paris: OECD, 27.

Notes to Appendix

Data for European countries and Japan is for residents with foreign nationality, and therefore excludes immigrants who have been naturalized. Data for Australia, Canada and the USA is for foreign-born residents, whatever their nationality, and therefore excludes children of immigrants born in the immigration countries.

[1]Data for the foreign population are from population registers except for France (census), the United Kingdom (labour force survey), and Japan and Switzerland (register of foreigners).

[2]1990 for France, 1992 for Ireland.

[3]1990 for France, 1992 for Ireland.

[4]Data for 1993 cover Germany, and for 1983 western Germany only.

[5]Census data (1980 and 1990 for the United States).

7 Modes of Incorporation: Toward a Comparative Framework

Aristide R. Zolberg

INTRODUCTION: THE STRANGENESS OF IMMIGRATION

Although demographers view migration as one of the three determinants of any human population, alongside birth and death, they envision it merely as relocation in physical space, as represented by a shift from one unit of statistical aggregation to another. From this perspective, international migration does not differ in kind from internal movement. However, this misses a large part of the point. The specificity of the process arises in the first instance from the organization of the modern world into sovereign states with clearly indicated *territorial* boundaries delineating mutually exclusive jurisdiction; it thus involves, in addition to relocation, a change from one state to another. Moreover, most of the states in question claim to be *national* states (or sometimes multi-national ones), and this claim constitutes a major foundation of their legitimacy. Nations are historical constructions centring on the delineation of a *cultural* boundary, denoting simultaneously inclusion and exclusion.[1] As the result of increased contact among populations within the confines of each state, and because of the efforts of each of them to make populations more alike within while emphasizing differences without, they are perceived by most of their members as family-like bodies, with a common ancestry and a common destiny. Consequently, whereas co-nationals take on the air of extended kin, even if they encompass several hundred million highly diverse individuals dispersed over continental spaces, as in the United States or Russia, non-nationals are considered "others", as forcefully evoked by the latinate English legal term "aliens".[2]

Population transfers *between* national states thus differ in kind from other forms of human migration, notably the wanderings of communities across space before the earth was carved out into mutually exclusive territories, and the movement of individuals within the confines of the state of which they are subjects or citizens. Whatever the reasons for the movement, and whether it is relatively voluntary or forced, it involves an irreducible *political* dimension. Concomitantly, immigration is an odd phenomenon in that it brings about an encounter between groups hitherto separated by the very boundaries that define their distinctive identities; and the settlement of aliens deviates from what most members of the receiving community take as the "natural" mode of reproduction of their nation. This is emphasized by the term "naturalization" used for admitting them into formal membership, a process that parallels adoption, whereby the law provides a fictional substitute for biological filiation.

Consequently, it is not surprising that immigration and the prospect of incorporating a significant body of aliens tends to provoke contentious confrontations: once the debate gets under way, it inexorably broadens to encompass a wide range of disparate issues, including law enforcement and the organization of economic life, the conduct of foreign affairs, the question of what obligations the members of an affluent national community have toward strangers who come knocking at their door, and ultimately the identity and cohesion of the receiving community. By the same token, it is a politically confusing subject because it provokes alignments that often cut across the usual line-up of interests and established political parties, and the relevant policy choices cannot be easily fitted in within the usual "Left-Right" framework. This is particularly visible in current American debates, where the right-wing *National Review* opposes immigration as undermining the integrity of the American nation, whereas the *Wall Street Journal* advocates an open door on free-market grounds, and Latino advocacy groups oppose punishing firms that employ unauthorized foreign workers because enforcement might lead to discrimination.

DIALECTICS OF THE TWO AXES

The confusion arises because immigration involves two very different dimensions of concern and interest, the one pertaining to its putative effects on material conditions, the other regarding its putative consequences for national identity. These can be represented by two cross-cutting axes, each with positive and negative poles, providing for a continuum of positions "for" or "against". Hence it is possible to adopt a positive position on immigration with respect to one dimension and a negative one in relation to the other.

To simplify somewhat, with regard to the first axis, immigrants – including refugees – are viewed primarily as "workers", so that alignments are closely related to the configuration of economic interests more generally. Immigrants are characteristically welcomed by employers as an addition to the labour supply that reduces the unit cost of labour; conversely, they are characteristically resented by resident workers as unfair competitors willing to accept lower wages and below-standard conditions. At worse, they may altogether displace natives. Some immigrants are entrepreneurs, and as such may be viewed variously as undesirable business competitors, or as welcome providers of unusual goods and services at lower prices. Beyond this, immigrants are also consumers of goods and services, both the ordinary kind one buys, and "public goods" that are automatically available to all residents, including many services provided by government. Hence immigrants may be simultaneously welcomed by businesses as buyers and by some branches of government as additional taxpayers who contribute to depleted social insurance funds, for example, while resented by other branches as burdensome extra clients who crowd existing facilities, such as schools or hospitals. The putative "balance sheet" of costs and benefits of legal and unauthorized immigrants to the welfare state figures prominently in current American debates. Matters are complicated by the fact that different units of aggregation can be used to draw up balance sheets, so that immigration may be deemed good for the whole economy, but bad for a particular locality or group; and similar considerations apply also to variation in the time frames employed in such calculations.

However, immigrants of any kind also constitute a cultural and social presence, and in that capacity evoke a distinctive set of conjectures regarding their putative impact on the receiving country's national identity. Although negative assessments of actual or potential immigrants along this axis are often specious and founded on conceptions of culture that are implicitly or explicitly ethnocentric, concern over the preservation of the host society's cultural character and social cohesion is not in itself illegitimate; hence an effort must be made to discuss "national identity" in a dispassionate and analytic manner. The question is what intellectual tools are most appropriate for tackling the subject, what information should be relied on, what are appropriate objectives, and what measures should be used in the evaluation of strategies to achieve them.

In keeping with the conceptualization of the nation noted at the outset, national identity can often be traced to the more or less explicit adoption by a ruling group at some turning point in a country's modern history of a formula that defines its distinctiveness in a world of competing states, and which is to be internalized by members of the society. Notable examples include the Tudor architects of modern England – well served by Shakespeare in this regard – the American Founding Fathers, the French Jacobins, the Bismarckian Reich-builders, the Bolsheviks in the wake of the Russian Revolution, or Jawaharlal Nehru and the Indian National Congress following the split of British India into India and Pakistan.

Although this process is common to all new or renovated states, national or multinational, the content of the formulas varies considerably. It ususally involves two components, in varying dosage: "ethnic" criteria, based on a myth of common ancestry, and political criteria, that is, commitment to a type of regime.[3] Whereas in the past Britain, Norway, Germany, or Israel relied almost exclusively on the former, the United States and France for some purposes attributed considerable weight to the latter as well, while the Soviet Union emphasized it exclusively, relinquishing the ethnic dimension to the level of its component republics. Although the national formula often takes into consideration some "objective" characteristics of the society, such as the language actually spoken by much of the population or the actual achievement of a relative political consensus, the culture and political orientation of the rulers themselves are always accorded pride of place.

But the national formula nearly always incorporates *negative* criteria of identity as well: We are who we are by virtue of who we are not. The negative "others" are commonly close neighbors with whom perennial wars are fought, or outsiders within one's own society, or remote aliens, regarding whom little is known and therefore much can be invented. Thus, in the Middle Ages to be Christian was not to be a heretic, a Jew, or a Muslim; in the sixteenth century, to be English meant not to be French, as Shakespeare demonstrates in *Henry V*, or Irish, as he insists in *Henry IV*, or yet a non-white "native", as emphasized in *The Tempest*. In the same vein, in the nineteenth century Germans identified themselves as neither Latin nor Slav, while the French became, in addition to "non-English", also "non-German". While the positive content of Indianness around 1950 was somewhat diffuse, on the negative side it was eminently clear – it meant not being Pakistani. The formation of politically-oriented identities involves a parallel dialectical process: to be a Soviet citizen meant not being a "capitalist", an outlook mirrored by the notion that Communists were "Un-American". Of special importance for present purposes is that in the course of the rise of the Europeans and their descendants to world hegemony, they elaborated in addition a common marker of identity as "white", with a sharply delineated negative counterpart encompassing the remainder of humanity.

In practice, markers of identity may focus on any one of a broad variety of characteristics, or combination of them, including not only religion, national origin, language, phenotype ("race"), but also more diffuse traits attributed to groups, such as their political culture or alleged "moral disposition", as denoted by their habits including often what they eat. Notoriously, every one of these was invoked at one time or another in American history as an objection to particular groups. The attributed cultural characteristics of immigrants weighed heavily in the world-wide movement to restrict immigration in the early decades of the twentieth century, not only among "immigration countries" such as the United States, Canada, and Australia, as well as a number of South American ones, but also in Europe, notably in Britain and Germany. In the United States a campaign was launched to exclude the "new immigration" from southern and eastern Europe on the grounds that they were intellectually inferior and of unsuitable character, as demonstrated by the most advanced "scientific" studies carried out in the best universities. As is well known, the campaign culminated after World War I in the imposition of a nearly absolute prohibition on Asian immigration and an unprecedented quantitative limit on annual admissions from Europe, considerably below the ongoing level, and distributed in a discriminatory manner according to national origins in an attempt to restore the American ethnic landscape to its erstwhile "Nordic" configuration.

However, it should be noted that the national identity axis also has a positive pole. One clear manifestation is the special arrangements for the immigration of what might be termed "external nationals".[4] Although the best known cases are Israel and Germany, which have somewhat different forms of a "law of return", nearly all other countries that had an extensive experience of emigration provide for some sort of special arrangements as well, including Italy, Spain, and the United Kingdom, which included the "patrial" category in the recasting of its nationality law in the early 1980s.[5] In the same vein, Canada attributes "points" to applicants who speak one of the country's two "founding" languages, English and French, and proposals along these lines have been set forth in the United States as well with regard to English. Another manifestation of "positive value" on the national integration axis is the intervention of immigrant communities to insure family reunion, or to block attempts to close the door – most effective, of course, where immigrants and their descendants have ready access to citizenship, as in the United States.

THE "WANTED BUT NOT WELCOME" SYNDROME

Not surprisingly, acute problems arise whenever any of the 'others' appear in a country by way of immigration. But how does that come about? The cases of the Irish, Chinese, and southern and eastern Europeans in the nineteenth century, as well as of Mexicans in the United States and Maghrebis in Europe today, highlight the paradoxical fact that the people objected to were usually induced to come in the first place. This highlights a perennial Catch-22: the very qualities that make a group suitable for recruitment as "labour" demonstrate its lack of qualifications for "membership". In a reversal of Groucho Marx's quip regarding his unwillingness to join any club that would have him as a member, these immigrants are wanted, but not welcome.

An acute manifestation of the dialectics of the two axes, the "wanted but not welcome" syndrome is a key source of the immigration-related tensions that have arisen among most of the postindustrial democracies today as a result of the massive recruitment of foreign workers during the "Bretton Woods" boom period (Zolberg 1991). In Europe, recruitment was initially limited to neighbouring countries with surplus population, notably Italy and Spain, and Finland (in relation to Sweden). However, as demand expanded, and some of the senders themselves joined the group of affluent post-industrial democracies, the domain of recruitment expanded to the eastern and southern Mediterranean, namely Turkey and the Maghreb: concomitantly, it crossed the traditional divide between Christian Europe and the world of Islam. The practice was widespread also in the United States where – in sharp contrast with Canada and Australia – in addition to the immigrants and refugees admitted through the "main gate" as permanent residents and future citizens, millions were brought in through the "back door" by way of a combination of special government programs (notably the "bracero" contract program with Mexico in effect during most of the 1941-64 period), and of "informal" recruitment of undocumented foreign workers by American employers with the benefit of "benign neglect" by US immigration authorities, and until 1986, the explicit assurance that these practices would not be sanctioned.

Selected according to economic criteria, notably willingness to work for very low wages and under harsh or dangerous conditions, immigrant labour is usually drawn from some less developed country or region, which belongs to the world of "others" in opposition to which the hosts have elaborated their identity; and the work they do in the country of immigration as well as the living conditions to which they are subjected ensures that the cultural gap between natives and immigrants even increases. Functioning as a self-fulfilling prophecy, this process of "differential incorporation" in turn provides plenty of grist for the alarmist mill (Portes and Rumbaut 1990).

Historically, the downside of labour immigration was dealt with by keeping the immigrants effectively out of the receiving society. Accomplished by way of extreme segregation, of which slavery is the archetype, this resulted in the formation throughout the colonial world of "plural societies", characterized by hierarchically stratified structures in which race functioned as class, and where it was taken for granted that the racial groups would remain apart (Furnivall 1948; Smith 1969). The tense legacy of these awkward ensembles persists throughout the "plantation belt", notably the Caribbean area (including the United States), Southern

Africa, and Southeast Asia. More recently, the pattern has evolved into milder forms of control designed to prevent settlement, such as limiting the intake to single men or single women, rotating recruitment, restricting them to the jobs for which they were imported, and confining them to residence in special hostels. Other devices include the erection of obstacles to naturalization, either by way of the categoric exclusion of certain groups, as with people of color in the United States from 1790 onward, or the imposition of long waiting periods and expensive procedures, as in Switzerland and Germany.

However, most of these practices conflict with contemporary norms regarding individual rights in liberal or social democracies, which usually apply to residents as well as citizens, and these are further reinforced by the adhesion of most of the states in question to international instruments in the same vein (Soysal 1994). These constraints on their hosts enabled many of the temporary workers recruited in the post-World War II period to turn themselves along with their families into "immigrants", and eventually into formal citizens. However, in most cases this did not resolve the matter of incorporation.

Although historically, refugees tended to be located on the positive side of the integration axis, more recently they have been subject to the "wanted but not welcome" syndrome as well. The concept of "refugee" as it is known in Western theory and practice emerged in the course of the European wars of religion, when Catholic and Protestant sovereigns extended protection and assistance to foreign co-religionists in need (Zolberg, et al. 1989). Albeit aliens, the refugees shared the religion of the receivers, which at the time constituted a central element of their identity, and therefore were not "strangers" but brothers and sisters in need; under these circumstances, the imperatives of Christian charity accorded with those of *Realpolitik*. Later on, the same sort of "likeness" principle was applied to other victims, from French aristocrats who escaped to conservative England during the French Revolution, to defeated Central European liberals and nationalists who fled to one of the small band of liberal states in the nineteenth century, and to European "defectors" from Communism welcomed by the West during the Cold War. However, states were not inclined to help victims who did not meet the test of identity: persecuted Spanish Jews were not welcomed in Christian States, the proletarian Communards of 1871 had no place to go after their defeat, and most Jewish victims of Nazism were denied havens as well.

In the post-World War II period the international community began moving toward a more universalist approach, extending refugee status to all those, anywhere in the world, who were outside their country and without government protection as a consequence of persecution; although the overwhelming majority remained in their regions of origin, some came knocking at the door of the affluent countries; and the fact that an increasing proportion of the latter were poor people of colour – and thereby akin from the perspective of the receivers to immigrant workers – triggered alarm bells and prompted a reconsideration of established policies. Although this revisionism antedated the end of the Cold War, as indicated by the response of the United States to the Mariel crisis of 1980 and of the Europeans to the escalation of asylum demands in the early 1980s, it was accelerated by the collapse of Communism, which eliminated at one blow the *Realpolitik* foundation of the post-war refugee regime.

INCORPORATION: CHALLENGE AND OPPORTUNITIES

Even if ongoing immigration into the western democracies were to be sharply reduced in the near future, as has already occurred in Britain and much of Continental Europe, the receivers face the challenge of successfully incorporating the large new wave of recent decades. What is the most appropriate balance between the obligation of the newcomers to respect the identity and cohesion of the host society, and the obligation of the hosts to respect the dignity and distinctive identity of the fellow human beings whom they have invited or at least authorized to live in their midst?[6] The quest for an answer must be informed by a realistic understanding of the scope of the task at hand, and this should also facilitate the elaboration of the best strategies for achieving the agreed upon objectives.

As illustrated by the late President Mitterrand's reference to a "threshold of tolerance", it is widely believed that nations have a limited capacity for incorporation, and that this is determined by objective factors, both quantitative and qualitative – i.e., the proportion of immigrants in relation to population, and their cultural distance from the hosts' national identity. In reality, however, these are highly subjective considerations. For example, in recent decades, the United States has received one of the largest waves of newcomers in its history, and certainly the most diverse with regard to certain attributes of "difference", notably "race". Quantitatively, the process of incorporation pertains to nearly one-fifth of the resident population, including some nine percent born abroad, and the U.S.-born "second generation" who make up another ten percent; these proportions are of course much larger in the metropolitan areas that serve as ports of entry, notably New York City, Miami, and Los Angeles.

Does this overtax America's capacity to incorporate newcomers, as argued, for example, by the distinguished former diplomat George Kennan (Kennan 1993: 151-156)? From one perspective, the load is relatively light: when population size is taken into consideration, the current US percentage of foreign-born residents is about half what it was at the beginning of the century, and considerably lower than that of other "immigration" countries today, Canada, Israel, and Australia. But from another perspective, the load is relatively heavy: the actual reference point for most Americans alive today is the recent past (1970), when the percentage foreign-born fell to around five percent, its lowest level since the early nineteenth century.[7] In the course of its construction as the core element of American national identity, the "nation of immigrants" was made into a sanitized memory, enshrined at the handsome Ellis Island Museum; and this idealized past is used by many as a foundation for invidious comparisons with the realities of the present.

Public pronouncements on the subject should be taken with a large grain of salt because opponents of immigration tend to exaggerate the difficulties of incorporation, whereas immigrant advocates tend to minimize them. This is true also with regard to the role of immigration in the host country's past. Although a receiving country's self-image as a "nation of immigrants" probably facilitates incorporation, in that it disposes the hosts positively toward the protracted process of negotiation this involves, this does not guarantee a trouble-free path and a happy outcome. For most of its existence the American self-image was constructed more precisely as a nation of *white* immigrants.[8] It is therefore quite possible for "European Americans" simultaneously to think of themselves as a nation that possesses a unique capacity for incorporating newcomers, and to believe that today's newcomers are more difficult to turn into Americans than their own ancestors – a belief which is not sustained by serious research on the subject.[9] On the other hand, a number of European countries have much more experience with immigration and the incorporation of newcomers than is recorded in their national memories. For example, as of the 1970s, nearly one out of every four French persons had at least one foreign-born grandparent; about ten percent of the white population of Great Britain was of immigrant descent, mostly Irish but also eastern or southern European; a substantial number of Germans were the descendants of French Huguenot refugees of the seventeenth century or Polish workers of the late nineteenth, and others would have traced their ancestry to Jewish immigration from eastern Europe had it not been for successful Nazi efforts to extirpate this from the national experience. Although French debates on immigration and incorporation are driven by the perception that recent immigrants are overwhelmingly Arab Muslims, who are especially difficult to absorb, this is questionable because in fact over one-third of today's immigrants originated in other countries of the European Union, and because most indicators suggest that the overwhelming majority of second generation Maghrebis become culturally French.

The extremist approach to the challenge immigration poses to national integration, set forth by the new right on both sides of the Atlantic, is wilfully and dangerously wrongheaded. Dangerously so, because its demagogic appeal to the deepest fears of the white majority is designed once again to foreclose the possibility of rational discussion of the subject. Willfully so, because it is hard to imagine that anyone writing at the end of the twentieth century is so deeply ignorant of the vast literature on the subject as to build an entire argument on the archaic notion that, notwithstanding their membership in a single animal species, as demonstrated most obviously by their ability to reproduce with any other member, human beings can be neatly categorized into mutually exclusive "races", that membership in such categories determines their "culture" and "character", and that race and behaviour are linked in a static manner that enables us to make projections into the future.

That being said, the settlement of a substantial group of people who diverge markedly from a country's established cultural norms does raise legitimate concerns, which should not be dismissed as *mere* xenophobia. For example, although the anti-Catholic agitation of the 1830s has been interpreted by the distinguished historian Richard Hofstadter as a manifestation of the "paranoid style" of American politics, there were objective grounds for worrying about the impact of this immigration since in their native Ireland the Irish appeared incapable of self-improvement, and in his encyclical *Mirari Vos* (1832) Pope Gregory XVI had condemned republicanism and democracy as vociferously and absolutely as any contemporary Ayatollah. As it was, the American Roman Catholic hierarchy emerged later on as a mainstay of the church's liberal wing, and in their new environment, many of the Irish acquired what sociologists term, following Max Weber, the Protestant ethic. Similar doubts were expressed about the capacity of Jews to overcome their "ghetto" ways; but the millions who migrated westward in the nineteenth century also underwent a fundamental cultural and social transformation, while nevertheless maintaining elements of their distinctive identity. Since the end of World War II, there has been a comparable massive exodus of Muslims from the Mashreq and the Mahgreb, so that Islam is now a presence throughout Europe and the New World, evoking analogous concerns, especially in the light of fundamentalist movements in their regions of origin. Although there is no a priori reason to doubt the willingness and capacity of these immigrants to adapt, one should not minimize the toil and trouble involved on both sides.

The constructed "pasts" invoked in contemporary debates must be taken with a large grain of salt. Paralleling much of what is going on today, earlier campaigns against immigration were coupled with dire warnings that the stranger invasion fostered an irremediable deterioration of the established national culture. In the United States, for example, the response in the early decades of the twentieth century was a concerted programme of forceful "Americanization", which imposed recitation of the Pledge of Allegiance on every school child, brought the national anthem to every baseball game and music-hall, and flags on every public building every day of the week as well as from private homes on holidays. Such an outpouring of patriotic rituals, which is now taken for granted as a routine feature of American life, would raise more than eyebrows throughout Europe and abroad were it to be encouraged, say, in Germany today, as a strategy for speeding up the Germanization of former guestworkers and their offspring,

The Americanization strategy was so successful that by the 1950s "the United States was at its most insular and provincial" (Bach 1993). Bowing to necessity, the immigrant communities adapted by taming their differences; while rejecting outright assimilation *à la française*, they accepted the "melting pot" and what contemporary critics of "multiculturalism" term, approvingly, "cultural pluralism". This resulted in an amalgamated "European American" identity, manifested by a high rate of intermarriage and the virtual disappearance of other European languages to the benefit of English monolingualism, and the waning of more particularistic self-designations (Alba 1990). Nevertheless, the immigrants also brought about changes in the mainstream culture, notably a broadening of the accepted range of diversity to encompass outsider religions and European pariah groups; the penetration of alien cultural production, such as a Jewish sensibility expressed for highbrows by Saul Bellow, middlebrows by Philip Roth and Woody Allen, and lowbrows by the deliberately vulgar comedian Jackie Mason; and the domestication of stranger foods such as pizzas, bagels, gyros, and wonton soup.

To approach the complex task of incorporation today on a sound basis, we must begin by correcting distorted views of the situation. A notorious example is the racial projection that forms the centerpiece of *Alien Nation*, a virulent book published to great fanfare in the United States in 1995 (Brimelow 1995). Based on calculations by the US Bureau of the Census, the chart projects the squeezing of the white majority to a bare 52.7 percent of the population in 2050 by way of a "pincer" whose upper jaw will consist of 26.2 percent "Asian-black other" and lower one of 17.1 percent Hispanics. But what do these categories signify? For example, "Hispanic" is a recently created artifact of the United States census, and one to which many of those so categorized object, along with many serious scholars; it covers such broad cultural and phenotypical diversity that one cannot easily imagine what it would mean for one-fifth of the United States to be "Hispanic" half a century hence, notably what languages these millions will speak. Brimelow further amalgamates Hispanics with the equally diverse Asians and Blacks into a single category of "non-whites", ignoring the fairly high and growing incidence of inter-marriage of both Hispanics and Asians with whites, the frequent catego-rization of the offspring of these unions as "white", and hence the evolu-tion of the category "white" itself into a more comprehensive one termed more accurately "non-black".[10] He insists that "race is destiny"; but the gratuitous attribution of agency to what are mere administrative-statistical categories is a dangerous exercise in self-fulfilling prophecy, which is un-fortunately in tune with recent writings on international affairs that raise the dire prospect of "the Rest against the West" and warn of the coming "clash of civilizations" (Connelly & Kennedy 1994; Huntington 1993).[11] "Race" might become "destiny", but only if we make so.

One of the major challenges the receivers face is the task of reconcep-tualizing the process of incorporation itself in the light of contemporary circumstances. The theoretical apparatus available in the social sciences for dealing with this subject world-wide is derived almost entirely from the American experience of the first half of the century, as developed by successive generations of sociologists, whose profession grew largely in the service of elites concerned with immigration as a "social problem". Using mostly the theoretical imagery of assimilation, the prevailing con-ceptualization posited "a basically unilinear process of immigrant adapta-tion to the host society" (Portes and Borocz 1989). Albeit now widely criticized as a "theory", the vision retains much of its validity if it is un-derstood as an interpretation of the American historical experience, which spread beyond the confines of academia and was amalgamated into a widely accepted doctrine after World War II, when immigration was passing into the realm of memory.

How do matters stand today? Much to the dismay of nostalgic tradi-tionalists, the terms of exchange between hosts and newcomers have shifted somewhat to the benefit of the latter. Because the new wave of American immigration was contemporaneous with the civil rights move-ment and its sequels, immigrants have a greater voice from the very out-set; consequently, the process of incorporation is unfolding in a some-what more confrontational atmosphere, a development which somewhat parallels the contemporaneous transformation of racial politics. Conse-quently, as suggested by an extensive study of the American landscape mandated by the Ford Foundation, "assimilation" of the newcomers by the hosts is giving way to a process of mutual "accommodation" (Bach 1993). This has been paralleled in Europe by the institutionalization of a human rights regime at the national and regional levels, with similar con-sequences (Soysal 1994). Although some deplore the "give" by the hosts as leading to unmanageable cultural diversity, such an outcome is very unlikely because the hosts retain overwhelming advantages: incorporation is taking place on *their* turf, within an institutional framework which *they* control. Despite the critics' lamentations over the triumph of "multi-culturalism", the burden of change and adaptation remains squarely on the immigrants' shoulders.

Another significant difference is that recent arrivals can much more easily maintain contacts with their erstwhile homeland because of revolutionary transformations in transportation, information, and international relations. This has fostered an unprecedented proliferation of "transnational communities". While it is too early to tell whether or not they will stabilize in that form after the second generation, should that be the case, it would significant modify the traditional configuration of the international political system as a congeries of mutually exclusive nation-states. The outcome depends in part on actions by states of origin and destination, which hitherto have tended to demand exclusive allegiances and to oppose ambiguous statuses such as dual nationality. Should that be changed? What are the costs and benefits involved?

These developments suggest the appropriateness of a more interactive model of incorporation, which envisions hosts and newcomers as agents seeking to maximize their respective objectives as individuals and as groups, leading to changes on both sides. The older unimodal conceptualization of identity-formation as a constant-sum game, whereby the acquisition of a new identity occurs at the expense of the original one, should give way as well to a multi-modal version, which acknowledges the uniquely human capacity for additive identities, as manifested by the capacity of any member of the species to learn and use more than one language, and for transforming many aspects of the self. Over time, most immigrants are likely to develop a mix of old and new elements of identity, some comfortably integrated, others less so.

Viewed in this interactive perspective, the outcome of the process of incorporation depends not only on the characteristics of the newcomers, as emphasized by Brimelow and other LePenists, but also on the environment in which they settle. Identity-formation is shaped by ongoing experiences in the host society, embedded in concrete economic, social, political institutions that generate opportunities and constraints. Whereas in Britain and the Continent the focus has been largely on race and religion – notably the presence of Islam – in the United States the more salient issues pertain to race and language notably the widespread use of Spanish. All three are important, but do not involve the same forms of institutional arrangements. For example, with regard to race properly speaking (i.e., phenotypical characteristics), it is relatively easy to prohibit discrimination and to back this up with law-enforcement and education of the public; however, with regard to religion, it is often necessary to revise established institutional arrangements, notably where religious practice entails different days of rest, food regulations, or dress codes (Bader 1996d). The most complex is undoubtedly language, because whereas the state or an employer can be made blind to race and even to religion, they cannot be made deaf and dumb. It is also noteworthy that whereas freedom of religious practice is a well established right within the framework of political liberalism, and hence implies an obligation to at least tolerate religious diversity, liberalism does not provide guidelines with regard to fairness in the realm of language, and one might therefore expect considerable resistance to the expansion of linguistic diversity (Kymlicka 1995).

Evidence from reliable research overwhelmingly indicates that the interactions between residents and newcomers are not undermining the cohesion of host communities on either side of the Atlantic. However, on the down side, there are disturbing findings that low-skilled immigrants, including especially those of tenuous legal status, tend to be recruited into secondary labour markets, and concomitantly display isolated patterns of settlement, with little or no contact with the host society. Less of the immigrants' making than a result of structures and policies of the host society, in the absence of remedial action such undesirable patterns might be reinforced. It is therefore evident that the task of incorporation cannot be left to the free play of market forces, but requires a major commitment of public action.

In this regard, one of the most ominous aspects of the present-day situation is the deterioration of the public sphere in the receiving societies, and particularly of institutions that hitherto played a major role in incorporating new waves of immigrants, as well as the lower classes more generally, into the body politic. Among the most important are the mass political parties that arose in the late nineteenth century on both sides of the Atlantic in response to the rapid expansion of electorates, as well as the labour unions. The decline of these organizations reflects major changes in the nature of work, notably the shrinking of the urban "blue collar" sector, which commonly provided to immigrants reachable rungs on the ladder of mobility (Zolberg 1995). As well, the universal military service institutions of the age of mass armies, which played a major role in incorporating male immigrants in the United States, the overseas Commonwealth, and France in the first half of the twentieth century, have been replaced by professional bodies except in Israel, where they continue to play a vital role in socializing immigrants. Given the waning of other institutions, much of the burden of incorporation will rest by default on the educational sector, which by the same token is likely to emerge as the prime arena of contention; however, there are many reports of decline in this sphere as well.

Some of these changes are probably irreversible, and others may be highly desirable: hardly anyone would advocate the revival of major international conflicts or of the iron discipline of taylorized River Rouge and Boulogne-Billancourt automobile assembly plants just so that immigrants might be turned more easily into Americans or Frenchmen. But if not these, what can take their place? Again, one thing is clear: the dismantling of the public sector, as advocated by new-breed conservatives is likely to be highly counterproductive. Democracies cannot survive as "separate and unequal" societies.

Notes

1   My approach is drawn from a somewhat heterodox mix of insights drawn from Clifford Geertz's classic essay on national integration (Geertz 1973), Fredrik Barth's concept of "boundaries" (Barth 1969), and Benedict Anderson's emphasis on "imagined communities" (Anderson 1983). However, I am placing greater emphasis on agency in the form of sustained action by political elites, as suggested many years ago by Leonard Binder in the course of discussions of the Committee for the Comparative Study of New Nations at the University of Chicago. See also in a similar vein the concept of "mytho-moteur" or "political myth" set forth in Bader 1995b: 87 *et passim*.

2   It is also noteworthy that "foreigner" is derived from the French "forain", which is itself derived from the Latin "foris", meaning "outside", and is also the source of "foire", i.e., "fair". "Foreigners" were thus outsiders who turned up in connection with fairs in which they exercised their activities.

3   The distinction is drawn from Rogers Brubaker (Brubaker 1992). However, I do not believe a country can be neatly categorized along these lines; in reality, all formulas involve both sorts of elements, in various doses. French identity may be political rather than ethnic, but there is no doubt that it is expressed in the French language, and that "soil", hallowed by the ancestors resting in it ("La terre et les morts") – as expressed for example in the writings of 19th century nationalist writers such as Maurice Barrès – play an important part. This is applicable also to the United Stats, whose "political citizenship" was constructed as exclusively white until the 1860s, and subsequently as white and black but not Asian, and where the domain of "whiteness" initially did not encompass southern and eastern Europeans. See for more models the contributions of Castles, Hoerder, and Juteau in this volume.

4   I am grateful to Long Litt Woon, an anthropologist working in the Norwegian Government's Department of Immigrant Affairs, for pointing out the distinctiveness of "patrials" as a special category of immigrants and for suggesting how they might fit into this framework.

5   Most Jews from Iberia found havens in Islamic states, where they were incorporated into the established "millet" system, as did persecuted Spanish Muslims. However, some were eventually allowed to settle in the Dutch Republic, whose Calvinist rulers were elaborating an identity derived in part from the Old Testament.

6   It is noteworthy that in his critique of multiculturalism, Richard Bernstein similarly objects to the notion of an undifferentiated "Asian culture" (Bernstein 1994). See also Bader 1996d.

7   Although at that time the "second generation" was somewhat larger than today (12 percent), these US-born children of the great pre-1925 immigration wave were thoroughly Americanized thanks to the national mobilization experiences of World War II.

8   The explicit whiteness of the "nation of immigrants" is illustrated by the "free and white" requirement for naturalization enacted in 1790, which remained in effect

well into the twentieth century, as well as by the protracted efforts to exclude Asians, which began in the 1870s and were fully realized in 1924; with minor modifications, the exclusion remained in effect until the late 1960s.

9 The relationship of African-Americans to the "nation of immigrants"is ambiguous. Although from a demographic perspective the slave trade constituted a form of international migration, the importation of slaves is generally not included in American constructions of "immigration". Having been excluded from the "nation of immigrants", and often by-passed in the labour market by newcomers, African-Americans are generally resentful of immigration. For example, New York City Mayor Dinkins, an African-American, refused to participate in the opening ceremonies of the Ellis Island museum on the grounds that "this has nothing to do with us". Although there has been significant black immigration from the Caribbean since the 1920s, the resulting communities have striven to maintain their distinctiveness; hence unlike Mayor Dinkins, General Powell *does* see himself as a member of the "nation of immigrants".

10 The latter point is drawn from a presentation by Mary Waters at a seminar of the International Center for Migration, Ethnicity, and Citizenship at the New School in October 1996.

11 Not so coincidentally, Connelly and Kennedy's article, "The Rest against the West", begins with an extended reference to the imaginary invasion of southern France by Third World hordes depicted in the reactionary novel *The Camp of the Saints,* originally published in France in 1973 (Raspail 1995).

8 The Arts of Forecasting and Policy Making*

Veit Bader

"Words that succeed, Policies that fail"

Recent normative discussions of "first admission" policies (migration, refugee and asylum policies) show much conflict and very little consensus. All possible positions are being promoted, from completely open borders, fairly open borders, bounded openness to strictly closed borders. Proponents of *fairly open borders* have constantly been faced with counter-arguments based upon ill predictions, fears and doom-scenarios (see Bader 1997). Furthermore, they have to admit that open borders put much pressure upon processes and policies of incorporation (see WRR 1979: XXXII ff.; WRR 1989: 10f.) Apart from the difficulty of bringing about a comprehensive policy that takes the (supposed) consequences of fairly open borders into account,[1] a lot of theoretical and empirical knowledge of incorporation processes in all their dimensions (see Engbersen/Gabriels 1995; Bader 1996c) is needed. This knowledge however is contested and uncertain.

With respect to a policy of *closed borders*, quite similar problems arise. Indeed, whatever the different objectives and means of migration policies may be, policy makers signalize an *increasing demand for knowledge of and information* about root causes, structural causes, motives ("reasons"), intermediate causes of migration and its effects. To narrow the *huge gap* between this demand and the *actual knowledge and information* we command, they set up a European Migration Observatory, ask for better coordination and for a better link between fundamental and applied research in this area.[2]

At the same time the scientific community of migration researchers (and, to be fair, most policy makers too, at least on the higher levels) know quite a lot about causes and consequences of migration and see *why actual migration policies*, particularly the more restrictive versions, *fail*:

155

they are dominated by shortterm interests from the perspective of receiving states, don't cover the full range of possible and necessary interventions, are poorly coordinated, encounter enormous implementation problems, are in more or less flagrant contradiction with legal obligations, are in serious tension with requirements of successful incorporation, do not fit easily in the constitutional framework of liberal democracy. The cry for *more comprehensive*, long-term, internationally co-ordinated migration (and refugee) *policies* is getting louder and louder. This growing quest for control *contrasts starkly with* our growing awareness of the *very limited capacities* of international and governmental organizations *to steer and control*.

In sum, we are confronted with two pressing problems: (i) the knowledge and information base with respect to migration and incorporation policies is limited, contested and uncertain; (ii) the political capacities to control and steer those processes are limited. Nevertheless we are *doomed to policy making*.[3]

In this programmatic article I will discuss these two issues: section I addresses problems regarding the limits of scientific knowledge and presents a model of critical scientific expertise; section II discusses the limits of politics.

I   FROM FORECASTING TO SCENARIO-MODELLING. CRITICAL SCIENTIFIC EXPERTISE AND DEMOCRATIC POLITICS

1   Limits of Prediction in Social Sciences

All proactive actors, huge organizations and governments in particular, are greatly interested to know the future, to learn about the effects of their actions and about unintended consequences and side-effects: "savoir pour prévoir, prévoir pour pouvoir" (from the French Enlightenment to "social engineering"). Increasingly, the social sciences have been enticed into *Zukunftsforschung,* in economics, demography, ecology, technology as well as in organizational science. Modelling the future is a hot topic and expanded enormously in the last two decades. For quite a while it has been difficult to resist the temptation scientifically to predict economic and demographic developments and at least some scientists still cling to forecasting. The Cassandric role is obviously tempting and the demand pressing. However, as we all know by now, prediction in general, and in the social sciences in particular, is impossible for a number of reasons:

(i) Prediction in a strict sense is only possible in *closed systems*[4]. If the actual complexities are drastically reduced, closed systems can be realized in theoretical models. But even in physics it is often extremely difficult to achieve experimental closure, let alone in social sciences and humanities. Even if it were possible to construct theoretical models of complex migration-systems and of their development (see below), actual migration takes place in a highly complex, contingent and open world.

(ii) Prediction presupposes *deterministic laws* or law-like generalizations and *closed futures*. Our social world does not match such a conception: contingency and open futures restrict the possibility of constructing theoretical models of closed systems of migration that have sufficient explanatory power.

(iii) Theoretical models presuppose a high degree of *reduction of complexity*. Actual migration is caused and influenced by a great variety of independent and dependent variables and characterized by their complex causal interaction and by retrograde and cumulative causation.

Apart from these general reasons, which hold for all sciences, strict prediction in the social world (by social science) is impossible for two additional reasons:

(iv) *Strategic interactions* have, in principal, unintended consequences (expectations of expectations of expectations) and unforeseeable side effects. The strategies and actions of the many actors involved in migration processes contravene each other and the result of their interaction is beyond the control and foresight of every party.

(v) *Predictions themselves* do influence and *change expectations and actions* and, in doing so, undermine their own validity: self-fulfilling as well as *self-destructing prophecies*. E.g., the discussion and announcement of restrictions in the Netherlands during the 70s "caused" a prompt and huge stream of migration.

As of the Seventies, the limits of forecasting became increasingly evident after "megamistakes" in demographic, economic, technological predictions had been recognized. *System-dynamic modelling* and the construction of *scenarios* made their entry in different disciplines.[5] Instead of extrapolating trends or simulating the possible effects of policies, scenario-research takes into account a heterogeneity of theoretical models and empirical methods, the insecurity of a lot of data (validity and sensitivity-analysis), different normative and political objectives and, perhaps most important, interactive and retrograde causality: path-dependent sequences of change in which policies do matter. Moreover, it presupposes an open and contingent future (Bader/v.d. Berg 1993: 70-4). This development results, on the one hand, in a much more modest role for the scientist, who resists implicit normative and political biases and accepts dissent within scientific communities. On the other hand, this type of research opens up political alternatives and paths that otherwise may be eliminated under the guise of "science"; it resists the danger of *Verwissenschaftlichung der Politik* as well as the opposite danger of *Irrationalisierung der Politik*.

2 Scientific expertise between expertocratic politics and armchair reflection

According to Benjamin Barber "the need for politics arises when some action of public consequence becomes necessary and when men must thus make a public choice that is reasonable in the face of conflict despite the absence of an independent ground of judgment" (Barber 1984:122). The *political situation* is one of high complexity, contingency, unpredictability and open futures. Action includes all forms of doing, not only deliberating, talking. It is necessarily "enmeshed in events that are part of a train of cause and effect" that cannot be stopped or bracketed (as in Habermasian discourses): non-decisions are decisions, waiting is doing. Consensus being absent, choices between different, often starkly conflicting options have to be made.

This pragmatist, democratic view of politics that presupposes the absence of an independent ground, of reason with the capital R,[6] does not entail irrationality or the fashionable praise of Will, Decision, Power and Aesthetics, but appeals to reasonableness and political judgement (see Barber 1988: 15, 194, 199). Uncertainty and contingency are not seen as the paramount danger but as the possibility and precondition for political freedom and action.

Such a concept of politics implies an *important but inherently limited role for science*, presupposing a critical reflection upon the specific character of scientific knowledge and its limits. In this respect it seems essential that scientists don't present themselves as normative experts; that they don't impose their own normative and political choices under the guise of scientific expertise; that they don't narrow but rather widen the scope of possible alternatives for democratic action; that they don't conceal but rather explicate the full degree of dissent within science; that they are always eager to say what they cannot or do not know, and what they do know with which degree of certainty. To elaborate this *minima moralia* of a democratic ethics of science, let me stress the following points.

2.1 Cognitive, normative, and expressive aspects of knowledge

If cognitive, normative and expressive aspects of knowledge are analytically distinguished, it will be evident that science is specialized in cognitive knowledge (see Bader 1988). Anyway, scientists cannot claim to have any superior knowledge in normative and expressive questions, and, given their self-understanding of the dominant intellectual division of labour, they don't openly claim such an expertise. However, this has never prevented them from a kind of hidden export of their own normative and political views, covered by the prestige of science. If scientists overstretch their case, this will usually only be revealed by outright attacks, be it by social movements and/or contra-expertise. In the normal working of social sciences a lot of unrecognized "truth-power" is at work.[7] Migration-researchers, evidently, are no experts with regard to moral problems concerning state sovereignty and borders and, consequently, should not behave like that.

2.2 Norms and interests in scientific research

The old myth of a completely neutral, impartial, objective science hides the fact that norms and interests play a considerable and important role in scientific research. They carry weight with:

- *Objectives* of research. Who determines the normative ends and chooses the subject? What is seen as a problem and by whom (scientists, governmental organizations, NGO's, migrants etc.)? "Who pays and who determines"?[8] What are the specific research questions: e.g. explain why specific policies of migration-control fail (in whose eyes?) A neutral answer to these questions is not even thinkable: *heterogeneity of normative and political ends*.

- Choice of *disciplines*. Mainstream paradigms in disciplines do have their - hidden or open - bias. If migration studies is a multi-disciplinary enterprise or an "art" (see below), is there a tacit or explicit hegemony of a specific discipline? *Heterogeneity of disciplines*.

- *Concept-formation*. Basic concepts (e.g. migration), in social sciences are highly contested. *Heterogeneity of concepts*.

- *Pro-theoretical frames* for theory-building and explanation. Highly complex social structures and developments cannot be unravelled on just one level or from one approach. The choice of frames is - implicitly or explicitly - informed and directed by normative perspectives.

- Choice of *theory*. Theories are answers to specific explanation-seeking-why-questions. How to explain actual decisions to move? There is no unified catch-all theory to explain everything: *heterogeneity of theoretical presuppositions*. The "choice of theory" has normative implications.

- Choice of *models* and modelling, e.g. highly detailed, disaggregated quantitative models under *ceteris paribus* conditions (constructed closure of systems) vs. global qualitative system-dynamic models.

- Hypotheses and operationalizations; choice of *methods* (quantitative, qualitative; "calibrating" and "fitting" of models; choice of times and paths of reference in comparative research). *Heterogeneity of empirical methods.*

- Judgement of *data* (choice of relevant information; examination of relevant data with respect to criteria like completeness, validity and reliability; if any extrapolation-techniques are used: sensitivity-analysis).
- *Stop* or *continuation* of research. Where, when and in which direction?
- *Application of results.*

I am strongly convinced that none of these choices can be made in a purely cognitive way. As already stated, ethics of science presses the scientist to spell out as explicitly as possible the respective normative and political considerations. But ethics in itself is not sufficient: it has to be complemented by internal and external democratic institutional safeguards and a critical democratic culture.

2.3 How to deal with complexity: pro-theory, theory, research, arts

Migration has complex causes and effects. Migration policy means to intervene in this complex situation. But scientific migration theories and research have to reduce this complexity in order to be possible at all. I propose a controlled approach to handle this complexity-problem in four steps (see Bader 1992):

(1) At a *pro-theoretical level* the problem is to generate a sufficiently complex frame of reference: *how to introduce sufficient complexity* in our scientific thinking about migration.[9] Its task is threefold: to criticize overgeneralizations and obviously undercomplex "explanations" (e.g. without "intermediate" variables); to stimulate the development of specific theories; to serve as a frame of reference for empirical research.

(2) At a *theoretical level* the problem is to *reduce complexity* and to choose the *adequate level of complexity* to spell out causal relations. To this end one has to have clearly delineated *explanation-seeking-why-questions* and to articulate *spaces of contrast.*[10] E.g., to explain the origin of migration-streams is not the same as to explain the ongoing of streams; to explain direct structural causes of migration-streams is not the same as to explain the reasons why people move (some move, others don't in similar/same situations (see Lonergan/Parnwell 1995)); to point out structural causes is not the same as to explain the specific destination of migration.[11] To indicate the direct structural causes in the sending and receiving countries is not the same as to analyse "root causes" (and again: how and when to stop the "chain of causes"?); Why do governments react differently in different times and countries? etc. The idea that one unified theory could answer all these different questions resembles the silly expectation that one map of the entire globe would do for planning a transoceanic flight as well as a climb on an extremely difficult mountain (see Christis 1993). To construct theories with causal, explanatory power, one

has to design closed systems ("thought-experiments") on different levels (macro, meso, micro; sending and receiving countries; intermediate structures etc.).[12]

(3) Although causal laws are decontextualized, in all *empirical research* "theories" are used to explain phenomena in specific contexts.[13] Theories should lead to specified explanatory hypotheses (reference-time and path added). They are to be tested (not "falsified") in research. Because of the "underdetermination of theory by data" no definitive confirmation or refutation is possible: true explanations always remain open for doubt and revision. This should not be misunderstood as scepticism: we have good and true answers for the time being and that is all we need (anyway, it is all we can have). The specificity of all empirical research-questions implies that not all aspects of migration can be analysed at one and the same time and from one perspective. Our empirical knowledge remains fragmentary, but this is no problem for science. We have time, we can go on, there is no necessity to act.

(4) *Arts of intervention, either as adviser or directly as policy maker.*[14] Here the reverse problem is *how to create sufficient sensitivity for the actual complexity* of the political situation and how to bridge the gap between "sciences" and "practices". Dichotomically presented, the differences can be summarized as follows:

- Sciences and practices each have their own, specific *problems*: for the sciences the problem is to find the truth. The contested and incomplete character of knowledge is not a problem but the source and fuel of *ongoing scientific research* (theoretical and empirical).[15] For practices, particularly for migration-policies, the problem is to arrive at a relative *successful intervention: ongoing decisions and actions.* Where scientific knowledge is not available, or is contested, uncertain, incomplete, fragmentary or whatever, one has to act in the "absence of truth".
- In science, the relevant criterion to judge knowledge is *truth*, in practices the criteria are *usefulness and effectiveness*. For practical problems (to be solved in time and under pressure) truth may be irrelevant or even counterproductive and it is always misleading to mix it up with effectiveness (don't disturb engineers building bridges with problems of non-classical mechanics).[16]
- Science has to reduce the complexity of the world (of migration) drastically, whereas practices cannot skirt this complexity. Practices usually *cut across scientific disciplines*; if they are informed by "practical" or "applied sciences"[17] these have to be *multi-disciplinary* and focused on the problems to be solved in practice, not on disciplinary problems of the respective sciences.

- Sciences usually concentrate on *propositionally articulated, abstract, general knowledge* and decontextualized theories, while practices have to rely on *tacit, specific, contextual, practical or personal knowledge and on experience* (good sense, feeling, virtues and traditions of judgement, ways of doing).[18] Only an arrogant, outdated version of "constructivist rationalism" may still hold that practical knowledge is not only a different, but also an inferior type of knowledge. Practical knowledge and experience may help as rules of thumb in highly complex and open situations where "certain" propositions definitively fail. If practical disciplines get institutionalized (in academic teaching and research) they have to bridge the gap between sciences/theories and "practice".[19]
- For lots of scientists openness and *contingency* still seem to be ultimate *challenges*, whereas for practitioners they indicate *freedom of action* and opportunities to change the future.

`Taken together these differences could nicely be illustrated by the old and ongoing quarrels between "pure sciences", "applied sciences" and "technai and artes". The latter, answering practical problems in a pragmatic, multi-disciplinary way, systematically try to bridge the gap between theories and practice, between propositional and practical knowledge. They have to open the eyes, ears and all other senses of practitioners for the complexity rightly excluded from scientific theories.

2.4   Types of policy research: critical analysis of ends? of means? of effects?

Policies, including migration-policies, are increasingly a legitimate subject of scientific inquiry. Sociologists and political scientists can be excellent in explaining why specific policies have been designed, implemented and, particularly, why they fail. However, this doesn't make them good policy-advisers or policy makers: policy-advising and making requires different knowledge, skills and experiences, as we have seen. Policyresearch, therefore, has clearly to be distinguished from policy-advising and making. Let me stress a few points:

The fact that social scientists as cognitive experts cannot claim any specific expertise in normative questions does not mean that *scientific analysis and critique of values*, norms, and ends would be impossible. Even from a strictly Weberian perspective ends (as articulated by governments) can be analysed and criticized cognitively: they may be *inconsistent or incompatible* with each other. Restrictive migration-policies and deflection-regimes in refugee-policies may be incompatible with proclaimed protection of human rights and with legal obligations; they may be incompatible with standards of justice (peace, security, fair international distribution); they may be incompatible with successful comprehensive incorporation-policies; they may be inconsistent with enlightened long-term interests (pensions, social security).[20] In addition, the *means* to realize these ends may be inadequate, counterproductive or *incompatible with other highly valued ends*: restrictive migration-policies may be infeasible, short-term oriented and lopsided; complete border-control and domestic inspection may be incompatible with global capitalist market economy and surely are incompatible with liberal-democratic constitutional norms.

Also, bracketing these moral problems, policy research can try to *describe and explain*: when and why migration became a problem; why specific ends have been chosen and changed (and when, by whom (coalitions of collective political actors), under which (economic, political, cultural) conditions); how comprehensive they are;[21] why and to which degree they succeed or fail.[22]

These kinds of research provide a lot of - contested and fragmentary - knowledge and detailed information highly relevant for policy-makers. But policy research can also try to answer difficult questions regarding *expected effects* of migration-policies. Given the restrictions and limits of our possible knowledge of the future, these answers are much more contested and piecemeal than those of descriptive and explanatory policy research. But in itself, the problems of scientific policy research do not significantly differ from the normal problems of empirical social science in general. Its specific problems result from the fact that this research is often ordered by governments and that its results are used in policy-advising and policy-making. This entails, firstly, that the results of scientific policy research are not "worthless" for the design of successful migration-policies: it can produce highly relevant causal knowledge and information and open up alternative futures. At the same time, policy research is anything but sufficient: policy-making is an "art" and a practice, not a science; and, secondly, that scientists enter into a different system or context in which different criteria and different power-relations prevail.

2.5 Policy research, policy advice and power

No extensive discussion of the tricky relation between science and politics is intended here. I confine myself to stress the different roles of scientists and "artists of intervention" (be they advisers or policy-makers, because advising is already policy-making): the one is an expert in dealing with scientific problems of truth, the other is an expert in tackling practical problems of successful intervention. These different roles interfere in different and not always harmonious ways.

To begin with: a lot of policy research is *ordered and paid for by governmental institutions*: who pays determines? To indicate only the most evident problems: (1) a (normative) critique of the ends of policies is often not welcome ("take it or leave it"); (2) the influence of scientists on the formulation of the problem is often limited; (3) the research is done under severe time and budget-restraints; (4) it is often difficult to defend the necessary cognitive autonomy in design and execution; (5) publication of the results is often restricted; (6) scientists are not in control of what is done with the results in bureaucracies and politics; even very prestigious and powerful scientists are generally unable to counter the use of "truth" in a completely distorted form; (7) many scientists have considerable difficulties to resist the temptations of "truth-power": they often cross the border between cognitive expertise and outright normative and political intervention.

These problems are the more pressing and evident when *scientists* play the part of *policy advisers and policy makers*. Scientists, then, play in a different game, whether they realize it or not. At stake is not truth but intervention, power to decide and act, and success. The specific role of scientific knowledge in policies can be elucidated by two simplistic models. At one pole one finds the adherents of a so-called *analytic-rational model*: policies are considered to be rationally designed and executed; problems can be rationally analysed and solved; more and better scientific knowledge leads to a consensus regarding the "one best way" of achieving objectives. At the other pole one finds the adherents of a *conflict or bargaining model*: problems don't have any natural order or hierarchy; they are constructed in the political realm by competing actors with differential powers and capacities to define; the design and execution of policies is a process of ongoing bargaining and conflict between competing collective actors (public, semi-public and private) with conflicting interests, power-bases, strategies and perspectives. There are no 'one-best-way' solutions, neither in principle nor in practice.[23] In the first model, scientific knowledge plays a paramount and undistorted role: scientific policies (*Verwissenschaftlichung von Politik und Verwaltung* and *End of Ideology*). In the second, scientific knowledge plays a minor and heavily politically moulded role: if it is effective at all, it is for political, not for 'scientific' reasons. The first model obviously fails for at least two reasons: First, it grossly overestimates the capacities of scientific knowledge and it underestimates its limitations, particularly its troubles in dealing with situations of high complexity; secondly, it completely neglects the different system-contexts of science and politics and is, as a consequence, awfully 'innocent' with regard to the transformation of truth into power. The second model, at least in its cynical and over-politicized versions, leaves no room for rational analysis and critique of knowledge and information used and processed in political problem-definition and decision making. Besides, both models are, normatively speaking, quite unattractive for good democratic policies.

The actual interplay is much more complicated than those two extremes suggest.[24] Quite roughly, it depends upon:

- the specific *structure of bureaucracies*: qualification, recruitment, career-patterns; relations between staff and line; internal decision-making powers; specific organizational cultures, etc.[25]
- the overall institutional and political *context* and dominant *style of politics*.[26]
- the structure and quality of *public discourse*.[27]

(4) the relative *balance of power* inside bureaucracies and of bureaucracies in relation to other collective political actors, including scientific institutions.[28]

(5) the specific *stage in the policy cycle*: what is an issue or 'problem', what are the possible alternatives to tackle it, which alternative is chosen, implemented, how to control and evaluate, how to change).[29]

(6) the *degree in which an issue is already politicized*. The potential influence of scientific or pseudo-scientific definitions of 'real issues' and 'true problems' will be obviously much higher, in case an issue is not yet politicized.[30]

Empirically, there are obviously *many options* between the polar extremes of *Verwissenschaftlichung der Politik* and a complete subsumption or neglect of scientific research.[31]

2.6 Towards a critical interaction between science and politics

Normatively, the preferred option requires a fruitful interaction between critical scientific expertise and democratic politics. In all political debate, in all political decision making, a huge amount of knowledge and information is used and processed. Critical scientists as cognitive experts in specific fields can and should play an important role both as critics (of priorities of issues, of misleading conceptualizations and framings, of evidently wrong causal claims and insufficient, irrelevant or false information) as well as in presenting alternatives (other links between issues, more fruitful concepts and frames, better and more relevant information, other possible ends, directions and means of policies etc.). A fruitful interaction presupposes, firstly, that scientists (including policy researchers), supported by a scientific culture that stimulates plurality, criticism and contra-expertise inside and between disciplines and arts, indicate with great scrutiny the limits of their cognitive expertise. Secondly, it presupposes conditions external to science, like a lively and critical public opinion, including politically mobilized contra-expertise, science hearings, 'performative' debates in which not only the different cognitive claims of disciplines are evaluated but also the conflicts and tensions between cognitive, normative and expressive claims. Essential facilitators and stimuli of such reasonable democratic talk are a democratic structure and culture of media, an effective use of all freedoms of political communication by social movements, NGOs, political parties, and structures and cultures of democratic governance. To the degree that these two conditions are fulfilled, a roughly symmetrical form of communication between sciences, the arts of intervention, and politics may develop,[32] the beginning of *reasonable politics* - opposed to 'rationalism in politics' (Oakshott) - urgently needed for realistic politics in the perspective of an associative democracy.

II   Limits of Politics: increasing 'quest for control' and limited capacities for control

Section I summarized the reasons why we are unable to predict the development of complex systems of migration. But even if a 'comprehensive scientific understanding' would be possible or available (as is suggested in v. Amersfoort a.o. 1995:5f), the scope and the effectiveness of politics and policies would not only be limited because of 'false and limited assumptions', and of ignorance of already available knowledge and information. Even if we (scientists, practitioners, policy-makers) could and did know all we want to know and if we had sufficient high quality information, we could not achieve what we want, for a number of well-known reasons. I confine myself to a summary of the most important ones without going into any detailed discussion.

(1) The old notion of controlling and *steering societies from one centre*, the state, has lost its credibility for reasons of principle and practice: (i) functional and institutional differentiation: with respect to autonomous 'autopoetic systems' and organizations, direct, operational control or steering from the outside is impossible; it would mean 'repressive de-differentiation' and the loss of all benefits of differentiation. (ii) The state-specific means of steering (law and legal violence) are not always effective and other means (like money and persuasion) are scarce, limited. (iii) States are not the only powerful actors interested in steering and control. In sum: states can promise comprehensive control but they cannot deliver. Many important causes of migration remain outside their span of control and cannot be influenced at all; or they cannot be influenced given the present institutional system (capitalist market economies, liberal-democratic constitutions, bureaucratic governance); or they cannot be influenced in the short- or medium term.

(2) *Politics* in itself is a highly *complex* and differentiated phenomenon, including many actors, many levels, many fields and arenas:

(i) The relevant *actors* for migration policies are: international organizations (e.g. UNHCR); supra-national units (EU); intergovernmental committees; foreign states (of sending and receiving countries); governments (different branches, departments and levels); NGOs; political parties; social movements and SMOs; organizations of migrants and refugees; the electorate; migrants; different kinds of "employers" and their organizations; trade unions. Actual migration policies result from strategic interactions between all these collectives and individuals,[33] and as such they are beyond the control of every one of them; they are volatile and lack consistency and continuity; they are unpredictable and have many unintended consequences and unwanted side-effects.

(ii) Official, authorized first admission policies are designed and executed on *different levels of government*: municipal, provincial, state, federal, intergovernmental, regional, international. Even within states this necessarily involves heterogeneity and lack of consistency (differences in objectives, timing, implementation) and limits of control. On an interstate level policies often directly contradict or contravene each other.

(iii) Different *branches and departments* are concerned with and affected by migration and refugee policies: judiciary, legislative and executive. Within the executive branch: departments of foreign affairs, of interior, economics, finance, social affairs, housing, education (no matter how Immigration and Naturalization Services may be institutionalized). These branches often block each other's business, constitutionally (judicial control) or otherwise; they have divergent objectives, perspectives, cultures and styles. As a result, a coherent migration policy across-the-board is extremely unlikely.[34]

Because of this differentiation, all possible policies are confronted with at least two general problems: coordination-problems and implementation-problems:

(3) *Coordination problems* of first admission policies recently draw much attention, particularly in the international arena.[35] The first problem is, of course, to find some minimal consensus regarding ends and objectives. Inside the EU this meant levelling down the normative standards of asylum-policies to the lowest common denominator: states can always legitimize their restrictive measures by pointing to other states. The second problem is to tackle the well-known dilemmas and *paradoxes of collective action*.

(4) To design a coherent migration policy is one thing, to *implement* it is quite another: (i) a lot of political talk and text is just "politics of symbolic action", not even meant to be realized in practice; (ii) all civil services have their official texts and onstage appearances as well as their hidden texts and normal offstage practices; (iii) implementation is not

only hindered juridically (see Hathaway, Groenendijk), by the fragmentation of civil services (levels and departments) and by inertia of cultures, habits and routines, but quite often also by unforeseen costs and restricted budgets. The well-known result of all this is that the actual policies at municipal and provincial levels often differ considerably and are not in line with the centrally proclaimed policy.

(5) The specific institutions of capitalist market society, together with recent neo-liberal politics (see Brodie/Gabriel 1995) limit and weaken the scope of possible intervention and control substantially. *States in capitalist societies* are relatively *weak and poor*. The weakness or even absence of governance is particularly evident *on a global level*. With the development of Keynesian Welfare- and Intervention States, internal mechanisms and means of steering as well as some transnational institutions and mechanisms of regulation evolved (Piore/Sabel 1984; Hirst/Thompson 1996). However, the "crisis of the welfare state" combined with neo-liberal reactions weakened both forms of governance. While states are getting weaker and multinational corporations are getting stronger and richer, lots of "global" problems ask for much stronger forms of international governance:[36] poverty and drastic "North/South" economic cleavages, ecological disasters, civil wars and ethnic cleansings. These "root causes" of migration are, of course, not "principally" and "forever" out of the reach of political intervention and control, but they surely are out of the reach of the existing institutions and mechanisms of governance.[37] Asking for more comprehensive migration-policies either entails a quest which self-consciously has to go far beyond the existing institutional settings, or it just means a very selective "comprehensiveness" in the mutual interest of the rich North-West-Atlantic states: keep the Unwanted out as long as possible. The latter, of course, is a much more sober and adequate description of most current governmental and intergovernmental initiatives. To outline the former goes far beyond the intent of this chapter.

CONCLUSION

The predominant division of intellectual labour has relegated "moral questions" from science to *moral and political philosophy*. Philosophers, of course, cannot solve our practical normative problems (see Bader 1997) and if only for this it would be silly to make them kings. Still they can contribute to the reasonableness of our normative debates: not by replacing citizens and politicians, but by participating *as citizens* (public or political intellectuals) in public discourse.

Social *scientists*, policy advisers and administrators can, and should, clarify the cognitive knowledge and information needed for democratic debate, decision making and action in the fields of first admission and incorporation policies. They too should participate in public discourse *as citizens* (see Barber 1988: 199, 201). Criticism of unfounded claims of philosophers and of scientists depends on a lively, plural and powerful public opinion. The gap between the normative requirements central to any elaborate concept of associative, strong or procedural democracy and the actual working of media and public opinion is enormous and disquieting.[38] However, this should not make us despair: there are important empirical differences regarding the degree of information, qualification and critical power of public opinions in different countries, fields, periods. And normatively too, most interesting questions are matters of degree.

If one distinguishes clearly between "comprehensive control", "comprehensive government" and "comprehensive governance" (Hirst 1994, Hirst /Thompson 1996), claims for more *comprehensive migration and incorporation policies* are neither impossible nor discredited, quite to the contrary. If "we" (even in the restricted sense of the governments of rich Northern states) prove to be unable to find convincing answers to the aforementioned global problems, our policies will be doomed to fail: muddling through from one crisis to the next. It is true that our quest for control is limited, but there are better or worse ways of dealing with these limits. The limits resulting from the predominant institutional structures (capitalist market economy, weak or absent institutions and mechanisms of international governance) should not cause apathy but concerted efforts to overcome these institutional limitations. The required changes are radical but so are the causes and symptoms of the "disease". A conclusion is not the place to discuss even the outlines of such institutional changes. In any conceivable model of feasible, multi-layered, comprehensive governance, states, particularly powerful states, still have to play a prominent role (see Hirst/Thompson 1996). At present, design and implementation of new institutions and mechanisms of governance are impeded by neo-liberal theory and politics. Realists tell us that such new governance is wishful thinking (and sociologist may join them in their scepticism). But practical and political beings have to act and change, and practical philosophers may tell us that we cannot do so without hope and some utopia. Reflective thinking can show us that we cannot know in advance what is possible and that we cannot find out without trying: if we trusted the sceptics, we wouldn't try and, thus, we would do the wrong thing anyway (see Bader 1991: 454).

Our insights into both the limits of scientific knowledge and into the limits to our quest for control are not without consequences for politics and policies. They do not directly lead us into conservatism (as Oakshott made us believe) or into neo-liberal politics of *dethronement of politics* (as Hayek thought). But they surely are incompatible with "scientistic" and "technocratic" politics and with many strong versions of republican *enthronement of politics*.[39] Something like *institutionalization of regret* into politics is minimally asked for (see Barber 1984:307-11). Once underway, we not only have to monitor and correct ourselves, but must also take care not to burn our bridges to avoid mega-mistakes and catastrophes as a consequence of mega-plans and mega-forecasting.

Notes

* I made ample use of unpublished manuscripts by Jac Christis whom I particularly want to thank for his critical comments and suggestions. I am also indebted to Ton Korver, Marja Gastelaars, Ewald Engelen, Klaske de Jong and Rinus Penninx.

1 This is not only empirically evident but it entails a normative conundrum as well: a good and comprehensive politics of incorporation is an internal moral requirement, owed to citizens and residents, and it may require at least some effective control of migration streams (see Bader 1997).

2 See de Jong 1995, Lonergan/Parnwell 1995, Goodwin-Gill 1994; Adelman 1995, Whitaker 1995; Amersfoort/Doomernik/Penninx 1995, Hathaway 1995.

3 In spite of neo-liberal claims to the contrary, *laissez-faire* politics, relying on "markets and social evolution" ("wait and see" and do not intervene), is not policy-free. It is - in apparent contradiction to libertarian assumptions - in favour of strict border controls and restricts the span of governance of democratic politics of international organizations as well as inside states. As is well-known and obvious by now, it works in favour of the rich, strong, and powerful. The recent dominant neo-liberal discourse tries to sell its ideology as an "End of Ideology", its planning (for a capitalist world market for multinational corporations) as "End of Planning", and its politics of "limiting democratic politics" as apolitical necessity of "free and efficient market allocation". Free flow of capital and information (as an ideology, not as a practice!) is evidently not accompanied by "free movement of people" (particularly not of the "unwanted migrants"). See Hirst/Thompson 1996.

4 See Bhaskar 1975; Sayer 1984: 182 ff.; Humphreys 1989.

5 See Dewulf 1991; Schnaars 1989. See Meadows (1972) as a forerunner. See also: Meadows 1991; CPB 1992; Luhmann 1990: 631. See Sayer 1984: 183f. for a critique of the "reductionist" and the "interactionist regress" in modelling. See Bader/v.d. Berg 1993: 70f. for system-dynamic modeling.

6 'Where there is certain knowledge, true science, or absolute right, there is no conflict that cannot be resolved by reference to the unity of truth, and thus there is no necessity for politics ... Where consensus stops, politics starts' (Barber 1984: 129). 'Where reason claims to speak, politics is silent' (Barber 1988: 205).

7 This normal working of science, stressed by "strong programme research", is neatly cleaned out in Luhmann's construction of the science-system as an autonomous, autopoetic system governed by the binary code true/untrue. What in the historical development of science was "Autoritätsverlust" is now presented as "Autoritätsverzicht". Science 'kann auf Anfrage nicht mehr antworten: so ist es, so macht es' (1990: 634, 641). But that is exactly what is still going on.

8 See Penninx 1992, Amersfoort a.o. 1995: 11f for evaluating judgments of "positive" vs. "negative effects" of migration: whose norms? whose perspective? whose definitions?

9 See Amersfoort/Penninx 1995: 12 ff. for a heuristic model of a "set of variables in migration processes" (including root causes, direct causes, intermediate structures in

sending and receiving societies), that should not be misunderstood as "theory". See Hoerder 1997 (in this volume).

10 See Garfinkel 1981. One has not only to ask "why x" but "why x and not y" to prevent the whole world of being relevant for a specific explanation.

11 As to historical explanations, there has to be enough room for the role of sheer contingency: e.g. the first place of settlement in an ensuing migration-chain. See Bader 1991: 334f. The role of contingency is nearly neglected by Sayer 1984: 190, 291 (note 33).

12 All causal explanations are confronted with the problem of the 'multiplicity, diversity and epistemic incompleteness of causes' (Humphreys 1989, ch.1). Because of the multiplicity of causes the world does not show empirical regularities. To test our causal laws we therefore design experiments in which we try to transform the world from an open system into a closed one. Although in the open system of the real world (of migration) the regularities may disappear, causes retain - at least for a realist account - their transfactual causal power. Otherwise we would be unable to make practical use of our knowledge of causes (which should not be interpreted as empirical regularities but as structures and tendencies). Because of the incompleteness of causes we have to distinguish between correct and complete explanations. Complete explanations of an event would involve the explanation of the whole world (the whole chain of causes). Causal laws should not be interpreted as universal regularities.

13 "Science-models", here understood as a specific combination from type of theory and type of method, play an important role on the route from "theory" to research. "Positivism" (a combination of a "deductive-nomological theory" and prediction), "hermeneutics" (understanding of meaning), "systems-theory" ("Problembezug" and functional analysis), and "realism" (causal structures and explanations) are well-known examples of such models. They also imply different relations between theory and practice.

14 See Luhmann's discussion of the outlines of a "generalized concept of therapy" and of a "general theory of interventions" which starts from three premises: (1) if the system in which "science" intervenes, is itself an autopoetic system, it has the same characteristics ("Selbstreferenz, Selbstorganisation, Autonomie"); (2) there is no "context free" knowledge which could be "transferred": (3) there are no "observers" which cannot themselves be "observed" (reiterative observations).

15 With regard to migration there remains a whole bunch of questions where policy research cannot give clear-cut and unambiguous answers, starting from: how can we influence "root causes" of migration, and if we can, with what chances of success? How to influence the different direct structural causes in sending countries? the migration-decisions of different classes or groups of potential migrants? the intermediate structures? etc. ending with: how to design relatively consistent migration-policies in a densely populated political arena where the collective actors and organizations do have conflicting interests and diverging strategies? How to overcome resistance inside governmental departments and how to streamline their different policies? How to prevent rightwing backlashes? How to overcome paradoxes of collective action in international co-ordination? etc.

16 See Christis 1995 for a very short outline. See Bader 1991: 172 ff.

17 The recently growing multi-disciplinarity inside academia (focused on practical problems: e.g. "migration and ethnic studies") creates a lot of strain with the existing institutionalization of disciplines and faculties.

18 Recently the insight is growing that sciences themselves are "practices" (see Bourdieu, Latour, Knorr-Cetina), but they are practices with a different goal! The awareness of the importance of practical knowledge has to be freed from a predominant

"conservative bias". It must be enough here to mention Gramsci, Wittgenstein, Michael Polany, Hayek (who really was not a "conservative"), Barber, Bourdieu, Schoen.

19 This is evident from all education and practice of engineering (civil engineering, chemical engineering, etc. see Sarlemijn 1984, 1995). If one compares the model of a good, reflective medical practitioner with other examples (e.g. in the field of public administration, management, socio-technology, ecology or migration/incorporation-studies) it is evident that the "ends" of the latter sciences are normatively much more contested ("health" vs. "closed borders"), that these sciences are much "softer", that the practical and institutional context is more conflict-loaded etc. See generally: Luhmann 1990: 642, 646: in all "output"-relations of science (normally conceived of as "pure" vs. "applied science") the focus is not on the "function of the system" but on its performance for other systems. It becomes increasingly clear that (1) all scientific knowledge is insecure. (2) Scientific experts become politicized; (3) the limits of technicization in the applications become clear; (4) keeping distance becomes crucial; (5) complexity of performances becomes evident.

20 See Bader 1991: 145f. for a short discussion of the "slippery slope" implicated in a direct normative evaluation of ends. See Keat (1981) for a lucid presentation of such a "Weberian" perspective.

21 At which points in migration-streams do they try to intervene? Why are they so often focused on control of entry of the receiving states? (See Korver 1997) In whose interest is this? When and how is the scope of intervention broadened? When and how is it aimed at inter-governmental and international coordination? How and why do they differ in different states as well as inside states (implementation on state, regional, local levels)?

22 To evaluate the effectiveness of policy-research in politics, Penninx has suggested a useful distinction between the different objects of research: (a) new or revised definitions of problems and normative objectives of policy; (b) knowledge and information regarding the "instrumentation of policies": which variables can be influenced in which way? (c) evaluate existing policies: why and to which degree do they succeed or fail? (4) exploration of new issues and processes. (Penninx 1992: 19).

23 See Penninx 1992: 4f. for references. See March/Olson 1989: 11f.

24 See Luhmann's illuminating critique of the old model of "transfer of knowledge" which neglects complexity-problems, treats the fields of interventions as black boxes and ignores the 'loss of authority of science' (1990: 649) on the one hand, and his critique of the metaphor of "negotiation" on the other. Compared to Luhmann's analysis I put much more emphasis on (asymmetries and shifts in) power relations.

25 It seems plausible that the potential influence of good policy-research and advice is much higher in departments with highly qualified professionals (similar background, same academic institutions, lots of formal and informal networks etc.), with flexible and open recruitment- and career policies, with a good overlap between competence and discretion, with a responsive, open and democratic internal culture.

26 It seems plausible that "enlightened autocracies" (from absolute monarchies to "real existing, scientific socialism") give more leeway to pseudo-science which "fits" into its line; scientistic and expertocratic styles of politics give more space to pseudo-scientific policies (e.g. the prominent role which is given to the CPB by Dutch political parties: politically caused 'de-politization of politics' (see Bader/v.d.Berg 1993: 77)). On the other hand: highly emotionalized and divisive styles (combined with subservient bureaucracies) prevent any effective influence.

27 A lively, open, plural and critical public discourse is an effective weapon against pseudo-science. It also provides optimal conditions for rational checks and scrutiny of knowledge and information which is used to ground and legitimize policies. At the same time "scientific advisers" get a chance to protest against and criticize the "misuse" of their advice.

28 Powerful bureaucracies, backed by strong governments (let's say: France) can as effectively use advice that "fits" as block uncomfortable, critical advice. "Bargaining" and "contracting bureaucracies" depend much more on divergent and conflicting knowledge and information of a variety of actors in their respective policy-fields: "scientific advice" tends to be contested much earlier and more directly. Inside bureaucracies: the effectiveness of scientific advice depends upon the homogeneity of the departments; if there are (hidden or open) factions: which faction ordered policy-research or asked for advice? Results can easily be (mis)used in the internal struggle as backing for specific policies.

29 It seems plausible that the earlier policy-research and "advice" takes place, the more weight it has (see Penninx 1992: 22f); if a specific policy is decided upon and already implemented, scientific influence has to wait for "crises of policies" to get another chance: when a more or less thoroughgoing revision or change of policies becomes unavoidable.

30 See Penninx 1992 for the Dutch "minority policy" from 1975-1983. But one has to realize that (1) many issues only become issues after they have been politicized (critical science follows social movements and collective action!); (2) whether this influence is healthy and fruitful depends completely on the quality of the scientific advice and on the different criteria of judgement (e.g.: the influence of quite a lot of "hard" scientists in judging the transscientific problem of risks of nuclear energy was a quite unhealthy one: they systematically ignored the limits of what they could know and tell as scientists).

31 Empirical research shows that political decision-makers are fairly independent from "scientific policy-advice": they are more interested in data and statistics than in scientific proposals on how to decide (see Knorr 1977; see for recent literature on social and science research and decision-making: Bulmer, Weiss/Bucuvales, Heller).

32 See Bader 1991: 150f. for similar problems in the relation between critical science and social movements. Ton Korver has rightly stressed the institutional aspect of a truly interactive form of cooperation between research and policy: 'there is no real common ground shared by policy and research (common definition of issues and problems in a shared organizational context - integrating commitments, responsibilities and competence - of budget-distribution, time-tables, publicity, and follow up. The very idea of policy research is its interactive status; since, however, an adequate institutional environment is lacking, the interaction is nominal at best'. The comparison with existing co-operation between researchers and the TUC in the Netherlands 'does not lead to optimism - to put it mildly'.

33 Some strategies are less obvious, e.g. those of employers in "illegal work" (see Amersfoort a.o. 1995: 3f, 44). See Zolberg 1987: 71 et pass for US.

34 See v. Amersfoort a.o. 1995: 28, 47; see Hathaway (1995), Goodwin-Gill (1994), Groenendijk. See for the different civil services: Adelman 1995. See for incorporation policies: Engbersen/Gabriël 1995 and Bader 1996d.

35 Burden sharing, homogenize deflection-regimes in asylum-policies inside the EU or on a transatlantic level; "safe third countries"; homogenize restrictive immigration-policies inside the EU (see d'Oliveira 1993 for many); coordinate more comprehensive approaches tackling root-causes; including states of sending countries (EU-Magreb conference).

See Streeck/Schmitter 1992; Lonergan/Parnwell 1995; Zolberg 1996; Gurr 1993 for many.

They are beyond the control of receiving states and beyond the resources and intervening capacities of sending states; they are beyond the reach of intergovernmental consultation mechanisms and beyond the intervention capacities of international economic organizations (IMF, World Bank, WTO) whose actual policies, as a matter of fact, only worsen the situation; they are beyond the intervention capacities of developmental agencies; of UN-security councils and peace-keeping forces; beyond Nato-interventions; beyond UNHCR; beyond international and intergovernmental ecological policies.

See Barber, Hirst, Cohen/Rogers, Offe/Preuß, Habermas. Critically: Bader 1994: 136-41.

Roberto Unger's project of empowered democracy is particularly vulnerable in this regard, but there is a broad range of positions compatible with this insight: from Popper's misleading metaphor of piecemeal "engineering" to Barber, Hirst, Cohen/Rogers and many others. Needless to say that the "Marxist-Leninist" claim of *Verwissenschaftlichung der Politik* didn't show the slightest awareness of both the limits of knowledge and of politics.

9 Conclusion

Veit Bader

Migration, first admission and incorporation are complex and contested social phenomena. Hence, it shouldn't come as a surprise that no comprehensive moral and social theories are available. No general practical answers, applicable at all times and in all societal context can be expected. In these concluding remarks I shall first try to summarize some important agreements, mention the main disagreements and explicate tasks for further theoretical and empirical research (I). Next I shall focus on central agreements and disagreements regarding practical ways out: what should we do? (II) I finish with a few remarks on the limited but important role critical philosophy and social science can play in this hotly contested political field (III): what can we learn from practical philosophy, history and social sciences?

I

I.1 Questions of first admission and incorporation are dealt with from a variety of competing approaches in moral and political philosophy and there is no consensus on theoretical strategies, let alone answers, even within specific traditions. A little reflection shows that this is not surprising. All the approaches are confronted with four impressive difficulties:

First, the constitutions of liberal, democratic welfare states are historical compromises between traditions of liberalism, democracy and socialism formerly thought to be absolutely incompatible. Practical philosophy, trying to explicate and critically evaluate the moral principles inherent in these constitutions, has to tackle tensions and *conflicts between fundamental moral principles*. We not only live in ethically plural societies with conflicting and probably incompatible notions of the good life, but moral principles themselves are in conflict.[1]

Secondly, each of the *principles*, be it autonomy, liberty, equality, participation or whatever, is itself *indeterminate*. On the one hand these principles limit the range of the morally permissible but, on the other hand, they leave considerable space for divergent institutions and policies

175

and do not prescribe what a morally just international economic and political order is or what a just first admission policy would be.[2]

Thirdly, practical judgement is a *complex* matter involving moral, prudential, ethico-political and realist arguments.[3] The *moral* point of view is universalist (however strong or weak) and requires that we treat (at least) all human beings as free and equal. *Prudential* arguments, however are particularist: one ought to do what is in the well-informed, long-term, rational interest of a specific unit in question (in our case the (nation) state). There may be good prudential reasons against comprehensive closure of borders (e.g. bottlenecks in specific labour-markets; long-term demographic developments and the future of pension-schemes). But prudential arguments always remain conditional and, at present, in all rich states of the North they seem to favor differentialist closure.[4] *Ethico-political* arguments are particularist: one ought to do what furthers the specific ethos, ways of life, culture of a specific community (in our case either an ethnic and/or a political community (the (nation) state). In my view, *Realist* arguments do not, of themselves, point into any specific direction: whatever one ought to do for moral or ethico-political reasons, one should always take care that "ought implies can": one should not ask for the impossible, and one ought to take into account the most probable and expected consequences of institutions and actions in order to avoid counter-productive outcomes. Realist arguments are clearly normative (of a negative kind: one "should not") and are particularly directed against moral arguments. In our case, realism is usually linked with the particularist perspective of the (nation) state and is often nearly indistinguishable from prudential or ethico-political arguments. Let me stress three points: (i) it may be difficult to distinguish these four kinds of "practical ought" and, admittedly, it is essential to combine them in all practical judgement. Nevertheless, it is crucial to *distinguish* between them *analytically* (see Nardin 1992: 277), otherwise their tensions and conflicts cannot be clarified. Moral requirements may conflict with particularist enlightened self-interest, they may contradict the values of ethnic, religious, national cultures, and they may not be feasible or counter-productive under present circumstances. Even if the outcome of such a practical judgement may be that one should not do, or at least not do now, what morally would be required, it remains crucial to know why.[5] (ii) In an imagined ideal world the four components of practical judgement may complement each other harmoniously. In the real world, in the case of first admission, their *tensions* are sharp and visible and it may prove extremely difficult to combine them. A wide gap between just principles, institutions and right actions on the one hand, and enlightened interests as well as entrenched cultures, on the other hand, indicates serious trouble for practical, "all things considered" judgements. The same kind of tension develops between moral and realist arguments "in contexts where existing arrangements are fundamentally unjust yet deeply entrenched" (Carens 1996: 169). (iii) If moral, prudential, ethico-political and realist arguments point in opposite directions, they have to be *balanced* one way or another. The should not be discarded: a morality which asks the impossible and clearly contradicts the most fundamental enlightened interests (*Gesinnungsethik*) does not live up to the demands of practical reason, is "not of this world", and the same holds for unqualified ethical particularism and ruthless *Realpolitik*. But how to balance them?

Fourthly, this indeterminacy of conflicting moral principles and practical judgement is reflected within theoretical approaches in moral philosophy. Most traditions allow arguments pro and contra open borders. They are *internally indeterminate*.[6] The complexity of practical judgement explains why *no* tradition is able to present a *comprehensive theory*.

If this is not an overly dramatized picture of the "state of the art", what, if anything, can we learn from practical philosophy in general, from moral philosophy in particular? Why waste our time with sophisticated technical language and complex theories of justice instead of directly participating as a partisan in political talk and action? "Whether or not we can find the theoretical resources" to handle these urgent practical questions (O'Neill 1991: 277) they will continually arise and come up for discussion.

Still, I think there is hope. If one opts for a non-foundationalist theoretical strategy, it may be possible to find some minimal but convincing moral principles and criteria, shared by different approaches, with regard to *first admission*. Of course there remain disagreements among participants in the debate. Should we link poverty and severe global inequality to first admission (as Goodin, Bader, Carens et. al. suggest) or not (as Pogge argues)? Do we really have to choose between policies addressing poverty and inequality directly, on the one hand, and fairly open borders, on the other hand, or can they be combined? Should we start our arguments from global moral obligations or stress domestic and transnational obligations of states (as Bauböck suggests)? How much weight should we give to legitimate arguments in favour of fairly closed borders? etc. However that may be, there is one major and important agreement among all participants who accept the legitimacy of moral as well as of ethno-political, prudential and realist arguments: however one may balance these countervailing views in general, in the present global contexts of severe poverty, inequality and violence, rich Northern states do not live up to their minimal global obligations. They fail to meet the two tests, mentioned by Bauböck: to fight poverty effectively and to engage in foreign and economic policies which enable other states to develop their own comprehensive systems of democratic citizenship. As long as, and to the degree that, this is the case, closure of their borders is morally wrong.

All practical philosophy has, in my view, to tackle two *major difficulties*:

(i) We cannot exactly compare and weigh the different moral, ethno-political, prudential and realist arguments in an abstract and general way, let alone quantify them. There is no algorithm. To me it is also evident that these arguments should not all count equally. We need, and we are able, to articulate minimal *priority rules* which limit opportunistic trade-offs: universalist considerations must - at least in cases of serious wrong - be able to trump self-interest or ethical priority for compatriots. The remaining gap has to be filled by *"theories of local justice"*. However, even these "theories", inevitably, leave considerable space. Widely diverging balancings are to be expected. It is fairly easy to claim that the different perspectives should be incorporated into practical judgements, but it is very hard to realize. There is no comprehensive practical theory at hand and we have many reasons to doubt that such a theory ever can be developed. In my view, this should not be deplored, because this indeterminacy of practical judgement even in highly specific contexts is the *Lebenselixier* of legitimate dissensus, *public talk* and democratic political decision making by all citizens who may be enlightened by moral philosophy and well-informed by critical social science.

(ii) Most moral and political philosophy is plagued by a *"terrible lack of institutional concreteness"*. This holds not only for the predominant theories of justice but also for more radical approaches which criticize the usual accommodations of moral principles to the predominant institutional settings of capitalist market economies and restricted party-democracy and which ask for institutional alternatives. The "design" of institutional alternatives for international, intergovernmental and national policies to eradicate poverty, to tame violence, to address the causes of forced migration, to coordinate humane refugee- and asylum policies, etc. is, in my view the *major bottleneck* in recent critical philosophy and social science.[7] Cooperation between critical philosophy and the social sciences would be essential for such projects but is painfully slow.

With regard to normative principles of *Incorporation* and with respect to living in a multi-national, -ethnic and -cultural society, a minimalist consensus, notwithstanding all the minor disagreements, seems to have developed in non-foundationalist political philosophy: "All different, all equal".[8] The interesting and important disagreements concern, again, institutional issues in different contexts and with regard to different ethnic and national groups (see below). Compared to the issues of a just global economic and political order and to first admission, however, it is interesting and important to note that here the gap between moral and political philosophy and empirically oriented social sciences is much smaller. More fruitful exchanges and border-crossings are taking place.

I.2 Among participating *critical social scientists* important agreements are evident: (1) all present, defend or argue within a pro-theoretical frame clearly spelled out by Hoerder: an interactive approach in migration and incorporation research, stressing unequal power relations and the need to connect a macro-level analysis of economic and political world-systems with a meso-level analysis of segmented labour markets and networks of families and groups, and a micro-level analysis of choices of individuals and families in a biographical and generational perspective. (2) All expect theoretically, and demonstrate empirically a huge diversity of national and ethnic groups, cultures and identities (pre-migration, dominant as well as national minority and ethnic cultures). The same goes for ways in which class, gender, race and ethnicity are "articulated"; for different forms of pluralism; and for legal, social, cultural, political regimes of in-corporation. This leads (3) to a shared criticism of predominant and heavily biased myths of unity and homogeneity of dominant as well as of minority groups, cultures and identities. It also leads to a shared criticism of "false necessities" in history and social sciences: history is much more contingent and open, and societies much less systemically integrated than grand sociological theories make us believe. In terms of their own re-search programmes this includes: (i) a need for conceptual *desegregation*: citizenship has to be conceived of as a multi-layered and multi-level con-cept (Stolcke, Bader 1996a); the container-concept of ethnicity has to be differentiated according to the many - mixed and shifting - criteria con-sidered to be constitutive (Juteau), and ethnic categories have to be dis-tinguished from ethnic groups (cultures, networks, identities) (Hoerder, Bader 1995b); normative pluralism has to be distinguished from struc-tural, cultural and political pluralism and the different patterns of their interaction have to be analysed (Juteau); various typical modes of incor-poration are predominant: pluralism, institutionalized domination, assimi-lation, syncretic integration (Esman, Juteau, Bader 1996d, Fig.3)) or: dif-ferential exclusion, assimilationism, pluralism (Castles), and their re-gional and local varieties have to be analysed (Hoerder);[9] differentiated policies of incorporation have to be expected (Zolberg, Bader 1996d); etc. (ii) If societies are better compared to "patch-works" than to systemic wholes, *comparative* studies have to describe this variety (Stolcke, Ho-erder, Juteau, Castles, Zolberg) and try to explain why the patterns are so different: why here other than there? (iii) If history is more contingent, *longitudinal* studies have to describe the - often unexpected - shifts and try to explain them: why then rather than now? Both comparative and historical studies are increasingly integrated and this ongoing research produces massive information and evidence of the huge variety of forms of migration, the responses of host countries, the reactions of national and ethnic minorities and the evolving interaction-patterns. (4) Critical analysis of implementation of policies, practices and results is urgent to counterbalance the rhetorical use of principles and politics of symbolic action (Castles, Castles 1996a, Bader 1997).

However, the reader should be warned. The fact that only minor disagreements among participating social scientists can be detected is more the result of selection than a reflection of some basic consensus in the social sciences in this area.

I.3 For a number of reasons a fruitful *cooperation between practical philosophy and social sciences* seems urgent: (i) to overcome historically and empirically uninformed moral speculations and pseudo-objective empirical research which do not spell out its normative and political presumptions; (ii) to critically assess claims in moral philosophy regarding the universal validity of moral principles by historical and cross-cultural anthropological research (see Barrington Moore) and to criticize historicist and anthropological particularism, relativism and claims that rules and practices are absolutely unique, cannot be compared or translated. We can compare, we can translate, we can understand, we live in an increasingly global context (see Waldron); (iii) most prominently in our case: to be able to "design" alternative institutions which are more in harmony with moral principles and can pass realist feasibility tests. However, such a "marriage" or, better, such a LAT-relationship seems difficult to realize even between critical practical philosophers and critical social scientists. Experiences during the expert colloquium in Amsterdam showed once more that the gap separating these disciplines is wide. As a result of a fargoing division of intellectual labour the differences in traditions, cultures, language games and ways of argumentation seem so great that it is sometimes difficult to understand each other, let alone to cooperate fruitfully. The gap seems insurmountable between foundationalist moral philosophy (radical abstractions, construction of models or islands of ideally just worlds without linking these utopias step by step to our "real world") and those historians and anthropologists who - rightly - stress the huge diversity of moral principles and practices and - wrongly - lapse into unfounded relativism. Crossing these boundaries seems to be easier if non-foundationalist political philosophy meets critical social science as is increasingly the case in discussion about multiculturalism. Historians and sociologists - rightly - stress that principles of multiculturalism did not come "naturally" nor as an application of philosophical principles of "the just society" (see Juteau); moral philosophers - rightly - stress that these principles have to be put to universalization tests to be rationally validated as just moral principles. Both could, in my view, agree that there is no view from nowhere, that all knowledge is historically, socially, culturally situated knowledge on the one hand, but, on the other hand, that this fact does not rule out the possibility of gradational judgements (there are better and worse forms of normative as well as cognitive knowledge) and of "relational" impartiality and neutrality.

II

We have an admirable set of human rights but still may be saddled with rotten moral theories to ground them. It is a remarkable fact, which cannot be reiterated often enough, that the degree of dissent on foundations is usually much higher than on principles and even practical solutions. My thesis is that even critical philosophers and social scientists disagree more on theoretical strategies than on what is practically urgent to do, particularly if one tries to articulate *minima politica*, minimalist political aims and ways to address urgent problems of forced migration and incorporation. I roughly sketch such a minimalist programme on which, in spite of all disagreements, most participants at the expert colloquium in Amsterdam could agree to and which, minimalist as it is, turns out to be still much too radical for governments and predominant political coalitions in rich Northern states.

(1) Even if a "comprehensive" policy to fight all *root causes of forced migration*, so fiercely advocated by moral critics, researchers and disappointed UN-officials may be far out of reach, a more minimalist politics, focusing on the fight against poverty and on efforts to stem gross violence and ethnic cleansings globally may be feasible. We may widely disagree about best policies and instruments, or - more soberly - on not totally ineffective or even counterproductive ways to achieve this but we all agree on the moral and political urgency of it.

(2) As long as, and to the degree in which we are unable to make progress, we have a weighty moral obligation towards all different types of forced migrants and we should rethink the old, rigid distinction between "political" and "economic refugees" (Zolberg for many). Rich Northern states (i) should minimally live up to obligations of fair burden sharing, (ii) should live up to humanly and extensively interpreted legal obligations following from the Geneva Convention, and (iii) should officially recognize that they are immigration-countries and should agree upon legally fixed (either by international treaties or by constitutional changes) minimal annual immigration ratios (say 1.5%) and fair, non-discriminatory immigration criteria (see Hoerder, Kymlicka 1996, Bader 1996a).

(3) Minimal moral and political requirements with regard to the *legal incorporation* of longterm residents in democratic, social constitutional states include: (i) so-called "illegal" longterm residents (asylum seekers rejected after overly long waiting periods, "wanted" undocumented unskilled workers, etc.) acquire moral rights simply as a consequence of sheer duration of stay - and, with it, growing social relations and expectations (see Carens for many) - and should therefore be "legalized". (ii) Differential exclusion and *Gastarbeiter*-regimes are clearly at odds with principles of liberal, democratic and social constitutions (see Walzer, Kymlicka, Castles, Zolberg for many). With regard to the legal incorporation of long-term residents, judged by two criteria - the fullness of rights and the security of the guarantee of rights - two morally permissible but conflicting options are defended: on the one hand many scholars are convinced that only a quick and easy access to full and equal citizenship which also may include the option of dual citizenship, is a relatively safe option to guarantee a full set of civil, political and social rights. On the other hand some scholars are convinced that, in our times, citizenship rights decline progressively in importance and can, eventually, be replaced by universal human rights and a kind of universalized denizenship status.

Historically, the guarantee of human rights and security has been intimately bound to states and citizenship. 'People without their own national government were deprived of human rights' (Arendt, 1951: 272)[10] and citizenship has been seen as 'the right to have rights'.[11] However, we have good moral, legal, and historical reasons to distinguish clearly between universal human rights (rights of all human persons) and citizenship rights (rights of citizens). *Morally*, it would be clearly indefensible to see state-membership as a precondition for human rights. In *legal* theory it is common knowledge to distinguish between *status personae, status libertatis,* and *status civitatis* and the respective rights.[12] *Historically*, during the 20th Century, particularly after the Second World War, civil rights and, increasingly, though much more contested, social rights have been understood not as rights of "citizens" but as universal human rights which we owe to each human person regardless of state-membership. This is evidently true for the many Human Rights Declarations but it holds also for mechanisms of enforcement (legally binding International and European Covenants on Civil, Political, and Economic, Social and Cultural Rights; European Courts etc.) however fragmentary and clumsy this development still is.[13] The growing importance of universal human rights can, in my view, be misunderstood in two ways. Both may have *politically* dangerous consequences.

First one may think not only, and rightly so, that citizenship rights lose importance when compared to human rights but one can declare them obsolete and thus replace citizenship by universal denizenship: *Why not universal denizenship?*[14] I think such an option is unattractive for two reasons: (i) even if denizens had the same *full* set of secure civil and social rights guaranteed to citizens which, still, is a long way to go,[15] and even if they had some political citizenship rights like local voting rights, such an 'extension of substantive citizenship' (Bauböck 1996a) has clear limits. The status of long-term denizens may be desirable for elitist liberals who are in favour of a kind of factual denizenship for most citizens, and for those calculating denizens who prefer the benefits of denizenship without the burdens of citizenship,[16] it is incompatible with any stronger notion of political democracy.[17] Restricted political rights and limited political participation, furthermore, prevent full and secure social and civil rights. The status, rights, and many opportunities of denizens depend upon political decisions in which they have no say. (ii) Rights of denizens are far *less secure* than rights of citizens even in our present world,[18] particularly if one not only looks at declarations, laws, statuses and rhetoric, but also on implementation and practice.[19] Not only long-term "undocumented residents", but denizens too are still in danger of being expelled.[20] Manipulation of the status of denizenship, furthermore, is an increasingly important strategic variable in the arena of influencing the future flow of migration.[21] Taking these two arguments together I think we have good political reasons not to opt for universal denizenship.

Secondly, one can try to get rid of the exclusionary aspects of citizenship by opting for "universal citizenship" and a "world constitutionalism" as a legal utopia: 'a system that finally denies citizenship: by suppressing it as a privileged status associated with rights not recognized to non-citizens, or instead by instituting universal citizenship, and thus in either case overcoming the dichotomy between "the rights of man and the rights of citizens"' (Ferrajoli 1995: 31; see Goodin 1996a). *Why not universal citizenship?* In my *Fairly Open Borders* (Bader 1997b) I've tried to summarize arguments against such a "strategy of replacement" of existing states, constitutions, citizenship rights and domestic obligations by a democratic world state, a world constitution, universal human rights and global obligations. Instead, I advocate a more sober, threefold strategy which also fits into the process of universalization of rights, on the one hand, but, on the other hand, takes clearly into account backlashes, serious problems of enforcement of international declarations and covenants as well as morally legitimate differences between countries. We should therefore, in my view, (a) shift the emphasis from citizenship to universal human rights of persons and to universalistically founded specific group rights over and against the state and, by this, continue the "domestication" of the state from the outside, which liberal constitutionalism started from the inside, without trying to replace citizenship rights by human rights. (b) With regard to political citizenship we should de-emphasize state-centred citizenship and shift the focus or the centre of gravity of political citizenship both upwards and downwards: let us be localists and "rooted cosmopolitans" simultaneously. If "post-national" or "trans-national citizenship" - not to be confused with "universal citizenship" - is meant to indicate such a shift, it should be welcomed and developed. (c) Alongside such a design for multiple political citizenship we should develop and strengthen different forms of social citizenship (many of them already quite "international" (see Cohen/Rogers 1995: 256) .

(4) A consensus seems to be growing not only among critical philosophers and social scientists but also in official proclamations of *policies in multi-ethnic or -national countries* (like Canada, Australia, Sweden, NL). "All different and all equal" minimally means: (i) taking equality of citizenship rights as a starting point; (ii) recognizing that legal equality does not necessarily lead to equality of respect, resources, opportunities or welfare; (iii) differential treatment for people with different characteristics and needs; (iv) establishing mechanisms for group representation and participation, particularly in cases of indigenous peoples and national minorities.[22] Particularly important has been the shift from mere symbolic and legal issues ("politics of recognition") towards material economic, social, and political issues ("politics of equality" of economic, social, cultural and political chances). This has not been the case in "cultural studies", which is still heavily moulded by the American model of *laissez-faire* pluralism (see Castles, Kymlicka 1996). But even in these more radical versions of policies of multiculturalism three are still three main practical limitations and areas of theoretical disagreement which have to be addressed. *First* the problem of the reach and *limits of multiculturalism policies*: they have originally been developed to address problems of integration of ethnically and culturally diverse immigrants, not to solve problems of incorporation of indigenous peoples and long-standing national minorities. Experiences in Canada and Australia clearly show that they are not calibrated nor able to do that successfully (see Juteau, Kymlicka 1996, Castles). Scholars and policy makers disagree about the further development and the specific targeting of policies of multiculturalism: should they include indigenous people, as the Australian Labor Party Government intended to (see Castles), or should they clearly be restricted to "ethnic minorities" (as Juteau 1997 and Kymlicka 1996 propose). *Secondly,* enforced cultural assimilation and enforced structural inclusion are morally wrong. This excludes some *types of incorporation policies*: assimilationism, institutionalized domination ("different and unequal" versions of pluralism like Guestworker regimes (Castles) and the structural pluralism of the "plantation-belt societies" (Zolberg)). However, the remaining range of morally permissible options is still quite broad: from

fairly free cultural assimilation without any structural pluralism to culturally diverse and structurally segmented societies. This space has to be
filled by widely differentiated policies of incorporation. Although this is
too simplistically stated, indigenous peoples and national minorities seem
to prefer structural pluralism (just short of secession) and cultural pluralism, while immigrant "ethnic" minorities seem to prefer far less structural
pluralism (see Juteau, Kymlicka 1995, 1997) and far greater forms of
cultural assimilation in the long run (see Hoerder). To find prudent and
context-sensitive balances between the countervailing tendencies of
structural inclusion or separation on the one hand, and cultural assimilation or retention on the other hand, a lot of specific information,[23] practical knowledge, and imagination is required. The "design" of incorporation policies is important but one should keep in mind that practical
judgement is an "art" and that the required balancing should take place in
democratic talk and decision making. *Thirdly,* societies differ widely as
to ethnic, national and cultural diversity, but all states developing multicultural and multi-national incorporation policies run against structural
limitations which follow from the fact that these societies are predominantly *capitalist market societies.* In times of economic crises and, particularly, of neo-liberal economic policies their capability for effective
policies of equality, particularly important to fight against the existence
or development of long-standing ethnic and racial underclasses (see Hoerder, Castles, Zolberg for many) is severely restricted.

(5) We have to find practical ways out of hard moral and political
dilemmas and our proposed policies may be not only inconsistent but incompatible: tolerant first admission put a lot of stress on fair incorporation policies and there is a trade-off between how many to let in and how
much to do for each; policies to fight global poverty and, particularly,
global inequalities may include more strain for policies to fight domestic
poverty and inequality; stressing strong democratic talk and action to find
ways out of these dilemmas may actually deepen the tension between
(global) justice and democracy if one does not succeed in shifting the
loyalties, solidarities and felt obligations from domestic to transdomestic
levels; accepting too much really "deep" cultural diversity may weaken
civil and democratic virtues and, as a consequence, weaken the will to
accept hotly contested and contingent majority decisions; etc. To me it is
plain that there cannot be one best way out, one optimal solution to these
hard questions and, furthermore, that the role of philosophers and social
scientists in "designing" such solutions is fairly limited. The quality of
the outcome of political decision making depends strongly on the quality
of democratic communication and institutionalized interactions among
critical philosophers as public intellectuals, social scientists, policy makers and the general public. *Vox populi* is clearly not *vox dei* but in these

times of lost certainties democratic public talk seems to be the best option to overcome the inevitable indeterminacy of moral principles and to find prudent and sensitive ways out of policy dilemmas.

III

The roles critical philosophers and social scientists can play in democratic politics may be limited, but they still are important:

(1) Even if practical philosophers cannot present clear answers to what we practically should do, they can demarcate the range of morally permissible institutional variation and tolerable politics and they can *stimulate critical distance and reflection* of the implicit or explicit rules and principles inherent in our institutions and politics.

(2) Critical historians and social scientists traditionally should play the role of *myth-hunters*. This is particularly important in this heavily politicized area which teems with powerful political myths like the myth of absolute state-sovereignty; of ethnically and culturally homogeneous nation-states; of so-called centuries or even millennia old, quasi-natural national traditions and identities; of the enormous cultural distance separating nationals and "aliens"; of the presumed impossibility that the latter acculturate; etc. Given the overwhelming historical and sociological counter-evidence and given any daily experiences, the stability of these myths is astonishing: Truth is, contrary to Milton, clearly not 'strong next to the Almighty' and she clearly needs 'policies, stratagems, and licensings to make her victorious'.

(3) Critical philosophers and social scientists as public intellectuals should introduce, in a critical and self-reflexive way, *new concepts, new ways of seeing and thinking* into public discourse and so broaden the range of imaginable and possible options.

(4) In my view the most urgent, as well as the most neglected role consists in the elaboration of *concrete utopias, institutional alternatives*. At present the modesty of democratic intellectuals in this regard is completely misplaced and nobody can really be afraid that "scientistic blueprints" will be imposed on tame politicians and on an innocent public. Radical democratic politics suffers from a severe lack of imagination of institutional alternatives to capitalist market economies, to the predominant global economic and political order, on the one hand, and from a serious memory gap as far as historical alternatives are concerned, on the other hand. It is my hope that the contributions in this volume will stimulate the cooperation of practical philosophers and social scientists and that they will bring an end to the "end of ideology" and "end of history" mood. This mood seems to have paralysed radical policies for quite a while now.

Conclusion   187

Notes

1   I believe that the tradition of radical egalitarian liberalism, or - as I prefer - of liberal, democratic socialism is particularly apt to explicate the public morality inherent in these constitutions, especially if it criticizes the predominant easy accommodations to capitalist markets and exclusively parliamentary democracy. Here are the main reasons for this credo: (1) it stresses and clarifies its inherent moral universalism and criticizes all illegitimate particularisms (versus communitarian ethics); (2) it strikes a reasonable balance between deontological and consequentialist arguments (versus purely consequentialist approaches like utilism and rigorous rights-talk like libertarianism; versus exclusive "care-ethics"); (3) it is restricted to public morality, contains no "comprehensive ethics" and leaves room for "ethical pluralism"; (4) it starts to recognize "moral pluralism" (see Larmore, Kekes, Becker), particularly a new balance of so-called "negative" civil rights, of political rights and of so-called "positive" economic, social and cultural rights. It is getting ever more critical towards the predominant focus in Anglo-American liberal "rights-as-shooting-guns" talk (see Unger, see Shue 1980) and, as a consequence, more plausible in those parts of the world where an exclusive focus on so-called "negative" rights has, rightly, a very bad record. However, my choice of such a radical egalitarian version of liberalism is not unconditional and I'm prepared to adopt better theoretical frames, if available, to explicate my strong moral intuition that closed borders are wrong. I'm prepared to elaborate on and qualify my moral conviction, not to sacrifice it on the altars of moral philosophy (see Williams).

2   See Carens 1995c:4, 1995a: 13; Perry 1995: 105; Shue 1980: 17; 1988: 704; Bader 1996c.

3   See Raz 1975, Habermas 1991. Two remarks on terminology seem to be in place: The distinction between *moral* and *ethical* argument follows Habermas' terminology and shows analogies with the distinction between the "right" and the "good" in the Rawlsian tradition. "Practical" judgement is used as a roof-concept covering different kinds of normative judgement, including moral ones. When I say that what is morally required may not be feasible, I do not say that it would be practically required and should be done. Quite to the contrary, if we can really show that it is not feasible, it cannot be practically required and should not be done (see my exchange with Bauböck 1996).

4   Prudential arguments in favour of more open borders (Goodin 1996, Pogge 1995: 205 for many) show that all prudential arguments are highly context specific and completely conditional. They depend on much contested information and, of course, on how the well-informed, well-understood long-term interests of a state are perceived and "calculated".

5   See Carens 1996: 166: "It is essential to distinguish between a regrettable but useful tactical concession to powerful political forces pursuing a morally objectionable path and a legitimate defense of an important and honorable value". See Bader 1996b.

6   Strong utilitarian arguments in favor of open borders have been developed by Singer, Goodin and others (see for indeterminacy of utilism: O'Neill 1991: 282f). The tradition of egalitarian liberals is severely divided on this issue (see Carens 1992: 25; Woodward 1992; Nardin 1992: 268f, 274 ff.)

7   "Design" should not to be misunderstood as "engineering" or traditional "blueprint": practical knowledge, imagination, practical tests and, most important, democratic deliberation and decision making are of utmost importance.

8   See Juteau, Castles, Zolberg, Kymlicka, Bauböck, Bader 1996d.

9   See also Castles/Miller 1993, Soysal 1995 (see Castles 1996a), see my short comparison in Bader 1996d.
10 See also Walzer 1977, 1985a, Aron 1974, Preuß 1995 for many.
11 See for a short critique of Earl Warren's phrase: Goodin 1996b.
12 See Bader 1995: 225f and 1996a. In a fine criticism of T.H. Marshall Luigi Ferrajoli (1995) has pointed out a confusing simplification in his treatment of citizenship. Whereas Marshall's definition: 'a status conferred on those who are full members of a given community', points, traditionally though not very clearly, to "political citizenship", i.e. membership in a democratic political unit, his much broader definition of "citizenship rights" include civil rights, political rights, and social rights. The second connotation is theoretically deceptive 'since not all these rights presuppose citizenship... In the legal tradition there has always been a distinction, alongside *status civitatis* (or citizenship), of *status personae* (personality or legal subjectivity)' (p. 3). Universalist rights of human persons as such (including children, mentally handicapped persons), completely irrespective of their specific citizenship status, are inclusive (p. 4) whereas rights of citizens as members of particular states are exclusive. In Ferrajoli's view this conceptual confusion is not just an innocent matter of words, it is politically regressive as well: the 'historical nexus between state and fundamental rights is contingent' (p. 27). Taking universal rights of human persons seriously today 'means having the courage to detach them from citizenship as "belonging" (to a particular national community) and hence from statehood. And detaching them from citizenship means recognizing their supra-national nature - in the twofold sense of their two guarantees, constitutional and international - and hence protecting them not only inside but also outside and against states, putting an end to the great *apartheid* that excludes the majority of the human race from enjoying them, in contrast with their proclaimed universalism.' (p. 29). To state it differently: civil rights and social rights do not refer, in their formulation, to specific political units and membership, whereas political rights: free and equal ballot and right to get elected in office, some of the freedoms of political communication and the right to citizenship, emigration and remigration, cannot even be thought of or articulated without such a reference.
13 See Goodin 1996b, Soysal 1995, de Lange 1995 for many.
14 As a strong tendency in Lange (1995: 100) and, particularly, Soysal 1995: 138 ff. See critically: Bauböck 1995b: 25 ff.
15 See Castles 1996a versus Soysal. See in detail for social rights: Meehan 1993.
16 Like military or other public services. In many cases, dual citizenship may provide outcome.
17 See Walzer 1983, Carens, Bauböck and many others.
18 Even granted citizenship can, of course, be revoked - as the predicament of German Jews under the Nazi regime clearly demonstrates - but compared to the quite "normal" manipulations with the legal and actual status of denizenship at present, this example shows that such policy involves a radical break with principles and practices of liberal-democratic constitutionalism. Citizenship is much more secure than denizenship.
19 Castles (1996a, point 6) versus Soysal. See my critical remarks: Bader 1995a: 137, 166. See Zolberg 1987: 73.
20 'Expulsion of the alien immigrant is still possible' (Groenendijk 1994: 11) discussing security and fullness of residence-rights and social and political rights in the four models: citizenship, quasi-citizenship, privileged treatment, and denizenship. 'Soysal probably overstates the degree to which some major groups in certain countries enjoy equal rights and protection from deportation' (Castles 1996a).
21 'Holland, in many respects not a harsh country at all, is exemplary in her new emphasis on the importance of influencing denizenship. A policy document, published

in 1994 (Entzinger/Van der Zwan, 1994) has since been accepted by the new Dutch government. The document lumps new and already established residents from non-European origin together and develops guidelines for integrating these residents into Dutch society. It is a workfare type of policy that is advocated here with two major sanctions to back it up. The first of these is the threat that non-compliance with the policy will have consequences for the option of citizenship. The second is that non-compliance may lead to eviction from the country, i.e. the withdrawal of the status of denizenship. Denizenship in this context is as a matter of principle a precarious status that may be withdrawn on grounds that previously did not exist. Undoubtedly, it will be a tricky affair to make it work, if only in a legally waterproof fashion. Leaving that for what it is, we still are faced with the message the policy contains for all "newcomers": even if you have passed the very complex, time-consuming and stringent procedures of first-admission, you had better realize that your "probationary" period in the country is far from finished.' (Korver 1996).

22 Castles, Juteau, Zolberg. See notes 75 and 78 in Bader 1996d. See the recent volume on group rights, edited by Juha Räikkä 1996.

23 Concerning the huge diversity between and inside of ethnic and national groups, and their respective position in society. At least the following criteria for judging the moral legitimacy of differentiated policies of incorporation in the different societal fields are relevant: (i) the degree of incorporation and of inequality in the respective field; (ii) the degrees to which incorporation or separation are *free or enforced*: enforced; (iii) the legitimate wishes and ends of ethnic minorities and/or their elites, with regard to the forms of incorporation; (iv) overall rough equality or inequality; (v) the - contested - effects of the different options and strategies upon minimal 'social unity' and 'cohesion' of the polity (see Bader 1996d).

Bibliography

ABS (Australian Bureau of Statistics) (1995) National Aboriginal and Torres Strait Islander Survey 1994: Detailed Findings Canberra: AGPS, ABS Catalogue No. 4190.0.

ACTU (Australian Council of Trade Unions) (1995) Combating Racism: Discrimination and Racism during 1994: How Far in Fact have we Come? Melbourne: ACTU.

Adelman, H. (1995) Control and Prevention: Canadian Refugee Policy. The Case of Rwanda. Conference Paper: Berg en Dal.

Adelman, H./Borowski, A./Burstein, M./Foster, L. (eds) (1993) Immigration and Refugee Policy: Australia and Canada Compared (two volumes) Melbourne: Melbourne University Press.

Alba, Richard (1990) Ethnic Identity: The Transformation of White America. New Haven: Yale University Press.

Ålund, A./Schierup, C.-U. (1991) Paradoxes of Multiculturalism Aldershot: Avebury.

Amersfoort, H.v./Doomernik, J./Penninx, R. (1995) International Migration: Processes and Interventions. A study of governmental interventions in migration processes. Commissioned by the secretariat of the commission of the European Union. Amsterdam.

Anderson, B. (1983) Imagined Communities. Reflections on the Origin and Spread of Nationalism. London: Verso.

Arendt, H. (1951) The Origins of Totalitarianism. San Diego/New York.

Aron, R. (1974) Is Multinational Citizenship Possible? In: Social Research 41: 638 ff.

Aubertin, A. (1939) Die Staatsangehörigkeit der verheirateten Frau. In: Zeitschrift für ausländisches öffentliches Recht 6.

Babu-Laban, Y. /Stasiulis, D. (1992) Ethnic Pluralism under Siege: Popular and Partisan Opposition to Multiculturalism. Canadian Public Policy 18 (4): 365-86.

Bach, R. (1993) Changing Relations. New York: Ford Foundation.

Bader, V.M. (1988) Macht of waarheid? In: Kennis en Methode 12(2): 138-57.

Bader, V.M. (1989) Max Webers Begriff der Legitimität. In: Weiß, J. (ed.) Max Weber heute. Frankfurt/M.: Suhrkamp, p. 296-334.

Bader, V.M. (1991) Kollektives Handeln. Opladen: Leske + Budrich.

Bader, V.M. (1992) 'Grand Theories', Empirismus oder Pro-Theorie? In: Forschungsjournal NSB 2: 9-21.

Bader, V.M. (1994) Eenheid van de communicatieve rede, recht en complexe maatschappijen. In: Recht en kritiek 2/94, 111-44.

Bader, V.M. (1995) Citizenship and Exclusion. In: Political Theory 23(2): 211-46.

Bader, V.M. (1995a) Reply to Michael Walzer. In: Political Theory 23(2):250-2.

Bader, V.M. (1995b) Rassismus, Ethnizität, Bürgerschaft. Münster: Westfälisches Dampfboot.

Bader, V.M. (1995c) Dilemmas of Affirmative Action. Benign State-Neutrality versus Relational Ethnic Neutrality. Part I. Paper for Conference 'Organizing Diversity' in Berg en Dal, November.

Bader, V.M. (1996) Auto-Comment on 'Citizenship and Exclusion'. Colloquium on Citizenship and Exclusion. Amsterdam April.

Bader, V.M. (1996a) A multilayered Concept of Citizenship. Response to Pogge's Comment. Colloquium on Citizenship and Exclusion. Amsterdam, April.

Bader, V.M. (1996b) Response to Bauböck's Comment. Colloquium on Citizenship and Exclusion. Amsterdam, April.

Bader, V.M. (1996c) The Institutional and Cultural Conditions of Postnational Citizenship. Paper for Conference 'Social and Political Citizenship in a World of Migration'. Firenze, February. To be published in Political Theory 1997.

Bader, V.M. (1996d) Incorporation and Egalitarian Multiculturalism. Paper for Conference 'Blurred Boundaries', Melbourne, July.

Bader, V.M. (1997) The Arts of Forcasting and Policy Making. In this volume.

Bader, V.M. (1997a) Introduction. In this volume.

Bader, V.M. (1997b) Fairly Open Borders. In this volume.

Bader, V.M. (1997c) Conclusions. In this volume.

Bader, V.M./Benschop, A. (1989) Ungleichheiten. Opladen: Leske + Budrich.

Bader, V.M./Berg, H.v.d. (1993) Simulatiemodellen en de maakbare toekomst. In: Berg/Both/Basset (eds.) Het Centraal Planbureau in Politieke Zaken. p. 63-79; Amsterdam.

Baier, A. (1995) A Note on Justice, Care, and Immigration Policy. In: Hypatia 10(2): 150-2.

Barber, B. (1984) Strong Democracy. Berkeley, LA, London.

Barber, B. (1988) The Conquest of Politics. Princeton, N.J.

Barrett, James R. (1992) Americanization from the Bottom Up: Immigration and the Remaking of the Working Class in the United States, 1880-1930. In: Journ. Am. Hist. 1992: 997-1020.

Barry, B. (1973)The Liberal Theory of Justice. Oxford, Clarendon Press.

Barry, B. (1989) Democracy, Power, and Justice. Oxford, Clarendon Press.

Barry, B. (1992) The quest for consistency: A sceptical view. In: Barry/Goodin 1992: 279-87.

Barry, B. (1994) Dirty work in the original position. Paper for conference 'The Ethics of Nationalism', Univ. of Illinois, April.

Barry, B. (1995) Justice as Impartiality. Oxford: Clarendon Press.

Barry, B./Goodin R.E. (eds.) (1992) Free Movement. Ethical Issues in the transnational migration of people and of money. New York, London etc.

Barth, Frederik (1969) Ethnic Groups and Boundaries. The Social Organization of Culture Difference. Boston: Little Brown and Co.

Barton, A. (1993) Cultural Interplay between Sweden and Swedish America. In: Swedes in America: Intercultural and Interethnic Perspectives on Contemporary Research, ed. by Ulf Beijbom (Växjö, 1993).

Bauböck, R. (1994) Transnational Citizenship. Aldershot: Edward Elgar.

Bauböck, R. (1994a) Changing the Boundaries of Citizenship. In: Bauböck (ed.) 1994b: 199-232.

Bauböck, R. (ed.) (1994b) From Aliens to Citizens. Redefining the Status of Immigrants in Europe. Aldershot: Avebury.

Bauböck, R. (1995) Gehen, Bleiben, Kommen. In: Offe, C. (ed.) Demokratietheorie. Fischer, Hamburg.

Bauböck, R. (1995a) Cultural minority rights for immigrants. Paper for 'Ethics, Migration and Global Stewardship', Washington D.C., Sept.

Bauböck, R. (1995b) Sharing the present, history and future. Paper for Second Vienna Dialogue on Democracy, November

Bauböck, R. (1996) Comment on Pogge's Realizing Rawls. Colloquium on Citizenship and Exclusion. Amsterdam, April.

Bauböck, R. (1996a) Comment on Stolcke's 'The Nature of Nationality'. Colloquium Citizenship and Exclusion. Amsterdam, April.

Bauböck, R. (1996b) Respons to Bader's Auto-Comment. Colloquium Citizenship and Exclusion. Amsterdam, April.

Bauböck, R. (1996c) Group rights for cultural minorities: justifications and constraints. Paper for Conference 'Multiculturalism, Minorities and Cititzenship. Firenze, April.

Bauer, O. (1907/1987) La question des nationalités et la social-démocratie. Montreal: Guérin Littérature et Paris: Études et Documentation Internationales.

Beck, E. (1933) Die Staatsangehörigkeit der Ehefrau. Zürich and Leipzig: Orell Füssli Verlag.

Beckert, S. (1995) Migration, Ethnicity and Working Class Formation. Passaic, New Jersey, 1889-1926. In: D. Hoerder and J. Nagler, eds. (1995) Cultural Transfer. German Migrations in Comparative Perspective. Cambridge, pp. 347-78.

Beitz, C. R. (1979) Political Theory and International Relations. Princeton.

Beitz, C. R. (1985) Justice and International Relations. In: Beitz et al. 1985: 282-311.

Beitz, C. R. (1991) Sovereignty and Morality in International Affairs. In: Held (ed.) p. 236-54.

Beitz, C. R. /Cohen, M./Scanlon, T./ Simmons, A. (eds.) (1985) International Ethics. Princeton.

Bell, D. (1975) Ethnicity and Social Change. In: Glazer, N. and D.P. Moynihan (eds.), Ethnicity. Theory and Experience. Cambridge: Harvard University Press, p. 141-76.

Bernstein, R. (1994) Dictatorship of Virtue. New York: Alfred A. Knopf.

Bhabha, J.F./Klug, F./S. Shutter, S. (1985) Worlds Apart. Women under Immigration and Nationality Law. London: Pluto Press.

Bhaskar, R. (1978) A Realist Theory of Science. Leeds.

BIMPR (Bureau of Immigration, Multicultural and Population Research) (1995) Immigration Update June Quarter 1995 Canberra: AGPS.

Bissoondath, N. (1994) Selling of Illusions. The Cult of Multiculturalism in Canada. Toronto: Penguin Books.

Block, M. (ed.). (1863) Dictionnaire Général de la Politique. Paris: O. Lorenz, Libraire-Éditeur.

Bodnar, J. (1985) The Transplanted. A History of Immigrants in Urban America. Bloomington, Ind.

Bonacich, E. (1972) A Theory of Ethnic Antagonism: The Split Labor Market. In: Am. Soc. Rev. 37: 547-59.

Bourdieu, P. (1990) The Logic of Practice. Oxford.

Boyd, M. (1994) Measuring Ethnicity: The Roles of People, Policies and Politics and Social Science Research. Lectures and Papers in Ethnicity No. 11 - Dept. of Sociology, University of Toronto.

Breton, R. (1964) Institutional Completeness of Ethnic Communities and Personal Relations of Immigrants. In: American Journal of Sociology, 70: 193-205.

Breton, R. (1974) "Types of Ethnic Diversity in Canadian Society". Presented at the VIIIth World Congress of the International Sociological Association, Toronto.

Breton, R. (1984) The Production and Allocation of Symbolic Resources: an Analysis of the Linguistic and Ethnocultural Fields in Canada. In: Revue canadienne de sociologie et d'anthropologie 21 (2): 123-244.

Breton, R./Isajiw, W.W./ Kalbach, W.E. /Reitz, J.G. (1990) Ethnic Identity and Equality. Varieties of Experience in a Canadian City. Toronto: Univ. of Toronto Press.

Breton, Raymond/Reitz, Jeffrey G./Valentine, Victor (1980) Cultural Boundaries and the Cohesion of Canada. Montreal.

Brodie, J. /Gabriel, C. (1995) Canadian Immigration Policy and the Emergence of the Neo-Liberal State. Conference Paper: Berg en Dal.

Brown Scott, J. (1934) The Seventh International Conference of American States. In: The American Journal of International Law 28.

Brubaker, R. (1992) Citizenship and Nationhood in France and Germany. Cambridge, Harvard University Press.

Brubaker, R. (ed.) (1989) Immigration and the Politics of Citizenship in Europe and North America. London: University Press of America.

Buchanan. A (1991) Secession. Boulder, San Francisco, Oxford: Westview.

Carens, J. H. (1987) Aliens and citizens: the case for open borders, in: Review of Politics, 49(2): 251 - 73.

Carens, J. H. (1989) Membership and morality: admission to citizenship in liberal-democratic societies, in: Brubaker (ed.) 1989: 31-49.

Carens, J. H. (1990) Difference and Domination. Reflections on the relation between pluralism and equality, in: Chapman, J.W./Wertheimer, A. (eds.) Nomos XXXII, 226-250.

Carens, J. H. (1990a) Immigration and the claims of community: the case of Fiji; Ms.

Carens, J. H. (1991) States and refugees: a normative analysis, in: Adelman, H. (ed.) Refugee Policy. Toronto, 18-30.

Carens, J. H. (1992) Migration and morality: A liberal egalitarian perspective, in: Barry/Goodin (eds.) 1992: 25-47.

Carens, J. H. (1992a) Refugees and the limits of obligation, in: Public Affairs Quarterly 6/1: 31-44.

Carens, J. H. (1995) Migration Controls and Democratic Diffidence. Paper for the Joint German-American Project on Migration and Refugee Policies.

Carens, J. H. (1995a) Immigration, welfare, and justice. In: Schwartz 1995: 1-17.

Carens, J. H. (1995b) Immigration, Political Community and the Transformation of Identity: Quebec's Immigration Politics in Critical Perspective.In: Carens (ed.) p. 20-81.

Carens, J. H. (1995c) Liberalism, Justice, and Political Community. In Carens (ed.), p. 3-19.

Carens, J. H. (1996) Realistic and Idealistic Approaches to the Ethics of Migration. In: International Migration Review 30, 1, p. 156-70.

Carens, J. H. (ed.) (1995) Is Quebec Nationalism Just? Montreal & Kingston etc., McGill-Queen's UP.

Castles, S. (1995) How nation-states respond to immigration and ethnic diversity. In: New Community vol. 21.

Castles, S. (1996) Auto-Comment on The Age of Migration, ch. 8. Amsterdam Colloquium, April.

Castles, S. (1996a) Comments on Yasemin Soysal. Amsterdam Colloquium, April.

Castles, S. (1997) Multicultural Citizenship: the Australian Experience. In this volume.

Castles, S./Miller, M.J. (1993) The Age of Migration: International Population Movements in the Modern World. London: Macmillan.

Christis, J. (1993) Stress and well-being: an environmental risk approach. Conference paper Tilburg 26/12.

Christis, J. (1995) Over kundes en hun wetenschappelijke status. Ms. NIA, Amsterdam.

Cohen, J./Rogers, J. (1992) Secondary Associations and Democratic Governance. In: Politics and Society, Vol. 20, 4. p. 393-472.

Cohen, J./Rogers, J. (1995) Solidarity, Democracy, Association. In: Cohen/Rogers (eds.), p. 236-67.

Cohen, J./Rogers, J. (eds.) (1995) Associations and Democracy. London:Verso.

Cohen, S.J.D. (1985) The Origins of the matrilineal principle in Rabbinic Law. In: Association of Jewish Studies Review 10.

Coleman, J.L./Harding, S. K. (1995) Citizenship, the demands of justice, and the moral relevance of political borders. In: Schwartz 1995: 18-62.

Collard, E. (1895) Die Staatsangehörigkeit der Ehefrau nach deutschem Recht. Erlangen: Diss. Friedrich-Alexander-Universität.

Colley, L., (1994) Britons. Forging the Nation 1707-1837. London: Vintage.

Connelly, M./Kennedy, P. (1994) Must It Be the Rest Against the West? In: Atlantic Monthly, December 1994, 61-91.

Conzen, K. et al., (1990) The Invention of Ethnicity: A Perspective from the USA. In: Altreitalie (April 1990): 37-63.

CPB (1992) Scanning the Future and Nederland in Drievoud.

Cranston, M. (1988) The sovereignty and the nation, In: C. Lucas (ed.) (1988) The French Revolution and the Creation of Modern Political Culture, vol.2: The Political Culture of the French Revolution. Oxford: Pergamon Press.

Crozier, B. (1934) The changing basis of women's nationality. In: Boston Univerity Law Review 14.

Cunningham, F. (1987) Democratic Theory and Socialism. Cambridge: Cambridge Univ. Press.

Danielson, J.B. (1985) Ethnic Identity, Nationalism and Scandinavism in the Scandinavian Immigrant Socialist Press in the U.S. In: C. Harzig and D. Hoerder, eds., (1985) The Press of Labor Migrants in Europe and North America, 1880s to 1930s Bremen, pp. 181-204.

Dasgupta, P. (1993) An Inquiry into Well-Being and Destitution. Oxford: Oxford University Press.

Davidson, A. (1993) 'Understanding citizenship in Australia' in: Public Affairs Research Centre Beyond the Headlines, Politics: Australia and the World Melbourne: Public Affairs Research Centre.

Delitz, (1954) Der Gleichberechtigunsentwurf im Staatsangehörigkeitsrecht. In: Das Standesamt 7.

Dewulf, G. (1991) Limits to Forecasting. Utrecht.

Diamond, M.J. (1990) Olympe de Gouges and the French Revolution: The construction of gender as critique", Dialectical Anthropology 15: 95-105.

Diner, H. R. (1983) Erin's Daughters in America. Irish Immigrant Women in the Nineteenth Century. Baltimore.

Dirks, G.E. (1995) Factors underlying Migration and Refugee Issues. Responses and Co-operation among OECD Member States. Conference Paper: Berg en Dal.

Dowty, A. (1987) Closed Borders. New Haven, London.

Dummett, A. (1992) The transnational migration of people seen from within a natural law tradition, in: Barry/Goodin (eds.) 1992: 169-80.

Dummett, A./Nichol, A. (1990) Subjects, Citizens, Aliens and Others. London: Weidenfeld & Nicolson.

Eder, K. (1996) Social Movement Organizations as a Democratic Challenge to Institutional Politics? Paper for Conference 'Social and Political Citizenship in a World of Migration'. Firenze, February.

Eisenstadt, S.N. (1951) Research on the Cultural and Social Adaption of Immigrants. In: Int. Social Science Bull. 3: 258-62.

Elias, N. (1991) La société des individus. Paris: Fayard.

Endemann, M. L. (1934) Zur Reform des Staatsangehörigkeitrechts der Ehefrau, In: Deutsches Recht 4.

Engbersen, G./Gabriëls, R. (1995) Sferen van integratie. Amsterdam: Meppel. Boom.

Esman, M.J. (1975) The Management of Communal Conflict. In: Glazer, N. and D.P. Moynihan (eds.), Ethnicity. Theory and Experience. Cambridge: Harvard University Press, p. 391-419.

Fanon, F. (1952) Peau noire masques blancs. Paris: Éditions du Seuil.

Ferrajoli, L. (1995) Dai diritti de cittadino al diritti della persona. In: Zolo, D. (ed.) La Cittadinanza (1994). Roma, Bari. English Translation by I.L. Fraser, 1995 EU Firenze.

Finkelkraut, A. (1987) La défaite de la pensée. Paris: Editions Gallimard.

Føllesdal, A. (1995) Do welfare obligations end at the boundaries of the Nation State? Manuscript, to be published in: Koslowski/Føllesdal (eds.) The Welfare State under siege. Springer Verlag.

Frideres, J. S. (1994) Edging into the Mainstream? Immigrant Adults and Their Children, unpubl. paper, Univ. of Calgary.

Furnivall, J.S. (1948) Colonial Policy and Practice. Cambridge: Cambridge University Press.

Gabaccia, D. R. (1988) Militants and Migrants. Rural Sicilians Become American Workers. New Brunswick.

Gabaccia, D. R. (1996) The 'Yellow Peril' and the 'Chinese of Europe': Italian and Chinese Laborers in an International Labor Market, 1815-1930. In: J. Lucassen and L. Lucassen, eds. (1996) Migrations, Migration History, History: Old Paradigms and New Perspectives. Bern: Lang.

Gagnon, A.-G. and D. Latouche (1991) Allaire, Bélanger, Campeau et les autres. Les Québécois s'interrogent face à leur avenir. Montreal: Editions Québec/ Amérique.

Gagnon, A.-G./Laforest, G. (1993) The Future of Federalism. In: International Journal 48: 470-91.

Gans, Herbert J. (1979) Symbolic Ethnicity: The Future of Ethnic Groups and Cultures in America. In: Ethnic and Racial Studies 2(1): 1-20.

Garfinkel, A. (1981) Forms of Explanation. New Haven/London: Yale UP.

Geertz, C. (1973) The Interpretations of Culture. New York: Basic Books.

Gellner, E. (1983) Nations and Nationalism Oxford: Blackwell.

Gellner, E. (1983) Nations and Nationalism. Oxford: Basil Blackwell.

Gerhard-Teuscher, U. (1986) Die Frau als Rechtsperson - über die Voreingenommenheit der Jurisprudenz als dogmatische Wissenschaft. In: Hausen, K. & H. Nowotny (eds) (1986) Wie männlich ist die Wissenschaft?. Frankfurt a.M.: Suhrkamp Verlag.

Gérin-Lajoie, P. (1967) "Québec, une société distincte." Rapport du comité des affaires constitutionnelles de la Commission politique de la Fédération libérale du Québec.Congrès annuel de la Fédération libérale du Québec, le 9 octobre 1967.

Glettler, M. (1985) The Acculturation of the Czechs in Vienna. In: Hoerder ed. 1985: 277-96.

Goldberg, D.T. (1993) Racist Culture. Philosophy and the Politics of Meaning. Oxford: Blackwell.

Goldberg, D.T. (1994) Multiculturalism: A Critical Reader Cambridge Mass.: Blackwell.

Goldlust, J./Richmond, A. H. (1974) A Multivariate Model of Immigrant Adaption. In: Int. Migration Rev. 8: 193-225.

Goldstein, J. E./Bienvenue, R. M. eds. (1980) Ethnicity and Ethnic Relations in Canada. A Book of Readings. Toronto.

Goodin, R.E. (1988) What is so Special about Our Fellow Countrymen? In: Ethics 98: 663-86.

Goodin, R.E. (1992) If people were money, in: Barry/Goodin (eds.) 1992: 6-21.

Goodin, R.E. (1992a) Commentary: The political realism of free movement, in: Barry/Goodin 1992: 248-63.

Goodin, R.E. (1996) Free Movement: Further Thoughts. Post-Script for Colloquium Citizenship and Exclusion, Amsterdam, April.

Goodin, R.E. (1996a) Why Citizenship? A Reply to Bauböck. Colloquium Citizenship and Exclusion. Amsterdam, April.

Goodwin-Gill, G. S. (1994) Asylum: The Law and Politics of Change. Amsterdam, Oct. 19.

Gordon, D. M./Edwards, R. /Reich, M. (1982) Segmented Work. Divided Workers. The Historical Transformation of Labor in the United States. Cambridge.

Government of Canada (1969)The White Paper. The Statement of the Government of Canada on Indian Policy. Ottawa: Queen's Printer.

Government of Canada (1984) Equality Now. Department of Supply and Services Canada. Ottawa: Queen's Printer.

Grant, J. P. (1993) The State of the World's Children . New York: Oxford University Press.

Gray, C. (1989) Speaking in Tongues. In: Saturday Night, Dec. 19, 1989.

Grayson, J. P. et al (1994) Racialization and Black Student Identity at York University and The Social Construction of 'Visible Minority' for Students of Chinese Origin and

Race on Campus: Outcomes of the First Year Experience at York University. York: York University, Institute for Social Research.

Green, N. L. (1996) The Comparative Method and Poststructural Structuralism–New Perspectives for Migration Studies. In J. Lucassen and L. Lucassen, eds. (1996) Migrations, Migration History, History: Old Paradigms and New Perspectives. Bern: Lang.

Guillaumin, C. (1972) L'idéologie raciste. Genèse et language actuel. Paris/La Haye: Mouton.

Gurr, T. (1993) Minorities at Risk. Washington.

Gutmann, A. (ed.) (1994) Multiculturalism: Examining the Politics of Recognition Princeton NJ: Princeton University Press.

Habermas, J. (1991) Erläuterungen zur Diskursethik. Frankfurt/M. Suhrkamp.

Habermas, J. (1994) Struggles for recognition in the democratic constitutional state. In: Gutmann 1994: 107–48.

Haddon, A.C. (1910) History of Anthropology. London: Watts & Co., 1910.

Hall, S. et D. Held (1990) Citizens and Citizenship. London: New Times, Laurence & Wishart, p. 173-88.

Hammar, T. (1985) 'Sweden' in Hammar, T. (ed.) European Immigration Policy: a Comparative Study Cambridge University Press.

Hammar, T. (1990) Democracy and the Nation State. Aldershot: Edward Elgar.

Hampe, K.A. (1951) Das Staatsangehörigkeitsrecht von Grossbritannien. Frankfurt a.M.: Wolfgang Metzger Verlag.

Hannum, H. (1990) Autonomy, Sovereignty, and Self-Determination. Philadelphia: Univ. of Pennsylvania Press.

Harel, L. (1996) Opening Remarks, presented at the Colloquium, "Citoyenneté et Pluralisme" organized by the Groupe de recherche GREAPE, Montréal.

Harzig, C. ed. (1996) Peasant Maids, City Women. Ithaca.

Hathaway, J.C. (1995) Fundamental Justice, International Comity, and the Deflection of Refugees from Canada. Paper for Conference 'Organizing Diversity', Berg en Dal, November.

Hawthorne, L. (1994) Labour Market Barriers for Immigrant Engineers in Australia Canberra: AGPS.

Held, D. (ed.) (1991) Political Theory Today. Cambridge UK: Polity Press.

Hendrickson, D.C. (1992) Migration in law and ethics: A realist perspective, in: Barry/Goodin 1992: 213-32.

Hirst, P. (1994) Associative Democracy. Cambridge.

Hirst, P./Thompson, G. (1996) Globalization in Question. Cambridge: Polity Press.

Hobsbawm, E.J. (1990) Nations and Nationalism since 1780. Cambridge University Press.

Hodson, R. /Kaufmann, R. L. (1982) Economic Dualism: A Critical Review. In: Am. Soc. Rev. 47: 727-39.

Hoerder, D. (1995) From Immigrants to Ethnics: Acculturation in a Societal Framework. In: D. Hoerder and L. P. Moch, eds. (1995) European Migrants. Global and Local Perspective. Boston, pp. 211-62.

Hoerder, D. (ed.) (1985) Labor Migration in the Atlantic Economies. The European and North American Working Classes during the Period of Industrialization. Westport, Ct.

Hoerder, D./Juteau, D. (1995) National Models and Societal Integration. From National Culture to National Diversity. Presented at the Conference "Organizing Diversity. Migration and Refugees: Canada and Europe", Berg en Dal, NL.

Hoerder, D.: Canadian Immigrants View Their Own Lives (research in progress).

House of Commons Debate (1971) Official Report, 115, 187, 3rd Session, 28th Parliament, October 8, 1971.

HREOC (Human Rights and Equal Opportunities Commission) (1991) Racist Violence: Report of the National Inquiry into Racist Violence in Australia Canberra: Australian Government Publishing Service.

HREOC (Human Rights and Equal Opportunities Commission) (1993) State of the Nation 1993: a Report on People of Non-English Speaking Backgrounds Canberra: AGPS.

HREOC (Human Rights and Equal Opportunities Commission) (1994) State of the Nation 1994 a Report on People of Non-English Speaking Backgrounds Canberra: AGPS.

Hughes, E. C. (1948/ 1971) The Study of Ethnic Relations. Repr. in idem: The Sociological Eye: Selected Papers. Chicago.

Humphreys, P. (1989) The Chances of Explanation. Causal Explanation in the Social, Medical and Physical Sciences. Princeton, New Jersey.

Huntington, S. P. (1993) The Clash of Civilizations? In: Foreign Affairs 72(3): 22-49.

Isajiw, W. W. (1981) Ethnic Identity Retention. Research Paper No. 125, Department of Sociology. University of Toronto.

Isajiw, W. W. ed. (1977) Identities. The Impact of Ethnicity on Canadian Society Toronto.

Jayasuriya, L. (1993) 'The idea of citizenship for a multicultural Australia' paper for Seminar on Ideas for Australia Sydney, March 1993.

Jong, C. D., de (1995) The Root Causes Approach. Conference Paper: Berg en Dal.

Juteau, D. (1993) The Production of the Québécois Nation. In: Humbolt Journal of Social Relations 19 (2): 79-101.

Juteau, D. (1996) Theorizing from the Margins. Ethnic Communalizations in the World System. In: Nations and Nationalism 2(1): 45-65.

Juteau, D./M. McAndrew (1992) Projèt national, immigration et intégration dans un Québec souverain. Sociologie et sociétés 24(2): 161-80.

Juteau-Lee, D. (1983) La production de l'ethnicité ou la part réelle de l'idéel. In: Sociologie et sociétés 15(2): 39-55.

Juteau-Lee, D. ed. (1979) Emerging Ethnic Boundaries. Ottawa.

Kamenka, E. (1976) Political nationalism - The evolution of the idea. In: idem. (ed.) (1976) Nationalism. The Nature and Evolution of an Idea. New York: St. Martin's Press.

Kant, E. (1977) Die Metaphysik der Sitten. Frankfurt a.M.: Suhrkamp Verlag.

Kaztauskis, A. (1904/1982) From Lithuania to the Chicago Stockyards - An Autobiography. In: Independent 57(4) Aug. 1904, 241-48. Repr. in: D. M. Katzman /W. M. Tuttle, Jr., eds. (1982) Plain Folk. The Life Stories of Undistinguished Americans. Urbana, pp. 99-114.

Keat, R. (1981) The politics of social theory. Oxford.

Keith, Sir A. (1919) Nationality and Race. From an Anthropologist's Point of View. Oxford University Press: Robert Boyle Lecture delivered before the Oxford University Junior Scientific Club on November 17, 1919.

Keller, F. v. /Trautmann, P. (1914) Kommentar zum Reichs- und Staatsangehörigkeitsgesetz. Munich: C.H. Becksche Verlagsbuchhandlung, Oskar Beck.

Kennan, G. F. (1993) Around the Cragged Hill: A Personal and Political Philosophy. New York: Norton.

Kerr, C. (1977) Markets and Other Essays. Berkeley, Ca.

Klessmann, C. (1985) Polish Miners in the Ruhr District: Their Social Situation and Trade Union Activity. In: Hoerder (ed.) 1985: 253-76.

Knorr, K.D. (1977) Policy makers' Use of Social Science Knowledge: Symbolic or Instrumental. In: Weiss, C.H. ed.) Using Social Research in Public Policy Making. Lexington, Mass. p. 165-82.

Kohn, H. (1948) The Idea of Nationalism. A Study in its Origins and Background. New York: The Macmillan Company.

Korver, T. (1996) Comment on Veit Bader: I see, I see what you can't see. Amsterdam Colloquium, April.
Koselleck, R. (1967) Preussen zwischen Reform und Revolution. Allgemeines Landrecht, Verwaltung und soziale Bewegung von 1791 bis 1848. Stuttgart.
Kymlicka, W. (1989) Liberal Individualism and Liberal Neutrality. In: Ethics 99: 883 -905.
Kymlicka, W. (1989a) Liberalism, Community, and Culture. Oxford: Clarendon Press.
Kymlicka, W. (1990) Contemporary Political Philosophy. Oxford: Clarendon Press.
Kymlicka, W. (1995) Multicultural Citizenship. A Liberal Theory of Minority Rights. Oxford: Clarendon Press.
Kymlicka, W. (1996) Update of Multicultural Citizenship, ch. 2. Amsterdam Colloquium, April.
Kymlicka, W. (1997) States, Nations and Cultures. Assen: van Gorcum.
Lange, R. de (1995) Paradoxes of European Citizenship. In: Fitzpatrick, P. (ed.) (1995) Nationalism, Racism, and the Rule of Law. Dartmouth: Aldershot, pp. 97-115.
Lessard, C. and M. Crespo (1990) L'éducation multiculturelle au Canada: politiques et pratiques. In: Repères 14: 125-83.
Licht, W. (1982) Labor Economics and the Labor Historian. In: Int. Labor and Working Class History 21: 52-62.
Lonergan, S./Parnwell, M.J.G. (1995) Assessing the Linkages between Environmental Degradation and Population Displacement. Conference Paper: Berg en Dal.
Lournoy Jr., R. W. (1924) The new married women's citizenship law. In: The American Journal of International Law 18.
Luban, D. (1985) Just War and Human Rights. In: Beitz et al. 1985: 195-216.
Luhmann, N. (1990) Die Wissenschaft der Gesellschaft. Frankfurt: Suhrkamp.
MacKinnon, C. A. (1982) Feminism, marxism, method, and the State: An agenda for theory. In: Signs 7.
Maguire, J. M. (1920) Suffrage and married women's nationality. In: The American Law Review, 54.
Makarov, A.N. (1947) Allgemeine Lehren des Staatsangehörigkeitsrechts. Stuttgart: W. Kohlhammer Verlag.
March/Olson (1989) Rediscovering Institutions. The Organizational Basis of Politics. Free Press.
Margalit, A./Raz, J. (1990) National Self-Determination. In: The Journal of Philosophy 87(9): 439-61.
Marshall, T. H. (1949/1965) Citizenship and Social Class. In: idem, Class, Citizenship, and Social Development. New York: Doubleday, pp. 71-134.
Meadows, D. et. al. (1972) Limits to Growth. New York.
Meadows, D. et. al. (1991) Beyond the Limits. London, Earthscan Publications.
Meehan, E. (1993) Citizenship in the European Community. London: Sage.
Meinecke, F. (1919) Weltbürgertum und Nationalstaat. Munich: R. Oldenburg.
Micone, M (1996) Marco Micone et le vote ethnique. Montréal Campus 16(10): 15.
Moch, Leslie Page (1992) Moving Europeans. Migration in Western Europe since 1650. Bloomington.
Moodley, Kogila (1983) Canadian Multiculturalism as Ideology. Ethnic and Racial Studies, 6(3), p. 320-31.
Mouffe, C. (1996) Pluralisme et démocratie: les limites du liberalisme politique. In: Gagnon, F., M. Mc Andrew and M. Pagé (eds.), Pluralisme, citoyenneté et éducation. Montréal: L'Harmattan, p. 81-92.
Multiculturalism Canada (1989) Rapport annuel (1988-1989): L'application de la Loi sur le multiculturalisme canadien. Ottawa: Supply and Services Canada.
Nardin, T. (1992) Alternative ethical perspectives on transnational migration, in: Barry/Goodin 1992: 267-78.

Nardin, T./Mapel, D. R. (1992) Convergence and Divergence in international ethics. In: Nardin/Mapel (eds.) 1992: 297-322.

Nardin, T./Mapel, D. R. (eds.) (1992) Traditions of international ethics. Cambridge University Press.

Nickel, H. (1915) Erwerb und Verlust der Staatsangehörigkeit seitens der Ehefrau und der ehelichen Kinder nach altem und neuem Recht. Erlangen: Buchdruckerei Louis Seidel Nachf.

NMAC (National Multicultural Advisory Council) (1995) Multicultural Australia: the Next Steps, Towards and Beyond 2000 (two volumes), Canberra: AGPS.

Noiriel, G. (1988) Le Creuset Français. Histoire de l'immigration XIXe-XXe siècle. Paris: Éditions du Seuil.

Nonini, D. M. (1993) Popular Sources of Chinese Labor Militancy in Colonial Malaya, 1900-1941. In: C. Guerin-Gonzales and C. Strikwerda, eds., Immigrant Workers. Labor Activism in the World Economy since 1830. New York, pp. 215-42.

Nordlinger, E. (1972) Conflict Regulation in Divided Societies. Harvard University: Center of International Affairs.

Nugent, W. (1992) Crossings. The Great Transatlantic Migrations, 1870-1914. Bloomington.

O'Neill, O. (1985) Lifeboat Earth. In: Beitz et al. 1985: 262-81..

O'Neill, O. (1991) Transnational Justice. In: Held (ed.) 1991: 276-304.

OECD (1995) Trends in International Migration: Annual Report 1994 Paris: OECD.

Offe, C./Preuß, U.K. (1991) Democratic Institutions and Moral Resources. In: Held (ed.) 1991: 143-71.

Oliveira, H.U. Jessurun d' (1989) Principe de nationalité et droit de nationalité. Notes de lecture au sujet du Droit civil international de Francois Laurent. In: Erauw, J. et.al. (1989) Liber Memorialis Francois Laurent 1810-1887. Brussels: E. Story-Scientia.

Oliveira, H.U. Jessurun d' (1994) Expanding External and Shrinking Internal Borders: Europe's Defense Mechanism in the Areas of Free Movement, Immigration and Asylum. In: O'Keeff, D./Twowmey, P. (eds.) Legal Issues of the Maastricht Treaty. London, New York etc.: Wiley Chancery Law.

Oliveira, H.U. Jessurun d' (1996) Comment on Stolcke. Amsterdam Colloquium, April

OMA (Office of Multicultural Affairs) (1989) National Agenda for a Multicultural Australia Canberra: AGPS.

OMA (Office of Multicultural Affairs) (1992) Access and Equity: Evaluation Report Canberra: AGPS.

Parekh, B. (1995) Cultural Diversity and Liberal Democracy. In: D. Beetham (ed.), Defining and Measuring Democracy. London, Thousand Oaks and New Delhi: Sage Publications, p. 199-221.

Parijs, P. v. (1992) Commentary: Citizenship exploitation, unequal exchange and the breakdown of popular sovereignty. In: Barry/Goodin 1992: 155-65.

Parijs, P. v. (1996) Justice and Democracy: Are they Incompatible?. In: The Journal of Political Philosophy, 4(2): 101-17.

Parsons, T. (1967) Sociological Theory and Modern Society. New York: Free Press.

Pateman, C. (1985) The Problem of Political Obligation: a Critique of Liberal Theory Cambridge: Polity Press.

Pateman, C. (1986) Feminism and participatory democracy: Some reflections on sexual difference and citizenship. Paper presented at the Meeting of the American Philosophical Association, St. Louis, Missouri.

Penninx, R. (1992) Wie betaalt en wie bepaalt? Onderzoeksbeleid van de overheid m.b.t. minderheden en de invloed van onderzoek op beleid. In opdracht van het ministerie van binnenlandse zaken, directie coördinatie minderhedenbeleid.

Perry, S. R. (1995) Immigration, justice, and culture. In: Schwartz (ed.) p. 94-135.

Pietrantonio, L./Juteau, D. /McAndrew, M. (1996) Multiculturalisme ou intégration: un faux débat. In: Actes du colloque Les Convergences culturelles dans les sociétés pluriethniques. Québec: Presses de l'Université du Québec, p. 147-58.

Piore, M. J. (1979) Birds of Passage: Migrant Labor and Industrial Societies. New York.

Piore, M.J./Sabel, C. (1984) The Second Industrial Divide. New York.

Pogge, T.W. (1989) Realizing Rawls. Cornell UP, Ithaca: London.

Pogge, T.W. (1989) Realizing Rawls. Ithaca: Cornell University Press.

Pogge, T.W. (1992) Loopholes in Moralities. In: The Journal of Philosophy, p. 79-98

Pogge, T.W. (1992a) Loopholes in Moralities. In: Journal of Philosophy 89: 79-98.

Pogge, T.W. (1992b) Cosmopolitanism and Sovereignty. In: Ethics 103: 48-75, and in Chris Brown (ed.), Political Restructuring in Europe. London: Routledge 1994, pp. 89-122.

Pogge, T.W. (1992c) O'Neill on Rights and Duties. In: Grazer Philosophische Studien 43: 233-247.

Pogge, T.W. (1994) An Egalitarian Law of Peoples. In: Philosophy and Public Affairs; p. 195-224.

Pogge, T.W. (1994a) John Rawls. München: C.H. Beck.

Pogge, T.W. (1994b) An Egalitarian Law of Peoples. In: Philosophy and Public Affairs 23: 195-224.

Pogge, T.W. (1995a) Three Problems with Contractarian-Consequentialist Ways of Assessing Social Institutions. In: Social Philosophy and Policy 12: 241-66, and in Ellen Paul et al., (eds.) (1995) The Just Society. Cambridge: Cambridge University Press.

Pogge, T.W. (1995b) How Should Human Rights be Conceived? In: Jahrbuch für Recht und Ethik 3: 103-20.

Pogge, T.W. (1995c) Eine globale Rohstoffdividende. In: Analyse und Kritik 17: 183-208, and in W. Kersting, (ed.). (1997) Die Ethik der internationalen Beziehungen. Frankfurt: Suhrkamp.

Pogge, T.W. (1996) Comment on Veit Bader. Colloquium 'Cititzenship and Exclusion', Amsterdam, April

Pogge, T.W. (1996a) Comment on Goodin's 'If People were Money'. Colloquium on Citizenship and Exclusion. Amsterdam, April

Pogge, T.W. (1997) Poverty and Migration. In this volume

Pogge, T.W. (1997a) Menschenrechte als moralische Ansprüche an globale Institutionen. In: Stefan Gosepath and Georg Lohmann(eds.): Die Philosophie der Menschenrechte. Frankfurt: Suhrkamp.

Pogge, T.W. (1997b) The Bounds of Nationalism. In: Canadian Journal of Philosophy Supplementary Volume.

Polanyi, M. (1962) Personal Knowledge. Chicago.

Porter, J. (1965)The Vertical Mosaic. An Analysis of Social Class and Power in Canada. Toronto: University Press.

Portes, A./Borocz, J. (1989) Contemporary Immigration: Theoretical Perspectives on its determinants and Modes of Incorporation. In: International Migration Review 23(3): 606-30.

Preuß, U. (1995) Problems of a Concept of European Citizenship. in: European Law Journal 1;3, 267-81.

Priest, Gordon E. (1990) Ethnicity in the Canadian Census. Toronto.

Proulx, J-P., (1993) Le pluralisme religieux dans l'école québécoise: bilan analytique et critique. In: Repères 15: 157-210.

Puskas, J. (1994) Consequences of Overseas Migration for the Country of Origin: The Case of Hungary. In: D. Hoerder, I. Blank and H. Roessler, eds., Roots of the Transplanted, 2 vols. New York.

Räikkä, J. (ed.) (1996) Do we need Minority Rights. Den Haag: Kluwer.

Raspail, Jean (1995) The Camp of the Saints. Petoskey, MI: The Social Contract Press.

Rauchberg, H. (1969) Die erste Konferenz zur Kodifikation des Völkerrechts. In: Zeitschrift für öffentliches Recht 10.

Rawls, J. (1971) A Theory of Justice. Cambridge/Mass.: Harvard UP.

Rawls, J. (1993) The Law of Peoples. In: Shute, S./Hurley, S. (eds.) On Human Rights. Basic Books, New York, p. 41-82, 220-30.

Rawls, J. (1993a) Political Liberalism. New York.

Raz, J. (1975) Practical Reason and Norms. Hutchinson.

Raz, J. (1986) The Morality of Freedom. Oxford.

Rehm, H. (1892) Der Erwerb von Staats- und Gemeindeangehörigkeit in geschichtlicher Entwicklung nach römischem und deutschem Staatsrecht. In: Annalen des Deutschen Reiches.

Reitz, J. G./Breton, R. (1994) The Illusion of Difference: Realities of Ethnicity in Canada and the United States. Toronto.

Renan, E. (1882/1992) Qu'est ce qu'une nation? Paris: Presses Pocket.

Resnick, P. (1993) Thinking English Canada. Toronto: Stoddart.

Rickards, M.(1994) Liberalism, Multiculturalism, and Minority Protection. In: Social Theory and Practice 20(2): 143-70.

Ritter, H. (1986) Dictionary of Concepts of History. New York: Greenwood Press.

Roosens, E. (1989) Creating Ethnicity. The Process of Ethnogenesis. London and New Delhi: Sage Publications.

Rorty, R. (1996) Who are We? Moral Universalism and Economic Triage. In: Diogenes 173.

Ruggie, J.G. (1993) Territoriality and beyond: problematizing modernity in international relations. In: International Organization 47(1): 139-74.

Sahlins, P. (1989) Boundaries: The Making of France and Spain in the Pyrenees. University of California Press.

Sarlemijn, A. (1995) Methodologie van Technologie-Management. In idem (ed.) Produkten op maat. Amsterdam.

Sarlemijn, A. (ed.) (1984) Tussen acadmie en industrie. Amsterdam: Meulenhoff.

Sarna, J. D. (1978) From Immigrants to Ethnics: Toward a New Theory of Ethnicization. In: Ethnicity 5: 370-78.

Sassen, S. (1996) Losing Control? Sovereignty in an Age of Globalization.

Sayer, A. (1992) Method in Social Science: A Realist Approach. London, Routledge

Scheffler, S. (1995) Individual Responsibility in a Global Age. In: Social Philosophy and Policy, 12/1: 219-36.

Schermerhorn, R.A. (1970) Comparative Ethnic Relations. New York: Random House.

Schnaars, P. (1989) Megamistakes. Forecasting and the Myth of Rapid Technological Change. New York.

Schoen, D.A. (1983) The Reflective Practitioner. New York.

Schuck, P./Smith, R.M. (1985) Citizenship without Consent. New Haven, London.

Schwartz, W. F. (ed.) (1995) Justice in Immigration. Cambridge/Mass.: Cambridge UP.

Seidman, L.M. (1995) Fear and loathing at the border. In: Schwartz (ed.), p. 136-46

Shapiro, V. (1984) Women, citizenship, and nationality: Immigration and naturalization policies in the United States. In: Politics & Society 13.

Shklar, J. (1991) American Citizenship: the Quest for Inclusion. Cambridge, London.

Shue, H. (1980) Basic Rights. Princeton, Princeton University Press.

Shue, H. (1988) Mediating Duties, in: Ethics 98:687 - 704.

Silverman, M. (1992) Deconstructing the Nation. Immigration, Racism and Citizenship in Modern France. London: Routledge.

Singer, P. (1972) Famine, Affluence, and Morality. In: Philosophy and Public Affairs 1(3):229-43.

Singer, P. (1993) Practical Ethics. Cambridge UP.

Smith, A.D. (1986) The Ethnic Origins of Nations. Oxford and Cambridge: Blackwell.

Smith, M. G. (1965) The Plural Society in the British West Indies. Berkeley: University of California Press.

Smith, M. G. (1969) Institutional and Political Conditions of Pluralism. In: Pluralism in Africa, ed. Leo Kuper and M.G. Smith. Berkeley: University of California Press.

Societé des Nations (1932) Nationalité de la Femme. In: Journal Officiel. Actes de la 13ème Session Ordinaire de l'Assemblée, Seances des Commissions, Procés-Verbal de la Première Commission, Genève.

Somers. M. (1993) Citizenship and the Place of the Public Sphere: Law, Community and Political Culture in the Transition to Democracy. In: ASR 58/5: 587 ff.

Soysal, Y.N. (1994) Limits of Citizenship. Migrants and Postnational Membership in Europe. Chicago and London: University of Chicago Press.

Soysal, Y. N. (1994) Limits of Citizenship: Migrations and Postnational Membership in Europe. Chicago: University of Chicago Press.

Staatslexikon -Recht, Wirtschaft, Gesellschaft (1962) Freiburg: Verlag Herder.

Stasiulis, D. (1985) The Antinomies of Federal Multi-Culturalism Policies and Official Practices. Paper presented in Montreal, at the International Symposium on Cultural Pluralism, UNESCO, 1985.

Stasiulis, D. (1995) Deep Diversity. Race and Ethnicity in Canadian Politics. In: Whittington, M.S. and G. Williams (eds.), Canadian Politics in the 1990s. 4th edition. Toronto: Nelson, p. 191-217.

Steiner, H. (1992) Libertarianism and the transnational migration of people. In: Barry/Goodin 1992: 87-94.

Stockle, V. (1996) The 'Nature' of Nationality. In this volume.

Stolcke, V. (1995) Cultural fundamentalism: New boundaries and new rhetorics of exclusion in Europe. In: Current Anthropology 36: 1-24.

Streeck, W./Schmitter, P. (1992) Social institutions and economic performance. London.

Strupp, K. (1925) Wörterbuch des Völkerrechts und der Diplomatie. Berlin and Leipzig: Walter de Gruyter & Co.e

Tamir, Y. (1993) Liberal Nationalism. Princeton New Jersey: Princeton University Press.

Taylor, C. (1992/1994) Multiculturalism. Examining the Politics of Recognition. Princeton: Princeton University Press.

Taylor, C. (1994) The politics of recognition. In: Gutmann 1994: 25–74.

Tilly, Louise A./Scott, Joan W. (1978) Women, Work & Family. New York

Tobin, James (1994) A Tax on International Currency Transactions. In: United Nations Development Program, Human Development Report. New York, Oxford University Press, p. 70.

Treblicock, M. J. (1995) The case for a liberal immigration policy. In: Schwartz 1995: 219 ff.

Turner, B., (1986) Individualism and Citizenship. In: idem, Citizenship and Capitalism, London: Allan & Unwin.

Tushnet, M. (1995) Immigration policy in liberal political theory. In: Schwartz 1995: 147-57.

Unger, R. (1983) The Critical Legal Studies Movement. Cambridge, Mass.

Unger, R. (1987) Politics. 3 Volumes. Cambridge.

United Nations (1962) Convention on the Nationality of Married Women. Department of Economic and Social Affairs, New York.

United Nations Development Program (1996), Human Development Report. New York, Oxford University Press.

United Nations. Nationality of Married Women. Commission on the Status of Women, Report submitted by the Secretary General, New York, 1950.

Valkenburg, F.C. /Vissers, A.M.C. (1980) Segmentation of the Labour Market: The Theory of the Dual Labour Market - The Case of the Netherlands. In: Netherlands Journal of Sociology 16: 155-70.

Vallee, F. G./Schwartz, M./Darknell, F. (1957) Ethnic Assimilation and Differentiation in Canada. In: Can. Journ. Econ Pol. Sci. 23: 540-49.

Van den Berghe, P. (1967) Race and Racism. New York: John Wiley and Sons Inc.

Vecoli, R. J. (1964) The Contadini in Chicago: A Critique of The Uprooted. In: Journ. Am. Hist. 51: 404-17.

Vogel, U. (1991) Is citizenship gender-specific? In: Vogel, U. & M. Moran (eds.) (1991) The Frontiers of Citizenship. London: Macmillan, pp. 58-85.

Wahnich, S. (1966) L'étranger dans la lutte des factions: Usage d'un mot dans une crise politique. In: Langages: Langue de la Revolution Francaise, Mots 16.

Walaszek, Adam et al. (1991) Conflict and Cooperation: Comparative Research on the East European Migratory Experience, 1880s-1930s. Manuscript , Labor Migration Project and Western Reserve Hist. Soc.

Waldron, J. (1987): Nonsense upon Stilts. Methuen, London, New York.

Wallerstein, I./Balibar, E. (1988) Race, Nation, Classe. Les Identités Ambigues. Paris: Éditions La Découverte.

Walzer, M. (1977) Just and Unjust Wars. New York, Basic Books.

Walzer, M. (1983) Spheres of Justice. New York: Basic Books.

Walzer, M. (1985) The Rights of Political Communities. In: Beitz et al. 1985: 165-94

Walzer, M. (1985a) The Moral Standing of States. A Response to Four Critics. In: Beitz et al. 1985: 217-37.

Walzer, M. (1994) Thick and Thin. Moral Argument at Home and Abroad. Notre Dame, London. Univ. of Notre Dame Press.

Walzer, M. (1995) Response to Veit Bader. In: Political Theory 23, 2, p. 247-49.

Weber, Max (1921/1971) Économie et société. Volume 1. Paris: Plon. Translated by J. Freund et al. from Wirtschaft und Gesellschaft, Grundriss der Verstehenden Soziologie, based on the 4th German edition, J. Winckelmann (ed.) Tübingen: J.C.B. Mohr (P. Siebeck) .

Weber, Max (1956/1978) Economy and Society. Volume. 1. Berkeley and Los Angeles: University of California Press. Translated by E. Fischoff et al. from Wirtschaft und Gesellschaft, Grundriss der Verstehenden Soziologie, based on the 4th German edition, J. Winckelmann (ed.) Tübingen: J.C.B. Mohr (P. Siebeck).

Weil, G. (1938) L'Europe du XIXe Siècle et l'Idée de Nationalité. Paris: Editions Albin Michel.

Weinstock D. M. (1996) Droits collectifs et libéralisme. In: Gagnon, F., M. Mc Andrew and M. Pagé (eds.), Pluralisme, citoyenneté et éducation. Montréal: L'Harmattan, p. 53-80.

Weiss, A. (1907) Droit International Privé. Paris: Librairie de la Société du Reveil J.B. Sirey et Du Journal du Paris, vol. I: "La nationalité".

Whitaker, R. (1995) Refugees: the Security Dimension. Paper for 'Organizing Diversity' Conference. Berg en Dal, November.

Wihtol de Wenden, C. (1987) Citoyenneté, Nationalité et Immigration. Paris: Arcantère Éditions.

Wihtol de Wenden, C. (ed.) (1988) La Citoyenneté et les Changements de Structures Sociales et Nationales de la Population Francaise. Paris: Edilig/Fondation Diderot - La Nouvelle Encyclopédie.

Willke, H. (1984) Zum Problem der Intervention in selbstreferentielle Systeme. In: Zeitschrift für systemische Therapie 2: 191-200.

Woodward, J. (1992) Commentary: Liberalism and migration. In Barry/Goodin 1992: 59-83.

Working Nation (1994) The White Paper on Employment Growth and Policies and Programs, Canberra: AGPS.

WRR (1979) Ethnische Minderheden. s'Gravenhage, SDU.

WRR (1989) Allochtonenbeleid. s'Gravenhage, SDU.

Young, I. M. (1989) Polity and Group Difference: A Critique of the Ideal of Universal Citizenship. In: Ethics 99, p. 250-274.

Young, I.M. (1989) Polity and group difference: a critique of the ideal of universal citizenship. In: Ethics 99: 250–74.

Yuval Davis, N. (1980) The bearers of the collective: Women and religious legislation in Israel. In: Feminist Review 4.

Zolberg A. R. (1991) Bounded States in a Global Market: The Uses of International Labor Migrations. In: Social Theory for a Changing Society. ed. Pierre Bourdieu and James S. Coleman. Boulder: Westview / Russell Sage Foundation.

Zolberg A.R. (1995) From Invitation to Interdiction: U.S. Foreign Policy and Immigration Since 1945. In: Threatened Peoples, Threatened Borders: World Migration and U.S. Policy, ed. Michael S.. Teitelbaum and Myron Weiner. New York: W.W. Norton.

Zolberg, A.R (1997) Modes of Incorporation: Towards a Comparative Framework. In this volume.

Zolberg, A.R. (1987) Wanted but not welcome. In: Alonzo, W. (ed.) Population in an Interacting World. Cambridge, Harvard University Press, pp. 36-73.

Zolberg, A.R/Suhrke, A./ Aguyao, S. (1989) Escape from Violence: Conflict and the Refugee Crisis in the Developing World. New York: Oxford University Press.

Index